UNDERSTANDING AMERICAN BUSINESS JARGON

UNDERSTANDING AMERICAN BUSINESS JARGON

A Dictionary

Second Edition

W. Davis Folsom

GREENWOOD PRESS
Westport, Connecticut • London

Library of Congress Cataloging-in-Publication Data

Folsom, W. Davis.
  Understanding American business jargon: a dictionary /
W. Davis Folsom.—2nd ed.
    p. cm.
  Includes bibliographical references.
  ISBN: 0–313–33450–1 (alk.paper)
  1. Business—Dictionaries. 2. Management—Dictionaries. I. Title.
HF1001.F65 2005
650′.03—dc22   2005016817

British Library Cataloguing in Publication Data is available.

Library of Congress Catalog Card Number: 2005016817
ISBN: 0–313–33450–1

First published in 2005

Greenwood Press, 88 Post Road West, Westport, CT 06881
An imprint of Greenwood Publishing Group, Inc.
www.greenwood.com

Printed in the United States of America

The paper used in this book complies with the
Permanent Paper Standard issued by the National
Information Standards Organization (Z39.48–1984).

10 9 8 7 6 5 4 3 2 1

To my wife and best friend, Kathy

CONTENTS

PREFACE

This book is designed to assist business people and students with the confusing and continually changing realm of American business English. Regardless of how you feel about it, global business has become a reality, and American business presence can be observed throughout the world. A few years ago, U.S. troops entering Somalia were greeted by young people cheering "Michael Jackson!" During the Gulf War the Saudi Arabian government restricted movement and interaction of American soldiers so its society would not be "corrupted" by American ideas. The sixteenth-century royal palace in Kirktipur, a village in the Kathmandu Valley in Nepal, has a large Coca-Cola sign hanging from it. In his book *Video Night in Kathmandu,* Pico Ivy depressingly describes seeing the movie *Rambo* dubbed in five South Asian languages. Trade treaties like NAFTA try to protect "cultural industries," but American companies, celebrities, and brands are recognized everywhere.

With this influence in the global marketplace comes the use of American business jargon. The major business media journalists in the United States are generally careful either not to use jargon terms or to explain them when used. But the headline writers for print media and business people interviewed by journalists use an abundance of jargon.

My interest in business jargon began innocently enough. A few years ago I walked into a classroom about one minute late. In the back row sat a group of four young men I knew well from previous classes. Walking by, I read the lips of one student saying, "Oh ____! He *is* here!" To which I replied, "How is my Group W Bench today?" The students smiled, but their expressions told me they did not know what I meant. Reaching the front of the classroom I asked if anyone could explain the meaning of "Group W Bench." No one knew. I offered a little extra credit to the first student who could answer the question. The next day a student came to my office and correctly identified the origin of the phrase.[1] When I asked how he found it, he confessed that his friend had told him but that he had started by looking in the business and economics dictionaries in the library. This got me wondering how often I used phrases, terms, and analogies that are not familiar to my audience, and it stimulated my interest and research into business jargon.

From this story it should be clear that I am not a lexicographer but instead a business professor with interest and experience in business communication. This dictionary is a compilation of business terms and expressions, and also of everyday American English phrases that are frequently used in the business environment. Native-born Americans use so much jargon that they are often not even aware that they are using it. Only when interacting with English-speaking foreigners do many Americans become conscious of their speech. Even then it is often difficult to limit the use of jargon. This can lead to many humorous experiences, but in a business setting, miscommunication can be costly. Take, for example, the two sayings *on the table* and *table an issue*. The first means something is open for discussion or debate, while the second means that discussion will be deferred to a later time. Imagine the misunderstandings that can be created by the use of jargon in business negotiations.

As any student of languages recognizes, languages constantly change. Sports, the military, government, science, and, today, technology are all sources of new words and phrases. It is difficult to keep up with changes in language and jargon. With the Internet providing global communication, the pace of change and the need for better understanding of English as used by American business people is greater than ever. Sample material from this book is available on the Internet at <http://www.islc.net/~folsom/language>. Please send me your questions or suggestions for future editions.

---

[1] "Group W Bench" is a phrase from Arlo Guthrie's 1967 antiwar ballad *Alice's Restaurant Massacre,* referring to grouping of inductees who might be "unfit" for military service.

PREFACE TO THE SECOND EDITION

So much has changed since the first edition of *Understanding American Business Jargon*. First, the Internet has become infinitely more user-friendly, and the World Wide Web has become the global business and communication giant predicted for so many years. When the first edition was created, search engines were in their infancy. Web sites were evolving from billboards (brochureware) into a functioning communication medium. With these changes, a plethora of new technology jargon has exploded into the business world. From e-commerce, to gigabytes, to spyware, technology jargon is the fastest growing area of American business jargon. Many terms took on new meanings in the world of business technology. Consider cookies, firewalls, hacker, and flame. An abundance of new acronyms have become accepted business language, including FTP, JPG, PDA, and HTTP. Text messaging has added to the use of abbreviations and jargon as part of communication short-hand.

With early leadership in the use and development of the World Wide Web, American business English—and with it, American business jargon—has expanded even further, dominating global business communication. Around the world, the demand for business English

xii PREFACE TO THE SECOND EDITION

and American business English flourished. Though a violation of intellectual property rights, a Rumanian Web site posted large portions of the first edition of this book as part of a promotion for its business English school.

Evolving financial markets with new products and new competitors have also been major sources of business jargon. Bubble burst, derivatives, burn rate, and fume date have become part of financial market jargon. In the past _____ gate was used to describe scandals. More recently Enronesque became the common label for corrupt business practices. A special area of financial jargon is Greenspeak, the terms and phrases of Federal Reserve Board Chairman, Alan Greenspan. For decades a small group of economists known as Fedwatchers, pored over the statements made by the Federal Reserve, looking for indications of change in Federal Reserve policy. Today, almost every investor and business person in the U.S. listens to the latest Fed pronouncements. From his 1999 description of the technology stock market as "irrational exuberance," to his "considerable period," "soft patch," and "short-lived" descriptions of the economy and monetary policy in 2003–2004, the words of Alan Greenspan have become common in American business jargon.

The military, a traditional source of an abundance of management jargon, continues to provide new jargon being used in the workplace. Collateral damage, a euphemistic description of civilian casualties associated with the Gulf War, has become a descriptor of the side effects or negative unintended consequences associated with a strategy or policy. Asset deployment and scorched-earth strategy are now used to describe business practices.

A British study found, not surprisingly, that workers often intentionally use business jargon in order to make them appear knowledgeable and up-to-date. For those who are not content to use the latest jargon, there are also business buzzword generators. Take any word from each of the three columns below and create your own important-sounding business jargon.

Column 1	Column 2	Column 3[2]
strategic	cost-based	core competency
interactive	logistical	alliance
responsive	discretionary	re-engineering
reciprocal	empowering	values
customer-oriented	visionary	benchmark

[2] "Business Jargon Hints," McGraw-Hill Web site, http://highered.mcgraw-hill.com/sites/007537892/student_view0/business_jargon_exercise.html.

What is a responsive, logistical alliance? Strategic, visionary values sure sounds important. How about the alliterative customer-oriented, cost-based, core competency? The fact is business people, consultants, and academics often repackage well-known business concepts using new business buzzwords. Customers and workers are sometimes confused, but other irreverent workers created a new game—business buzzword bingo, where a predetermined list of buzzwords they expect their supervisor to use in a meeting or seminar is arranged on bingo cards. Bored workers, forced to attend the meeting mark their cards as the speaker uses the buzzwords; the winner is the first person to connect the words on his or her card.

As stated in the first edition, the goal of this book is to help reduce communication problems, not to add to the use of business jargon. Since the publication of the first edition, I have maintained a Web site (www.islc.net/~folsom/language), offering to try to interpret business jargon. Hundreds of people have sent requests, in the process creating additional material for the second edition. Requests have come from editors and translators, students (particularly international students taking courses with American professors), and individuals learning about financial markets.

Reflecting changing business dynamics and the creative talent in marketplace, American business jargon will continue to evolve in the twenty-first century.

W. Davis Folsom
Beaufort, South Carolina

ACKNOWLEDGMENTS

Many kind people contributed to this book. First, I would like to thank USCA students Kim Pressley, Pam Digesare, Jodi Redd, Thomas Fuss, John Dotson, Chris Walden, Tara Green, Audra Smith, and Joe Tucker for their business jargon contributions. Second, I want to thank friends and colleagues who also contributed to this dictionary, including Julianne Morgan, Tom and Betty Pritchett, Jami and Leah Martin, Chet and Mary Grace Allenchey, Brendon Hanna, Brian and Gae Chilla, Robert Botsch, Murray Kaplan, Al Beyer, and Jerry and Faye Rosenthal.

I want especially to thank my mother Myrtle Folsom for proofreading this book, and my wife Kathy and son Bradley for tolerating with humor the many times I lapsed into jargonese instead of English while working on this book!

Special thanks to my University of South Carolina Beaufort colleague and friend, Professor Rick Boulware for his assistance. His many suggestions, proofreading, and criticisms greatly enhanced the book's quality. Thanks also to Conrad Hartz for his assistance in updating this book.

STYLISTIC GUIDE

Abbreviations   Common business jargon abbreviations are included in the dictionary.

Acronyms   A separate list of acronyms is included at the end of the dictionary.

Alphabetization   Because so many business jargon terms are multi-word phrases, all terms are alphabetized by letter rather than by word.

Brackets   Brackets indicate clarifying information provided by the author with quotations.

Cross-references   The reader is directed to synonyms and related terms in the dictionary. Terms that appear within an entry and are themselves main entries in the dictionary are designated in all capital letters. Those that are acronyms (which would ordinarily be capitalized) are specially designated with an asterisk.

Examples   A unique feature of this dictionary is examples of business jargon as used in American media. The examples were selected to enhance understanding of the term and of the context within which business jargon is frequently encountered.

Parentheses   Parentheses are used for three purposes: to indicate acronyms; to indicate the origin of a term or phrase; and to include introductory or concluding words or phrases that may accompany an entry.

Semicolons   Semicolons are used in definitions to indicate two or more distinctly different meanings of a term or phrase.

UNDERSTANDING AMERICAN BUSINESS JARGON

A

AAA. American Automobile Association; top rating given by U.S. bond rating services.

ABANDONMENT RATE. The percent of marketing calls that are abandoned by telemarketers. When consumers answer a telephone and there is no one at the other end of the line, it is often because a telemarketer has closed the call because he or she has found someone else to talk with.

"Members of the telemarketing industry praised the California Public Utilities Commission last week for delaying a reduction in the state's maximum abandonment rate that had been scheduled for Jan.1." (*DMNews,* December 9, 2002, p. 3)

ABEND. The sudden termination of a computer program or system. From abnormal ending.

ABOUT-FACE. To reverse direction or to reverse a decision (military).

"In About-Face, Dell Will Sell PCs to Dealers." (*Wall Street Journal,* August 20, 2002, p. B1)

ABOVE AND BEYOND. More than required.

ABOVEBOARD. Visible; honest.

"Here's why. It was baseless that I, as chairman of the New York Stock Exchange compensation committee from 1999 to June, 2003, had somehow failed to inform the NYSE board of a benefit they themselves had approved. Having been there, I know the records will prove it was all above-board, well-vetted and fair. It is absurd to suggest that the brightest minds and keenest thinkers on Wall Street were befuddled by the complexity of Richard Grasso's compensation package—especially one composed just like their own. Might as well say NASA couldn't launch a Goodyear blimp." (*Wall Street Journal,* June 10, 2004, p. A12)

ABOVE THE FOLD. The part of a Web page that is visible without scrolling. Banner ads are usually placed at the top of a Web page so they are visible and not "below the fold," in the part of a Web page that requires the viewer to scroll.

ACCELERATION CLAUSE. A stipulation in a contract stating that the unpaid balance becomes due and payable if specific actions transpire, such as failure to make interest payments on time.

ACCELERATION PRINCIPLE. Hypothesis that investment varies with the rate of change in aggregate demand. First introduced by John M. Clark in 1917, the principle was developed to explain the large variations in investment over the course of a business cycle. Keynes incorporated the acceleration principle into his General Theory.

ACCOUNTABLE. Responsible for.

ACCOUNTING INFORMATION SYSTEMS (AIS). Computerized information retrieval systems.

"These conclusions, taken together, demonstrate the need for accounting researchers to become more focused on ethical considerations in the design of accounting information systems, performance measurement criteria, and financial reporting models." (*Business Ethics Quarterly,* July, 2004, p. 399)

ACCREDITED. A term used by the Securities and Exchange Commission to define investors who are financially sophisticated and have no need for the protection provided by certain government filings. Also known as a qualified purchaser.

ACCRUAL BASIS. In accounting, the practice of accounting for expenses and income as if they are earned or incurred, whether or not they have been received or paid.

ACE. Expert; to achieve a perfect score.

ACE IN THE HOLE/UP YOUR SLEEVE. Hidden advantage.
"There was no crisis. Mr. Pollakowski found that Cambridge deregulation was followed by a boom in housing investment. Mr. William Tucker says that 50-years of pent-up housing demand is an 'ace in the hole' in reviving the city." (*Wall Street Journal,* May 19, 2003, p. A17)

ACID TEST. Final, decisive test; proof.
"Revulsion over this corporate excess isn't simply some populist screed. The 'acid test' of corporate reform is CEO compensation and accountability, says Warren Buffett, America's foremost investor. A board challenging CEO pay, warns the sage of Omaha, 'is like belching at a dinner party.' Bill McDonough, former head of the New York federal reserve and now running the SEC's new accounting and oversight board, says the current level of executive pay cannot be 'justified economically ... or morally.'" (*Wall Street Journal,* Sept. 18, 2003, p. A17)

ACID TEST RATIO/QUICK RATIO. Financial test of solvency that compares a firm's liquid assets and liabilities.

ACROSS THE BOARD. Equal for everyone.
"While we agree that Mr. Bush has a lousy first-term spending record, he is now saying that in a second term he'd restrain non-defense increases. Mr. Kerry's stated agenda is increased spending nearly across the board and tax hikes. The voters can decide which of these better constitutes 'fiscal discipline.'" (*Wall Street Journal,* Aug. 9, 2004, p. A12)

ACT IN CONCERT. Work together.
"Speaking out against the Kyoto initiatives in a 1997 speech in China, he said that costly regulations and restrictions are a bad idea, especially when 'their need has yet to be proven, their total impact undefined, and when nations are not prepared to act in concert.'" (*Wall Street Journal,* Aug. 29, 2001, p. B1)

ACTIONABLE. Something that can be activated or accomplished.

ACTION ITEMS. To-do list.

"To boost accountability, the blackout report said North America's reliability standards must be made mandatory. It also said some standards should be reconsidered. For example, FirstEnergy's transmission operators were certified and its summer planning was in compliance with existing standards. 'There were no action items that ECAR had ordered us to do where we sat back and said, nah, we're not going to do it,' said Mr. Jones." (*Wall Street Journal,* April 13, 2004, p. A1)

ACTIVE INCOME. Income earned from a business activity the investor is actively involved in. Active income is taxed differently from passive investment income according to the U.S. tax code.

ADDER. An addition or increment.

ADHOCRACY. An organization with minimal structure, few rules, and delegation of authority to professionals within the organization.

AD IMPRESSIONS. How often people see an advertisement.

AD INFINITUM. Until infinity (Latin).

ADJUSTED BASIS. Price of an asset from which to calculate and derive capital gains or losses upon sale. Actions such as stock splits that have occurred since the initial purchase must be accounted for.

ADJUSTED GROSS INCOME (AGI). A measure of personal income used by the INTERNAL REVENUE SERVICE. AGI includes all sources of personal income minus allowances for contributions to INDIVIDUAL RETIREMENT ACCOUNTS, KEOGH PLANS, alimony payments, and other adjustments.

AD LIB. Improvise.
"Mr. Jimmy Carter will use the million-dollar award to carry on the work of his Carter Center in Atlanta, for such purposes as monitoring elections where people are trying to win democracy and building houses for the poor through Habitat for Humanity. Mr. Gunnar Berge's ad lib notwithstanding, Mr. George W. Bush thoroughly approved of the committee's choice and called Mr. Carter to tell him so." (*Wall Street Journal,* Oct. 15, 2002, p. A21)

ADMINISPHERE. The rarified air that administrators operate in above the rank-and-file employees.

ADMINISTERED PRICES. Prices controlled by government.

ADMINISTRATIUM. Humorous reference to an organization with many administrators.

ADMINISTRIVIA. The trivial activities and reports required by administrators.

"As a project manager, I thoroughly enjoy the responsibility of coaching, supporting and managing people and projects but then there is the administrivia." (Mary Grace Allenchey, AT&T, 1996)

AD NAUSEUM. To the point of making people sick (Latin).

ADOPTION. The merger or acquisition of a mutual fund by another fund.

"In the mutual-fund world, 'adoption' is the shortcut by which fund companies can plug gaps in their portfolio lineups by taking over funds run by other investment companies." (*Wall Street Journal,* December 3, 2003, p. R1)

ADOPTION PROCESS. The steps consumers go through in accepting a new product, including awareness, interest, evaluation, trial, and rejection or adoption.

AD VALOREM. Value-added (Latin).

ADVANCE-DECLINE RATIO (A-D). The ratio of the number of stocks trading above their previous closing prices compared to the number trading below their previous closing prices over a particular period.

ADVERSE SELECTION. A situation in which buyers or sellers lack relevant information about some aspect of product quality.

ADWARE. Software that displays advertising on computer screens.

AFFILIATE. Local market television and radio station that agrees to carry programming and commercials provided by a network (national broadcasting company).

AFFILIATE MARKETING. A revenue-sharing agreement where businesses pay other firms (affiliates) for referrals. Affiliate marketing is widely used on the Internet, where e-commerce businesses pay other Web sites based on click-throughs or sales resulting from referrals. Before it became a dominant destination Web site, Amazon.com grew rapidly through affiliate marketing.

AFFIRMATIVE ACTION. Policies enacted to redress barriers or discrimination seen as limiting access to resources and opportunities, usually in employment and education.

"In the campaign for the 1998 vote that brought the BJP into power, the party's leadership called for a ban on cow slaughter, the conversion of a number of Islamic mosques into Hindu temples, and the scraping of affirmative action policies they charged favored India's 150 million Muslim population, the world's second-largest." (*Wall Street Journal,* May 14, 2004, p. A1)

AFFLUENZA. Combining the words affluence and influenza, affluenza describes thoughtless materialism in which consumers overwork and accumulate high levels of debt to purchase more goods. *Affluenza* is the name of a Public Broadcasting System film.

AFFORDABILITY INDEX. National Association of Realtors' index of housing costs in different regions of the United States.

AFTER MARKET. Market for stock after its initial offering; market for maintenance materials and parts.

AFTER-TAX BASIS. Comparison of corporate taxable bonds with municipal tax-free bonds.

AGE THE ACCOUNTS. Arrange accounts receivable in order of the days they are past due.

AGING SCHEDULE/THE AGING. A list of accounts receivable in order of how many days they are past due. The aging schedule is used by lenders when considering loans to businesses.

AHEAD OF THE CURVE. In advance of others. A person or product that is new and unique.

AIR (TO). Broadcast on television or radio.

AIRBALL. A total miss (basketball).

AIR COVER. Taking responsibility for an unpopular decision.

AIR IT OUT. Discuss openly.

AIR ONE'S DIRTY LINEN/LAUNDRY. Talk about one's problems.

AIRPLANE RULE. As something becomes more complex, the possibility of failure increases.

AIR TIME. Broadcast time on television or radio.

"To compete against 24-hour cable news channels accustomed to showing news all the time, CBS aimed to avoid going to TALKING HEADS and, instead, give more air time to its embedded reporters, equip them with better technology and present a vast array of graphics. In the past, embedded reporters often had to show a story to the military before broadcasting; this time, they can report live." (*Wall Street Journal,* March 24, 2003, p. B1)

ALL-BLUE. All IBM. IBM is referred to as BIG BLUE.

ALL EARS. Very eager; listening intently.

ALL-HANDS MEETING. A meeting, usually called by senior management, that everyone is expected to attend.

ALL HELL BROKE LOOSE. Things got out of control.

ALL OR NONE (AON). Stock market order prohibiting partial sales or purchases.

ALL-OUT. Full effort, holding nothing back.

ALL SYSTEMS GO. Ready to act or proceed.

ALMA MATER. Nourishing mother (Latin); school from which a person graduated.

ALPHABET STOCK. Categories of stock within a larger corporation.

ALPHA GEEK. A firm's technology expert.

ALPHA PUP. Market research label for the "coolest kid in the neighborhood."

"If alpha pups go for it, we'll sell millions of them." ("25 Hot Buzzwords" Kate Lorenz, MSNCareerbuilder.com, July 21, 2004)

ALPHA STAGE. In finance, the first stage of venture capital, also called seed money.

ALSO-RAN. Loser; a product or person who is not among the most successful.

AMAZONNED. To lose a significant portion of your business to a dot-com company. Many BRICKS AND MORTAR companies are losing business to Internet competitors.

AMBULANCE CHASER. Lawyer who specializes in personal injury claims; unethical lawyer.

"His 'divisive' populism and liberal votes are at odds with mainstream values, party chairman Ed Gillespie added yesterday. White House strategist Karl Rove, with instincts honed in Southern brawls pitting trial lawyers against business, believes in the power of 'ambulance chaser' as a political epithet." (*Wall Street Journal,* July 7, 2004, p. A4)

AMERICAN COWBOY. Executive in American workplace who is dynamic but also somewhat out of control.

AMERICAN DEPOSITORY RECEIPT (ADR). Certificate backed by shares of a foreign company.

"Yesterday's deal was announced after the close of stock trading in New York, where both AngloGold and Ashanti's American depository receipts trade on the New York Stock Exchange. AngloGold rose 40 cents, or 1.24%, to $32.55 a share. Ashanti rose 12 cents, or 1.5%, to $8.12 a share." (*Wall Street Journal,* Aug. 5, 2003, p. C14)

AMERICAN DREAM. Widely held perception that each generation of Americans will be better off than the previous generation.

"'The jump in prices was very unexpected,' she said. 'I don't know if I can afford one now.' Inadvertently, the economic development project that is MassMoCA may have ended her American dream." (*Wall Street Journal,* July 7, 2004, p. D10).

AMERICANS WITH DISABILITIES ACT (ADA). 1992 federal legislation requiring businesses to provide equal access for customers and also accommodation for employees with special needs.

AMPED. Excited; high-energy.

"Never mind that luge is nothing more than an amped-up version of an age-old American pastime—'it's just sleigh riding, only our sleighs go 100 miles per hour,' says retired three-time Olympic luger Duncan Kennedy. For years, U.S. luge fell largely into the 'who cares' category." (*Wall Street Journal,* Dec. 19. 1997, p. 1)

ANCHOR (TO)/ANCHOR TENANT. The largest, best known tenant in a shopping mall; to hold in place; symbols used in HTML to indicate the beginning and end of hypertext links (< >).

"The 21-year-old mall, which will lose its Foley's anchor store to nearby North East Mall in Hurst, is spending $100 million to become an indoor/outdoor mall with a new movie theater, lakes and an ice rink." (*Wall Street Journal,* Oct. 18, 2000, p. T1)

ANGELS. Investors in start-up companies who contribute a small amount of capital and provide advice to the new entrepreneur.

"Control also becomes an issue when many friends-and-family investors sit on a board, said Joanna Rees Gallanter, managing partner of Venture Strategy Partners, a San Francisco venture firm. 'You could have three or four angel investors on the board,' she said. Try to get them off, and there's trouble." (*Wall Street Journal,* July 16, 2003, p. B7C)

ANGLE. The emphasis or slant presented in a proposal or news story.

ANGRY GARDEN SALAD. A poorly constructed Web site with incorrect links to other pages and sites.

ANNUAL TRAIL RATE. Mutual fund reporting of annual broker's commission.

"Jargon: Annual trail rate. Translation: annual broker's commission." (*Wall Street Journal,* Jan. 4, 1999, p. R8)

ANOINTED. Chosen by top company executives (biblical).

"Mr. [Eliot] Spitzer is going after British-based Glaxo for 'concealing' information about its popular antidepressant medicine, Paxil. According to America's new self-anointed drug czar, Glaxo's crime is that it publicized one study showing Paxil had positive results in adolescents, but didn't advertise four studies that showed inconclusive results or suggested Paxil may increase the risk of suicidal thoughts." (*Wall Street Journal,* June 21, 2004, p. A16)

ANTE BELLUM. Before the war (Latin).

ANTENNA SHOP. A retail store that introduces new products to consumers but does not sell the product.

ANTE UP. Pay up one's share.

"The U.S. will help lead a donors conference in Madrid later this month, but other wealthy countries have hinted that they are unlikely to ante up anything close to the $20.3 billion that President Bush has asked Congress to provide as the U.S. share for next year." (*Wall Street Journal,* Oct. 2, 2003, p. A4)

ANTI-NUKE. Someone opposed to nuclear weapons or energy.

A-OK. Operating smoothly (the early NASA program).

APOLLO SYNDROME. Secretly working to delay the development of a project as long as possible in order to put off the end of the work and employment. A reference to the American space program.

APPLE POLISH (TO). Flatter; BROWN-NOSE.

APPLICATION SERVICE PROVIDER. A provider, from a remote server, of business computer applications.

ARB. Abbreviation for arbitrageur, an investor who tries to profit by small differences in market prices for the same security or commodity.

ARCHIE BUNKER. A bigoted, lower-class American; REDNECK. Archie (played by Carroll O'Connor) was a character in the *All in the Family* television series.

"Not surprisingly, Mr. [Carroll] O'Connor's death set off a spate of media discussions about 'All in the Family' and its significance, few as memorable as the one starring actor/director Rob Reiner. On 'Hardball' it fell to Mr. Reiner, who portrayed [Archie]'s son-in-law Michael, aka Meathead, to answer questions about the fears people like Archie Bunker might have—the sort of people living in changing, crime-plagued neighborhoods, and who, like Archie, didn't like it." (*Wall Street Journal,* July 2, 2001, p. A14)

ARM AND A LEG. Expensive.

"Both AT&T and Verizon charge an arm and a leg for monthly data plans. Both favor plans that force you to estimate how many megabytes of e-mail and Web pages you'll use in a month, and then charge you extra for going over." (*Wall Street Journal,* Dec. 11, 2003, p. B1)

ARMCHAIR GENERAL/QUARTERBACK. Critic who does not have experience in the area he or she is criticizing; know-it-all.

ARMPIT. A very undesirable place.

ARMS-LENGTH TRANSACTION. Transaction that complies with the legal requirements to avoid any conflict of interests. See CHINESE WALL.

ARM WAVING. Excitement, sometimes exaggerated or irrational.

AS IS. Sold with no warranty. Most used products are sold as is.

ASK PRICE. The price at which a stock, bond, or other security is offered for sale.

ASLEEP AT THE SWITCH. Not awake; not focused on one's duties (early U.S. railroad era).
   "Perhaps the real reason behind the latest announcement is that Chinese authorities don't want to look like they're asleep at the switch while technology races past them, even if they realize the futility of their task." (*Wall Street Journal,* July 6, 2004, p. A22)

ASSESSED VALUE. The value assigned to property by a city or county for the purpose of tax assessment.

ASSET DEPLOYMENT. The allocation of a firm's assets. The term comes from the military, where an officer would deploy his or her troops.

ASSET PLAY. Takeover of a company whose assets are undervalued on the balance sheet.

ASSET STRIPPER. A CORPORATE RAIDER who buys a company intending to sell all or most of the company's prized assets to pay off the debt incurred in purchasing the company. An asset stripper calculates that the remaining parts of the company will be valuable.

ASS-KISSER. One who flatters superiors. See also BROWN-NOSE.

ASSMOSIS. Sarcastic description of the process by which some people advance in a corporation.

ASSOCIATE. An employee. The term is intended to convey the impression that employees are partners in the organization.

ASTROTURF MOVEMENT. An artificial grassroots movement where "spontaneous" letters or calls to politicians are a coordinated effort to influence policy.

ASYNCHRONOUS LEARNING. Courses or training programs that are self-paced, often provided over the Internet.

AT FACE VALUE. On initial inspection or on the surface.

ATTENTION, INTEREST, DESIRE, AND ACTION (AIDA). The four stages of a marketer's concept of a consumer's mental buying process.

AT THE BELL. At the opening or closing of the market. The New York Stock Exchange uses a bell to start and end trading. Politicians and celebrities are often photographed ringing the NYSE bell.

AT THE END OF THE DAY. After everything has been discussed or considered.

AT THE 11th HOUR. At the last minute possible.

AT THE HELM. In charge (military).

AT THE MARKET. At the current market price.

AT THE MONEY. An option with a strike price (price at which the asset can be purchased or sold) equal to the current price of the asset.

AT THE OPEN. Stock market order to buy or sell at the first traded price.

ATTRIT. Abbreviation for attrition. To attrit is to cut back the number of employees slowly by not replacing people who leave the company.

AUDIT TRAIL. Accounting method to document the source of a data entry.
    "In our report, delivered this week, we recommend specific actions to resolve the privacy issues raised by government programs in which personally identifiable information about U.S. persons is used by our government. These include: 1) technical standards for data mining using anonymized data where possible; 2) appointing privacy officers to insure supervision through audit trails and congressional oversight; 3) exempting data searches based on particularized suspicion, non U.S. persons, foreign intelligence, and emergencies; and 4) requiring, under certain circumstances, permission from the Foreign Intelligence Surveillance Court." (*Wall Street Journal,* June 3, 2004, p. A14)

AUNT MILLIE. Derogatory term for an unsophisticated investor. See also BLUE-HAIRS.

AVERAGE DOWN. To continue to buy shares of stock or a mutual fund as the price decreases, thereby lowering the average cost per share.

AVERAGE UP. Stock market strategy of continuing to buy shares of stock or a mutual fund as the price rises, adding to a profitable position.

AX OR AXE (TO). Terminate from a job; eliminate. See also GET/ GIVE THE BOOT.

AX TO GRIND. Something a person is angry or upset about; a personal agenda.
"State law now permits corporate by-laws to set minimum experience requirements for directors, and to bar business competitors or corporate fraudsters from serving on company boards. In the name of 'shareholder democracy,' the SEC now proposes to let any group of dissidents with an ax to grind blow right past these sensitive limitations and place their advocates on the corporate ballot." (*Wall Street Journal,* Dec. 30, 2003, p. A10)

B

BABY BELLS. Nickname for the seven regional telephone companies created with the breakup of AT&T (MA BELL) in 1984.

BABY BOOMERS. The first generation of people born in the United States after World War II (1945–1964).
"The withdrawal of HH issues will create planning problems for many EE and E bondholders, especially as more baby boomers with these bonds start to retire, said Daniel Pederson, author of "Savings Bonds: When to Hold, When to Fold & Everything In-Between." (*Wall Street Journal,* July 29, 2004, p. D2)

BABY-BUST GENERATION. The low-birth-rate generation after BABY BOOMERS.
"Little wonder a lot of people shuddered at a widely quoted 1989 study, by Harvard's Gregory Mankiw and David Weil, that suggested real, or inflation-adjusted, home prices would fall 3% annually in the 20 years to 2007 as the baby-boomer demand crests and the smaller baby-bust generation comes to dominate the market." (*Wall Street Journal,* Nov. 29, 1999, p. 22)

BACK (TO). Support financially.

BACK AGAINST THE WALL. No place to go; a difficult situation.
"With his party's back against the wall, Liberal cabinet minister Pierre Pettigrew plays the ethnic card in Quebec, saying the Bloc Quebecois considers 'others' a threat to their identity. Gilles Duceppe counters that his party is inclusive, but sounds a strident separatist message." (*Macleans,* June 7, 2004, p. 23)

BACKBONE. Courage; in computing, the central parts of an electronic communication network.

BACK BURNER (ON THE). Kept in reserve; delayed, holding back.
"Bryant L. Van Brakle, secretary of the FMC, said the petitions to allow the NVOs to sign confidential contracts with shippers remain 'under active consideration. They're not on the back burner.'" (*Journal of Commerce,* August 3, 2004, p. 1)

BACKDOOR. Of questionable ethics; dishonest; a security vulnerability installed by a virus or Trojan that gives an attacker easier access to the computer system, often bypassing the installed security systems.
"Bush left for Europe and meets with an antiwar Pope John Paul II today. Berlusconi appealed for Iraq protesters to stay peaceful. Kerry accused the president of instituting a 'backdoor draft' by forcing troops to stay on duty longer than their enlistment." (*Wall Street Journal,* June 4, 2004, p. A1)

BACKDOOR SELLING. Secretive actions by a salesperson to influence other members of a buying center.

BACK END. The part of a business concerned with production and distribution. Consumers see the FRONT END but not the back end.

BACK-END LOAD FUND. A mutual fund that charges investors a fee to sell shares. Contingent deferred sales charges is the formal name for back-end fees.

BACK-END STRATEGIES. Operational decisions regarding how responses to direct marketing offers will be fulfilled. Also called fulfillment.

BACKFILL. The person brought in to replace someone on a job.

BACKFIRE. Produce results opposite of those expected.

"Most people tend to underestimate others' willingness to be generous in the workplace, so people are often reluctant to ask for assistance, Mr. Flynn adds. And spending too much time helping others can backfire by cutting into one's own productivity or hurting relationships." (*Wall Street Journal,* August 31, 2004, p. B6)

BACKFIRED. A plan that did not work and hurt the originator.

BACK IN THE SADDLE AGAIN. In control again.

BACKLASH. A negative reaction.

"Carriers who fail to invest in the proper network technology will face a customer backlash in today's competitive environment." (*America's Network,* Feb. 1, 1996, p. 2)

BACK OFF. Slow down; moderate.

"The Irish rock star's advocacy group runs radio ads in Rep. [A Nussle]'s Iowa district to protest his fiscal 2005 budget's cuts in global aid and AIDS relief. Bono aides call the ads a warning to White House and Congress not to back off [Bush]'s promised increases." (*Wall Street Journal,* April 30, 2004, p. A4)

BACK OUT OF. Cancel a deal previously agreed upon.

BACKSEAT DRIVER. Constant critic; person giving unwanted advice.

"Drive Buys/Audi A8L—Limousine Luxury, Even for Back-Seat Drivers." (*Wall Street Journal,* July 21, 2000, p. W11C)

BACK TAXES. Taxes that are owed or overdue.

BACK TO SQUARE ONE, BACK TO THE DRAWING BOARD. Starting over.

"Now it's back to square one. Our allies, the Poles and Spaniards, had expected to win the $500 million deal and complained publicly about the award. Both had lobbied for the contract at the highest levels; both had assured their domestic publics that pork-barrel bounty would flow in excess from their countries' participation in the Iraq war." (*Wall Street Journal,* April 7, 2004, p. A19)

BACK TO THE SALT MINES. Back to work.

BACKYARD BARBEQUE THEORY. Monetary policy theory where additions to the money supply become "fuel" which suddenly flares up, overstimulating the economy.

BAD BLOOD. Distrust or ill will between people or groups based on past experiences.

BAD DEAL. Poor business transaction.

BAD EGG. A troublemaker.

BAD-MOUTH (TO). Be critical of someone who is not present.
    "It is not simply Mr. Clinton's China policy that has him in hot water. It is the way it illuminates his very idea of policy. Whether as a handy foil to berate Mr. Bush for insensitivity to human rights, a convenient source of campaign cash or, now, a vehicle to bad-mouth the Reagan and Bush administrations, the Clinton China policy from the first has been subsumed into the permanent campaign." (*Wall Street Journal,* March 17, 1999, p. 1)

BAD PAPER. Worthless money or checks.

BAG OF SNAKES. A business situation that has been full of unfavorable surprises.

BAIL OUT. Sell an investment without regard to the price.
    "Under the plan, expected to be announced next week, China Huarong will bring in outside auditors to help sort out D'Long's web of investments and debt, the central banker said. He said authorities haven't decided how to reorganize the company and haven't earmarked any specific amount of loans to bail out the group. 'No one has a clear idea about how many assets D'Long still possesses and how much money is needed to restructure the company,' the central banker said." (*Wall Street Journal,* August 26, 2004, p. A11)

BAILOUT. Financial support or rescue.
    "Daiei Inc. will present its latest revival plan to its main lenders later this week, in what might lead to the third major bailout in less than four years for the debt-burdened retailer." (*Wall Street Journal,* August 25, 2004, p. 1)

BAIT-AND-SWITCH. An unethical sales technique wherein low-priced goods are advertised but not available when customers come to the store. On the Internet, bait-and-switch techniques involve the use of keywords such as free, sale, or sex in order to get search engines to list a site and trick viewers into purchases of the site's offerings.

"Sen. Rick Santorum (R., Pa.), a leading critic, joked darkly of becoming 'roadkill' in the bill's path. But fellow Republicans accused a 'suddenly righteous' White House of using 'bait and switch' tactics to make Mr. Bush look tough at their expense." (*Wall Street Journal,* Feb. 13, 2004, p. A2)

BAKE-OFF. Competitions among securities firms to gain the investment banking business of companies.

"The rule would curtail the common practice of securities firms having star analysts appear at pitch meetings, sometimes known as bake-offs, where corporate executives choose which of several competing securities firms will lead their company's initial public offering or other stock issue." (*Wall Street Journal,* June 6, 2002, p. C1)

BAKER'S DOZEN. Thirteen instead of twelve.

BALDRIGE AWARD. 1988 federal government—sponsored award to companies that excel at improving the quality of their products; named after former Secretary of Commerce Malcolm Baldrige. Corporations sometimes promote the fact that they have won a Baldrige Award in their marketing efforts.

BALLGAME. The overall business situation.

BALANCED SCORECARD. Management accountability system providing objectives and performance review.

"With a balanced scorecard approach, CEOs and boards of directors can communicate their strategy throughout the organization, the strategy can be measured and monitored, and any necessary operational changes can be identified and implemented on a timely basis." (*Best's Review,* Jan. 2005, p. 82)

BALLISTIC (TO GO). Become very angry.

"The shop also crafted the much-maligned Coke campaign in 2000, which featured a crotchety wheelchair-bound grandmother going ballistic at a family reunion when she discovers there's no Coke." (*Wall Street Journal,* June 16, 2004, p. B5)

BALL OF FIRE. Highly energetic.

BALL OF WAX. Everything included.

BALLOON NOTE / PAYMENT. A loan with a large final payment. Some mortgage loans are made on a 15- or 30-year payment basis, but come due in a shorter period with a large single payment.

BALLPARK ESTIMATE / FIGURE. A quickly calculated estimate of costs.
"I do think members of the administration have willfully deceived the public and Congress about the costs of the Iraqi war and its aftermath. And they continue to do so. Just last week, the administration's new budget director, Joshua Bolten, refused to give Congress even a ballpark estimate of costs for fiscal-year 2004—which begins in less than two months. 'Why?' asked Democratic Sen. Joe Biden of Delaware. 'Simply because we don't know what they will be,' Mr. Bolten said. 'Oh, come on now!' Sen. Biden replied." (*Wall Street Journal,* August 5, 2003, p. A4)

BALLS. Nerve, courage.

BALONEY. Nonsense; boastful language.

BANANA PROBLEM. Not knowing when to stop, derived from the story about a child who knew how to spell banana but did not know when to stop; technology slang for a problem that does not require a great deal of expertise; something even a gorilla could handle.

BANDWIDTH. A measure of electronic transmission capability. Bandwidth dictates the amount of digital information or data that can be transmitted.

BANG FOR THE BUCK. The most impact or results for one's money.
"'With a better tone to the overall market, the feeling was the correction had run its course,' said Michael Metz, chief investment strategist at Oppenheimer & Co., 'and you'd get your biggest bang for the buck by going into small stocks, which still haven't given up their leadership.'" (*Wall Street Journal,* Nov. 13, 2003, p. C10)

BANG-UP JOB. Very good performance.

BANKER'S ACCEPTANCE. A short-term credit instrument commonly used in international transactions. A bank guarantees the future payment for an international sale, creating a security sold at a discount against the value of the future payment.

BANKROLL. To finance a business deal; a sum of money.

BANK RUN. See RUN.

BANNER. A small ad appearing on a Web page.

BANNER YEAR. Best year ever.
"Stuart Miller, Lennar's president and chief executive, said strong demand and constraints to supply, along with favorable interest rates, were setting up a banner year for Lennar and other home builders. The company increased its earnings forecast for the year to $5.30 a share from $5.25 a share." (*Wall Street Journal,* March 17, 2004, p. 1)

BARBELL STRATEGY. The balancing of small margins on hot-selling products with higher margins on slower-selling products.
"Now, however, a couple of trends seem to be converging, analysts say, that appear to be cutting away at the 'barbell strategy' Wall Street has hoped computer makers would pull off." (*Wall Street Journal,* March 2, 1999, p. C1)

BAR CODE. Computerized electronic-scanning label on products.

BARE-BONE. Lean; without any extras.
"Cut to the bare-bone in the late 1980s and the early 1990s, corporate/institutional advertising programs that promote the name, image and reputation of the company rather than specific products or services, are undergoing a fundamental rethinking that appears to be positioning the programs for a strong rebound." (*Business Marketing,* Aug. 1994, p. 20)

BAREFOOT PILGRIM. A novice investor who has depleted his or her assets through poor stock market investment decisions.

BARGAIN-BASEMENT. Cheap, inexpensive. Macy's department store in New York City was famous for bargains that could be found in its basement store area.
"But unlike Wal-Mart, Carrefour didn't build its reputation in its home market as the retailer that offered the lowest prices, analysts say. Rather, Carrefour's claim to fame for years was a massive array of quality goods in one place—at reasonable, rather than bargain-basement prices." (*Wall Street Journal,* Feb. 26, 2004, p. B2)

BARGAINING CHIP. Something else that can be offered in business negotiations. For example, in stalled negotiations, a seller could offer owner financing to entice the buyer to make the purchase.

"Four U.S. oil companies—Marathon Oil Co. and ConocoPhillips of Houston, Amerada Hess Corp. of New York and Occidental Petroleum Co. of Los Angeles—greeted yesterday's statement with enthusiasm. All have been chafing to return to Libya since they were forced to abandon lucrative operations when sanctions were imposed in 1986. Libya has held the U.S. assets in trust the past 18 years as a bargaining chip in its efforts to get sanctions lifted." (*Wall Street Journal,* Feb. 27, 2004, p. A7)

BARKING UP THE WRONG TREE. Asking or speaking with the wrong person or with someone who has already made his or her decision.

BARNBURNER. Exciting contest.

BARNEY DEAL. A business transaction that does not make sense, done to appear to be doing something.

BARN RAISING. A cooperative effort to help neighbors or colleagues.

BAROMETER STOCK. A stock whose price movements are representative of general market conditions.

BARON COMPANY. A technology company located in a rural area.

BASELINE. Parameter against which a project can be evaluated.

BASE-TENDING. Protecting one's interests.

BASH. Big party. See also SHINDIG.
"At the 1996 Summer Games in Atlanta, Mattress Mac, a.k.a. Jim McIngvale, lobbied IOC members in his hospitality suite. The flamboyant Houston furniture-store owner invited the IOC members to a big bash attended by Carl Lewis and other well-known athletes." (*Wall Street Journal,* Feb. 26, 1999, p. B1)

BASIS. The cost of an investment. The basis includes the price paid plus any expenses associated with the purchase and is used to determine capital gains or losses.

BASIS POINTS. Fractions of 1 percent. One hundred basis points equals 1 percent.

BASKET CASE. A hopeless situation or person.

"Thus Mr. Paternot describes [Ace Greenberg] performing card tricks for his new prize Bear Stearns client on the day of Wall Street's hottest IPO ever. Elsewhere he refers to a prominent internet CEO as an emotional basket case." (*Wall Street Journal,* August 27, 2001, p. A13)

BAT AROUND. Discuss.

BAT A THOUSAND. Be successful every time; in baseball to bat a thousand means to get a hit every time at bat.

BATH (TO TAKE A). Lose a lot of money.

BATTING AVERAGE. Percentage of the time one is successful (baseball).

"What if a ballplayer's strikeouts didn't count against his batting average? Well, that's pretty much what's happening with many stock mutual funds." (*Wall Street Journal,* August 1, 2004, p. 1)

BAUD. The speed of a communications line, expressed in changes per second.

BAUD BARF. The screeching sound produced when a computer is connecting to a network or when a telephone line is connected to the Internet.

BEAMER, BEEMER. A BMW car; an IBM employee.

BEAN COUNTER. A low-level clerk; negative reference to an accountant.

"The 2002 farm bill opened the CSP to all eligible farms, just as programs like Medicare are open to all eligible. 'If implemented as originally envisioned ... the CSP could cost as much to operate in any given year as do traditional farm programs now,' Department of Agriculture Economic Research Service economist Katherine R. Smith (speaking for herself, not the agency) told a conference last month. Bean counters initially put the price tag at $2 billion over 10 years, then upped it to $7 billion." (*Wall Street Journal,* July 22, 2004, p. A2)

BEAN TOWN. Boston, Massachusetts.

BEAR. Investor who thinks the stock market will decline.

"Furniture makers are moving production overseas as quickly as they can, but it is unlikely they can close the pricing gap. Labor costs are such a large part of the business. Exacerbating the situation, furniture makers have been neglecting information technology investment, bears argue." (*Wall Street Journal,* Oct. 22, 2003, p. C1)

BEARDING. The practice by investors attempting to take over a company of hiding their purchases of the company's stock by dividing the orders into smaller lots and using multiple stock brokers.

BEAR HUG. The rescue of a company from a hostile takeover by a WHITE KNIGHT.
"By Friday afternoon, rumors were swirling in Las Vegas that a deal was in the making, says Joe Greff, an analyst with Fulcrumb Global Partners LLC, who was in Las Vegas then. MGM Mirage's Mr. Terry Lanni sent Mandalay a so-called bear hug letter—an unsolicited offer proposing terms for a sale—and the companies put out terse press releases." (*Wall Street Journal,* June 7, 2004, p. B1)

BEAR MARKET. A stock market in general decline.
"Buyers on WALL STREET have gone into hibernation and technology stocks are approaching bear-market status." (*Wall Street Journal,* August 20, 2004, p. C1)

BEAT A DEAD HORSE. Continue to argue/discuss an issue that cannot be resolved.

BEAT AROUND THE BUSH. Avoid getting to the point.

BEATING THE GUN. Gaining an advantage through a quick response.

BEATS ME! I do not know.

BEAT THE BUSHES. Search everywhere; aggressively market even in rural or unlikely places.
"How to Sell How-To Books—Market Them as Instruction For Idiots and Dummies; Beat the Bushes for Topics" (*Wall Street Journal,* March 14, 2001, p. B1)

BEAT THE LITTLE GUY. Take advantage of a smaller competitor.

BEEF UP. Expand, make stronger.
"GM Chief Financial Officer John Devine, speaking at an industry conference in Traverse City, Mich., said the test is more extreme

than the tests GM uses. GM recalled the Saturn vehicles voluntarily to 'beef up their suspensions,' he said. 'We are moving aggressively,' Mr. Devine said." (*Wall Street Journal,* Aug. 6, 2004, p. A3)

BE FLAT. To have sold all. See also WORK OUT.

BEGGAR-THY-NEIGHBOR. An international trade strategy
based on frequent currency devaluations designed to make exports
cheaper and imports more expensive.

BEHIND THE EIGHT-BALL. Under pressure (billiards); in a
highly disadvantageous position.
    "Let's make this simple. Aside from scandals, the one remaining
domestic issue that packs real political punch this year is patient
rights. And patient rights—particularly the struggle between
health-maintenance organizations and those who rely on them for
health care—happens to be the one issue on which Republicans
have planted themselves squarely behind the eight ball." (*Wall
Street Journal,* July 15, 1998, p. A1)

BELL COW. Someone who influences others. In a dairy herd, the
bell cow is the lead cow that the other cows follow.

BELL-RINGER. Exciting, new high; door-to-door salesperson.

BELLS AND WHISTLES. Features, details.
    "While the firm counts large corporations and law firms among its
clients, 'we find many smaller trials are using technology,' Mr. Paul
Neale says. 'You don't have to have 12 flat screen monitors or all
the bells and whistles to use the technology. Some savvy plaintiffs
and criminal defense lawyers representing clients in minor cases
just use a document camera and a projector.'" (*Wall Street Journal,*
May 26, 2004, p. A1)

BELLWETHER INDUSTRY. An industry whose performance
serves as a leading indicator for the overall economy.
    "OPIC has provided financing or insurance for more than $900
million in current foreign direct investment in Venezuela, he said.
'We are generally a very important catalyst for investment ... and
a bellwether for political risk in a country.'" (*Wall Street Journal,*
July 15, 2004, p. A9)

BELLY UP (TO GO). Bankrupt.
    "They're limited partnerships and other direct-participation pro-
grams are again. Before you buy, here's what you need to know. Sold

mainly by financial planners. Minimum investments can be as low as $1,000 in an IRA. Easy to buy into but can be tough to exit, making them suitable only for investors who can stomach illiquidity. Many limited partnerships went belly-up in the '70s and '80s." (*Wall Street Journal,* April 7, 2004, p. D1)

BELOW BOOK. Less than list price; less than the value of a company's assets.

"CNA, a property and casualty insurer, could be reviving from a few years of poor financial performance. Last week, its shares rose by more than two points, to $28, on news of solid fourth-quarter profit, but it still trades below book value of $33 a share. Haggar, a maker of men's pants, has been near $20, below book value of $24." (*Wall Street Journal,* Feb. 15, 2004, p. 4)

BELOW PAR. Less than face value. Bonds selling at less than maturity value (usually $1,000) are selling below par.

BELOW THE BELT. Nasty; unfair. In boxing, a punch below the belt is illegal and can lead to disqualification.

BELT-TIGHTENING. Cost-cutting. See also DOWNSIZING.

"Dow Chemical said a 12% increase in sales prices and an 8% increase in volume helped make up for a 15% rise in costs for the natural gas and crude oil used to produce plastics and chemicals. As part of its belt-tightening program, Dow Chemical slashed some administrative and other expenses in the latest quarter by 14% from a year earlier." (*Wall Street Journal,* Jan. 20, 2004, p. A1)

BELTWAY BANDITS. Consultants working in the Washington, DC, area, technically with offices inside the Beltway (Interstate 495 and a section of I-95).

BENCHMARKING. Measuring performance by comparing to industry leaders.

"Other recent reports also found fault with peer reviews. A report issued last August by former Securities and Exchange Commission Chairman Richard Breeden, as part of his duties as the corporate monitor of WorldCom Inc., now known as MCI, warned about the implications that benchmarking can have for executives' pay. 'Excessive compensation often results from "benchmarking" exercises, which seek to identify certain percentiles of pay, Mr. Breeden's report says.'" (*Wall Street Journal,* April 12, 2004, p. R4)

BENCH STRENGTH. Other personnel available to assist or take over from current leaders (baseball).

"Other CEOs who are shopping for COOs—often at the behest of boards concerned about building bench strength for succession choices—are having more difficulty than they expected." (*Wall Street Journal,* May 11, 2004, p. B1)

BENCH WARMER. A person who is not among the top performers (baseball).

BEND OVER BACKWARD. To do whatever is necessary or possible.

BEN FRANKLINS. One-hundred-dollar bills, which show the face of Benjamin Franklin.

BENT HIS OR HER PICK. Made a mistake.

BEST PRACTICE. Leading methods or strategies used in an industry.

"Best Practices LLC (BP) has perfected a strategy for stealing the effective business practices of successful companies. BP, a consultancy and benchmarking group in Chapel Hill, North Carolina, routinely plunders other companies' ideas and adapts them for its own use." (*Inc.,* July, 2001, p. 62)

BETA FACTOR / COEFFICIENT. Stock market measure of price variability. A statistical measure of the relative risk of a common stock compared with the market for all stocks.

"A similar concern is a fund's expenses. The higher they are, the higher the annual fees you will pay. Past performance is another key issue. You should also consider a fund's beta factor. Beta measures a fund's volatility relative to the overall market." (*Medical Economics,* April 11, 2003, p. 59)

BET THE FARM / RANCH. To risk everything.

"It's hard to find anyone opposed to the idea of replacing factories of failure like Bushwick High. But activists who favor school 'accountability' through testing and tougher academic standards warn that New York's approach could be a distraction. 'I wouldn't bet the farm on small schools,' says Michael Cohen, president of Achieve Inc., an advocacy group backed by corporations and state governors concerned that U.S. students aren't learning the skills they'll need in college and the workplace." (*Wall Street Journal,* Sept. 4, 2003, p. B1)

BETTING ON THE OUTCOME. Not knowing the end result but wagering on what one believes it will be.

BETWEEN A ROCK AND A HARD PLACE. A difficult situation that presents impossible or unpleasant options for escape.
"Now a proposed biotech research park threatens to drive a wedge between Dr. Becker and some community leaders, including the Rev. Tuggle. Hopkins officials support the idea of creating a 22-acre research park in East Baltimore; the Rev. Tuggle opposes it. Community activists are against the park, proposed for a site north of the Hopkins campus, because many residents have been evicted and others must move to make way for it. Such disputes 'put me in between a rock and a hard place,' says Dr. Becker. 'It's very hard being the person who worked on pulling all this together with the pastors.'" (*Wall Street Journal,* August 9, 2004, p. B1)

BETWEEN JOBS. Unemployed.

BIBLE BELT. A region populated largely by people of conservative, religious-oriented values. Geographically, the area bounded by Virginia, Florida, and Texas is generally considered the Bible Belt in the United States.
"Stumping on behalf of his tax hike, Mr. Bob Riley, a Southern Baptist, has tried to appeal to the spiritual side of voters in his Bible Belt state. 'According to our Christian ethics,' he's fond of saying, 'we're supposed to love God, love each other and help take care of the poor.'" (*Wall Street Journal,* August 25, 2003, p. A10)

BID-TO-COVER RATIO. The ratio of the number of bids for Treasury securities compared to the number accepted at Treasury auctions.

BIG APPLE. New York City.

BIG BITE. Large amount.
"Sony's operating income—revenue minus the cost of sales as well as administrative and advertising expenses—fell 41%, as a strengthening yen against the dollar and restructuring charges took a big bite out of profit." (*Wall Street Journal,* July 29, 2004, p. B4)

BIG BLUE. International Business Machines, IBM.
"IBM has been a big booster of Linux since 2000, viewing open-source programs as a way for its consultants to sell more of Big Blue's hardware and software programs. The new program for Brazil

standardizes the service in what IBM views as a large potential market." (*Wall Street Journal,* June 14, 2004, p. B5)

BIG BOARD. New York Stock Exchange.

"Selling was broad. Transportation stocks fell on concerns about oil prices and higher fuel costs. AMR, parent of American Airlines, lost 46 cents, or 5.8%, to 7.52, on the New York Stock Exchange. Continental Airlines fell 58 cents, or 6.4%, to 8.52, Delta Air Lines slid 19 cents, or 4.1%, to 4.50; and Alaska Air Group shed 79 cents, or 3.8%, to 19.91, all on the Big Board. Northwest Airlines lost 29 cents, or 3.4%, to 8.32." (*Wall Street Journal,* August 6, 2003, p. C3)

BIG-BOX STORE. A large-format store, typically one that has a plain, box-like exterior and at least 100,000 square feet of retail space.

BIG BROTHER. Powerful authoritarian force, usually the government, that monitors and directs people's actions. The term is derived from George Orwell's classic book, *1984.*

"On June 13, Michel Staszewski, a high-school history teacher who is opposed to electronic voting, paraded along a voting line in a Brussels school. 'This system is like Big Brother,' he said. 'You never find out if your vote is ever counted.' He handed out pamphlets and requested signatures on a petition. But the citizens he was courting didn't pay much attention." (*Wall Street Journal,* July 28, 2004, p. 1)

BIG BUCKS. A lot of money.

BIG CHEESE. Important person.

BIG D. Dallas, Texas.

BIG ENCHILADA. Significant person.

BIG FISH/CHEESE. Important person or company.

"They have an unusual status at the agency. Their authority is magnified because the agency's lawyers and accountants 'won't second-guess them,' a former SEC official said. They are big fish in a little pond." (*Wall Street Journal,* March 12, 2004, p. C1)

BIG FOUR. The four largest accounting firms in the United States.

BIG LEAGUES. Important people; large, dominant organizations (baseball).

"TOM is heading for the main board as early as next month, with three other top-10 GEM-listed companies also preparing to head to the big leagues." (*Wall Street Journal,* June 10, 2004, p. C16)

BIG PICTURE. The overall view of things.

"Generally, though, when wealthy donors budget how much to give to charity, they are 'not adjusting upward for the fact that they have more assets,' says Tim D. Stone, NewTithing's executive director. 'A lot of people, when they think about how much they are donating or want to donate to charity, they aren't really thinking of the big picture of all their wealth,' adds Claude Rosenberg, a retired money manager who founded and is chairman of NewTithing." (*Wall Street Journal,* April 22, 2004, p. D21)

BIG SIX. Six largest U.S. accounting firms, now down to the BIG FOUR.

"Leading accountants Ernst & Young have called for an independent regulator of auditors, breaking rank with the remainder of the Big Six which would rather continue with the existing system of self-regulation." (*Management Today,* Aug. 1995, p. 12)

BIG THREE. The three largest U.S. automobile manufacturing firms: Ford, General Motors, and DaimlerChrysler.

"Reading the News: S&P Downshifts Ford's Debt Rating; Move Reflects Skepticism About a Big 3 Turnaround; Still, Investors Are Relieved" (*Wall Street Journal,* Nov. 13, 2003, p. A3)

BIG-TICKET ITEMS. High-priced goods.

BIG-TIME SPENDER. Extravagant consumer.

BIG WHEEL/SHOT. Manager; important person; a person who thinks he or she is important.

BILLED AS. Advertised as.

BIMBO. An attractive woman not known for her intellect.

"Not merely Monica [Lewinsky]. But all the other women who've passed through the Clinton vortex. The Clinton camp itself long ago dubbed these incidents 'bimbo eruptions,' suggesting mere dalliances." (*Wall Street Journal,* Oct. 26, 1998, p. 1)

BINDING ARBITRATION. A legal dispute resolution mechanism where people who have a conflict present their evidence to an independent authority, the arbitrator (not a judge), and agree in advance to abide by the ruling of the arbitrator. Many contracts now contain binding arbitration clauses as a means of avoiding the legal costs and lengthy delays associated with litigation.

BINGO CARD. Reader's enquiry card in a magazine.
"A simmering controversy is bubbling to the surface on the roll of bonus leads derived from bingo cards." (*Advertising Age's Business Marketing,* April 1995, p. 1)

BIRD DOG (TO). Track down; stay focused on a project.

BIRD DOG FEE. Payment for information leading to a sale.

BIRD DOGS. Spotters. People who identify potential customers for salespeople.

BIRD IN THE HAND. Accessible or available now. Short for the old saying, "a bird in the hand is worth two in the bush."
"It's a 'bird in hand' strategy that is spreading its wings." (*Wall Street Journal,* July 28, 2004, p. C1)

BIRDS (FOR THE). Worthless.

BIRDYBACK. Transportation system using both airplanes and trucks.

BIT BARFING. Overwhelming Web site visitors with extensive information regardless of whether the information is needed or asked for.

BIT BUCKET. A fictional bottomless pit into which vital electronic messages and files fall when something in the system fails.

BITCH SESSION. Meeting where employees express their complaints. Management rarely encourages bitch sessions, but sometimes meetings turn into them.

BITE THE BULLET. Go ahead with a difficult task even though it might be expensive.
"Technology and media investors have a dearth of companies in their universe growing as rapidly as Google, which doubled its revenue in the past year. Many may elect to bite the bullet and pay the expected high price for Google shares next month." (*Wall Street Journal,* July 29, 2004, p. C1)

BITE THE DUST. Fail; die.

"When he scrolled upon breaking news that Tim Koogle will give up his job as Yahoo! Inc. chief executive, Mr. Paternot shot his fists in the air like a sports fan, yelling, Yeah! Another one bites the dust!" (*Wall Street Journal,* May 2, 2001, p. A1)

BITE YOUR TONGUE. Be quiet, say nothing.

BLACKBALL/BLACKLIST (TO). Refuse to allow someone to work, join, or gain access to a group.

"Russia's mini-crisis was sparked in May when regulators used a new money-laundering law to revoke the license of medium-size Sodbiznesbank. The move sparked panic, as rumors of blacklists swirled and banks stopped lending to each other, provoking a liquidity squeeze." (*Wall Street Journal,* July 16, 2004, p. C1)

BLACK BOX. Unknown, complex technology or a situation where decisions are made without full information.

"One reason: The company's AHL division, which uses a 'black box' quantitative investment strategy in several different funds, is believed to have about $7.5 billion in assets, though the company doesn't disclose its size." (*Wall Street Journal,* March 5, 2004, p. C3)

BLACK HOLE. A project with significant cost overruns (astronomy).

BLACK KNIGHT. Bad guy; initiator of a hostile takeover.

BLACK MARKET. Illegal buying and selling of products. See also PARALLEL ECONOMY.

BLACK MONDAY. October 19, 1987, when the DOW JONES INDUSTRIAL AVERAGE fell 508 points, or over 20 percent.

"The Dow Industrials' plunge of 684.81 was their worst-ever point drop, but it ranked only 14th among the average's worst percentage declines, falling well short of its 22.61% plunge on Black Monday, Oct. 19, 1987." (*Wall Street Journal,* Sept. 18, 2001, p. A1)

BLACK TUESDAY. The October 29, 1929, stock market crash. The stock market crash symbolized the beginning of the Great Depression, though a downturn in the economy had already started.

BLAMESTORMING. Sitting around discussing why a deadline was missed or a project failed and who to blame. A play on the word brainstorming.

BLANK CHECK. Total freedom of action; money provided without restrictions.

"In a second ruling, the Court said that Yaser Esam Hamdi, an American citizen seized by U.S. allies in Afghanistan in 2001, was entitled to 'a meaningful opportunity to contest the factual basis' for his incarceration, though it ruled that the president was authorized to seize and hold him and other prisoners under a congressional resolution passed in the wake of Sept. 11. 'A state of war is not a blank check for the President when it comes to the rights of the nation's citizens,' Justice Sandra Day O'Connor wrote in the case." (*Wall Street Journal,* June 29, 2004, p. A1)

BLANKET (TO). Cover an area thoroughly and in detail.

"The deal signals an eagerness to blanket the credit-card market, filling consumers' wallets with cards, whether or not they carry the Citigroup name. In turn, Citigroup will then attempt to cross-sell such cardholders other Citigroup products such as mortgages and consumer loans." (*Wall Street Journal,* July 16, 2003, p. A13)

BLEED. Extract large amounts of money from someone.

BLEED AD. A newspaper or magazine ad with graphics that go to the edge of the page.

BLEEDING EDGE. A more extreme cutting edge or leading edge.

"So new, its creators aren't entirely sure where it's headed." ("25 Hot Buzzwords," Kate Lorenz, MSNCareerbuilder.com, July 21, 2004)

BLEM. Abbreviation for problem.

BLIND AUCTION. Sealed-bid auction.

BLINDSIDE (TO). Surprise an opponent.

"Mr. Baucus took pains not to blindside his GOP colleagues, as Democrats complain Republican leaders did to them in the House." (*Wall Street Journal,* Oct. 24, 2001, p. A2)

BLIND TRUST. Financial management agreement wherein the trustee has complete control over investment of funds. Politicians in the United States frequently put their assets in a blind trust in order to avoid a conflict of interest when making government policies that affect business.

"Sen. Bill Frist's purportedly blind trust is in fact quite transparent since the documents showing his immediate family's holdings in HCA are publicly available. The disclosure shows investments in the range of $10.1 million to $30.3 million or more." (*Wall Street Journal,* April 20, 2004, p. A21)

BLING. Expensive or extravagant jewelry worn in excessive amounts; a gaudy or tasteless display of wealth.

"Many of today's popular TV shows, from 'Entertainment Tonight' and 'Access Hollywood' to practically anything on the E Channel, suggest we've become a bling-bling society. TV specials showcase the opulence of our favorite entertainers—Ben Affleck, Jennifer Lopez, Will Smith, etc. Newscasts report the price of diamonds and other jewelry worn by stars at popular award shows. Davey. D, 'Fixation on bling-bling isn't limited to hip-hop,'" (*San Jose Mercury News,* August 8, 2003)

BLISTER THE COMPETITION. Outsell the other firms in a market.

"This is the way we can blister the competition." (Jami Martin, USC Corp. Nov. 23, 1995)

BLIVET. An unsolvable or out-of-control problem. The term is derived from World War II term meaning ten pounds of manure in a five-pound bag.

"An embarrassing bug at a sales pitch is a 'blivit.'" (*Wall Street Journal,* May 5, 2002, p. B1)

BLOCKBUSTER. A huge success.

"Late last month, St. Paul Travelers Cos., the insurer formed in April when Travelers closed its puzzling $17.8 billion deal to buy a shaky St. Paul Cos., announced what Morgan Stanley termed a 'blockbuster reserve charge' of $1.625 billion." (*Wall Street Journal,* August 4, 2004, p. C1)

BLOCK TRADE. The selling or buying of shares of stock in 100 share units. Trades of less than 100 shares are called odd-lot transactions.

BLOG. Web log.

"Blogs mostly catalog their creators' musings, with links to related sites, and as such they can be as hard to categorize as the people behind them." (*Wall Street Journal,* Nov. 18, 2002, p. R8)

BLOW BY BLOW. In complete detail (boxing).

BLOW HOT AND COLD. Waver, change one's opinion back and forth.

"John Hansen, president of the Nebraska Farmers Union, allows that the union, known for its populist bent, does have some criticism. One is that his experience, and that of some members, in Nebraska has been that the Farm Credit System blows hot and cold in its interest to make loans." (*ABA Journal,* Nov. 2003, p. 107)

BLOW-IN. An advertising piece inserted in but not bound into a magazine.

BLOW SMOKE. To attempt to deceive.

BLOW THE WHISTLE. Attempt to stop something by reporting it to authorities. See also WHISTLE-BLOWER.
"Executives aren't required to tattle on their own companies, but 'if you did something you know was wrong, you may want to go to the government and get immunity or leniency,' says Seth Taube, the Securities and Exchange Commission's former enforcement chief for New York. 'The earlier you blow the whistle, the better deal you get.'" (*Wall Street Journal,* April 21, 2004, p. C1)

BLUE-BOOK VALUE. Market value of automobiles. Refers to Kelley's "Blue Book" of automobile prices.

BLUE-CHIP. Top quality, highest. In poker, the blue chip is the highest-valued chip.
"The Dow industrials, meanwhile, rose 110.32 points, or 1.1%, to 10083.15, marking the 22nd time the blue-chip index has crossed 10000 at closing since it first topped that mark in March 1999. The average still is down 3.6% for the year." (*Wall Street Journal,* August 19, 2004, p. C1)

BLUE-COLLAR WORKER. Laborer, usually in manufacturing or services, where traditional dress codes often called for blue shirts or uniforms. Often used, or misused, to make a general social class distinction with WHITE-COLLAR.

BLUE-HAIRS. Elderly women consumers.

BLUE IN THE FACE (TO TALK UNTIL) Exhausted and frustrated.

BLUE LAWS. Local or state regulations restricting some types of business activities on Sunday. Foreign visitors to the BIBLE BELT are often bemused to find they cannot buy liquor on Sunday in some parts of the region. The term is derived from the nineteenth-century, when "blue" meant drunk or lewd.

"A proposal to end South Carolina's blue laws, which restrict business on Sundays, would solve a hairy problem at the Columbiana Centre mall in Columbia." (*Wall Street Journal,* Oct. 23, 1996, p. S1)

BLUE RIBBON PROGRAM/COMMISSION. Top quality; highly regarded.

BLUE SCREEN OF DEATH. A blue screen error message that appears on computer monitors when a fatal error occurs.

BLUESHIRTS. IBM employees. See also BIG BLUE.
"The blueshirts from Armonk (N.Y.) descended on the personal-computer division in Boca Raton (Fla.), crushing its autonomy and, by default, turning the market over to a multitude of competitors." (*Wall Street Journal,* May 30, 1996, p. A11)

BLUE-SKY LAWS. State securities laws requiring sellers of new stock issues to register and provide financial information about the company.
"Unlike Mr. Blum, they haven't demonstrated that investors relied on the research, leaning instead on state 'blue-sky laws,' which require brokerage firms to fairly disclose material facts to investors. The term stemmed from the belief that if investors weren't adequately protected, they could be sold anything—including the 'blue sky' itself." (*Wall Street Journal,* March 17, 2004, p. C1)

BLUE STREAK. Very rapid.

BLUETOOTH. Name of a wireless technology which, like Wi-Fi, allows wireless connection to computers over a short distance.
"Originating from a Danish king's name, the term Bluetooth describes another wireless technology, different from Wi-Fi." (*Wall Street Journal,* December 4, 2002, p. D5)

BLURB. A brief announcement about a product.

BOAT ANCHOR. Something, usually a piece of equipment, that is useless.

BO DEREK. A perfect stock or investment. The term comes from the 1979 film *10,* in which actress Bo Derek portrays the "perfect" woman.

BODY LANGUAGE. Nonverbal communication.

BOGEY. A target; also a budget bogey, which is a budget limit.

BOGUS. False, fraudulent.
"'Who am I kidding?' says an unemployed chief financial officer. 'Everyone knows that I'm looking for a job. It's bogus to pretend that all I really want is information.'" (*Wall Street Journal,* August 10, 2004, p. B4)

BOHICA. Bend over, here it comes again.
"Eileen C. Shapiro discusses how to determine if one's organization is being hurt by 'bohica,' which she defines euphemistically as 'bow out, here it comes again,' and refers to an increasingly common employee coping strategy for dealing with the steady stream of new and improved programs and slogans. Shapiro argues that poor employee attitude might indicate that managers have failed to ensure that the newest program or slogan could pass the bohica audit." (*Wall Street Journal,* Feb. 26, 1996, p. A12)

BOILERPLATE. Standard legal language used in contracts.
"United Policyholders, a 12-year-old advocacy group that represents consumers and commercial-insurance buyers, maintains the boilerplate disclosures brokers provide aren't enough, given a broker's role as a buyer's representative. 'If you're going to tell me I've got to read the fine print, that's not what people are paying for,' said Amy Bach, executive director of the San Francisco group." (*Wall Street Journal,* August 11, 2004, p. C3)

BOILER ROOM. A questionable sales organization, usually in telephone marketing.
"Your May 10 editorial 'Headline Risk at the SEC' suggested the SEC has proposed mutual fund reforms merely for their 'headline value.' Unfortunately, since fraud at mutual funds was pervasive, far more than headlines are at stake. The funds called into question were not boiler-room operations: Fraud occurred at some of the biggest and most reputable fund companies. Anything less than a forceful response from policymakers would be irresponsible." (*Wall Street Journal,* May 17, 2004, p. A21)

BOILS DOWN TO. Essence; most important considerations.
"No matter how many 'issues' the GOP uses as bait, the party's underperformance among blacks is likely to continue so long as the negative perceptions do. 'What it boils down to,' says Mr. Nadler, 'is that Republicans don't have the guts to run the kind of hard-hitting program attacking Democrats on Democratic turf.'" (*Wall Street Journal,* July 28, 2004, p. A12)

BOIL THE OCEAN. To attempt something too ambitious.

BOMB (TO). Fail horrendously.

BOMBSHELL. Big surprise.
"With strong U.S. economic numbers—including the bombshell 8.2% gross-domestic-product growth number in the third quarter and November's brisk manufacturing survey, 'we are quite certain that rates are going up,' says Scott Hetzer, senior vice president and treasurer at Dominion Resources Inc., a Richmond, Virginia, energy producer." (*Wall Street Journal,* Dec. 4, 2003, p. C1)

BONA FIDE. In good faith (Latin); authentic.
"Instead, eBay is one of the bona fide hits of the Internet era and, in some ways, a global economy unto its own. Under Ms. Whitman's direction, the company has expanded into more than two dozen countries, creating a vast online marketplace where users sold $24 billion of electronics, appliances and other goods last year." (*Wall Street Journal,* August 5, 2004, p. B1)

BOOK ENTRY. Registration of stock ownership without issuing stock certificates.

BOOKS. Financial records.

BOOK THE GOODS. Place an order.

BOOK TO MARKET. The ratio of the BOOK VALUE to the market value of a company's equity.

BOOK VALUE. The value at which an asset is carried on the firm's balance sheet. Book value is calculated by subtracting liabilities and intangible assets (GOODWILL) from a company's assets.

BOOMERANG METHOD. Sales technique where the salesperson turns a buyer's objections into reasons to purchase the product.

BOOMERS. See BABY BOOMERS.

BOONDOGGLE. A special deal; questionable public spending.
"The demonstration projects for competition are really simply 'fig leaves' (as some of my former colleagues have privately admitted). I was in Congress long enough to know how demonstration projects really work. For liberal spending boondoggles, they become entrenched parts of the federal government. But, on needed reforms,

demonstration projects mean a quiet, obscure death." (*Wall Street Journal,* Nov. 21, 2003, p. A12)

BOOSTER SHOT. Stimulant or support.

"Positive statements by stock market analysts about a stock can boost the price of the stock. SEC Chairman William Donaldson called the new rules 'an important milestone' and predicted they will combat conflicts of interest that have plagued Wall Street's leading firms. 'Booster shot' reports will be banned by the new rules, preventing analysts from releasing upbeat research near the expiration of lock-up periods for stock holdings." (*Wall Street Journal,* July 30, 2003, p. C5)

BOOT (TO GIVE SOMEONE THE). Terminate, fire someone.

BOOT CAMP. Training facility or program (military).

"A new spa, the Mountain of Youth, opened in February outside of Atlanta. Weeklong 'boot camps' run $1,100 and include 12 hours of lectures on diet, nutrition and supplements as well as white-water rafting and horseback riding." (*Wall Street Journal,* August 13, 2003, p. D1)

BOOTH BUNNY. A sexist description of the attractive women hired by technology firms for industry trade shows.

"CTAM has not seen the dramatic collapse in attendance that most other industry trade shows have experienced. But other conventions more dependent on attendance by vendors and their booth bunnies, such as NCTA and NATPE, have seen attendance plunge 25–50%." (*Broadcasting & Cable,* July 21, 2003, p. 16)

BOOTSTRAP BUSINESS. A venture started with very little capital.

BOOTSTRAPPING. Starting or operating a business with very few resources.

"The problem: How to know when to ditch the bare-bones bootstrapping practices and behave like a grown-up business." (*Wall Street Journal,* August 3, 2004, p. B8)

BOOT UP (TO). Start a computer.

"The messages you got suggest that the computer isn't seeing the drive, and so it can't find Windows and can't boot up from the drive. This might mean the drive is corrupted, but it doesn't necessarily mean your data are lost or irretrievable." (*Wall Street Journal,* August 19, 2004, p. B4)

BORROWED UP. Having taken out loans up to the lender's limit.

BOTH SIDES OF THE AISLE. Involving both parties.

BOTS. Automated search robots.
"The bots collect the information and return it to be posted on the company's Bargain.com Web site." (*Wall Street Journal,* September 16, 2002, p. R13)

BOTTLENECK. Something that slows the production process.
"Higher inventory levels now could lead to slower growth later. Once companies have built enough of a buffer against supply shortages and production bottlenecks, they don't need to build it again." (*Wall Street Journal,* July 30, 2004, p. C1)

BOTTOM FISHING. Buying stocks that have significantly declined in value.
"'The rally we saw late in the day was nothing more than some bargain hunting and some bottom-fishing,' said Tim Smalls, senior stock trader at brokerage firm SG Cowen." (*Wall Street Journal,* Feb. 14, 2003, p. C1)

BOTTOM LINE. An accounting profit or loss; the main idea.
"If you hold company stock in your 401(k) and retire or change jobs, gains will be taxed at the lower capital-gains rate if you take the shares as a lump-sum distribution. Downside: You immediately have to pay income taxes—and possibly a tax penalty—on the stock's 'cost basis,' the value at which you acquired the shares.— Bottom line: This maneuver is worthwhile only if you have a big gain on the stock." (*Wall Street Journal,* August 18, 2004, p. D1)

BOTTOM OF THE BARREL. Last resort, last option available.
"The savings rate, which has had a sudden and sharp drop from an already low 2.7% in July to a near-bottom-of-the-barrel 1.2% in December, likely was flat in January." (*Wall Street Journal,* March 1, 2004, p. C1)

BOTTOM OF THE LINE. Least expensive; lowest quality. See TOP-OF-THE-LINE.

BOTTOM OUT (TO). Reach lowest point or price.
"'We should see a recovery in 2007 to 2008. Rents can't fall much further in new buildings, because if they do, the developers will go bust,' says Leslie Chua, an associate director at Jones Lang LaSalle, a real-estate services firm. 'I think we'll see rent prices

bottom out in 2005 to 2006,' says Mr. Chua." (*Wall Street Journal,* Dec. 10, 2003, p. B1)

BOTTOM-UP. Business analysis method where the whole is the sum of the individual parts.

BOUNCEBACK. An undelivered e-mail message.
"A bounceback is a message that has not been delivered. Non-delivery may be for reasons like a full in-box, address changes, new size limits on in-boxes, or e-mail address blocks." (*DMNews,* December 2, 2002, p. 2)

BOUNCE-BACK CARD. In marketing, a card prospective buyers submit to the company. Bounce-back cards provide leads for sales-people.

BOUNCE IDEAS. Share new ideas with others.

BOUTIQUE. A visible, specialized subdivision of a business.

BOXED IN. Having few or no choices; to narrow the possibilities.
"Help Wanted: How Much Longer Can Consumers Keep The Economy Afloat?—A Key Prop Is Threatened By Rise in Joblessness; Inventories Look Better—Boxed In at the White House." (*Wall Street Journal,* Sept. 10, 2001, p. A1)

BOXING PEOPLE. Placing people in categories, stereotyping.

BOZO FILTER. An e-mail filter that deletes messages from people or groups the recipient does not want to receive messages from.

BOZON. Stupidity; not genuine.

BRACKET CREEP. The tendency of inflation to push people into higher tax brackets.
"To prevent bracket creep, in which taxpayers are pushed into higher brackets simply because of inflation, Congress requires annual cost-of-living adjustments. Those adjustments are tied to the consumer price index." (*Wall Street Journal,* Sept. 18, 2002, p. D1)

BRADY BONDS. Dollar-denominated bonds issued during the George W. Bush administration, and used to assist Latin American countries in debt restructuring. The securities are named after Bush's Secretary of Treasury, Nicholas Brady.

"Before Mexico became the first sovereign borrower last month to adopt collective-action clauses in a bond subject to New York law, a unanimous agreement by bondholders was required in the U.S. to make payment adjustments. However, bondholders could alter nonpayment terms via exit consents where a simple majority could render the old bonds too unattractive for holdout creditors to keep. Such consents were used in Ecuador's Brady bond debt restructuring in 2000, which garnered a 97% participation rate." (*Wall Street Journal,* March 12, 2003, p.1)

BRAIN CHECK. A mental error.

BRAIN DRAIN. The loss of talented people to other countries or areas where there are better opportunities.

"There was no significant difference in the number of articles published from 1985 to 1989 by researchers now based in the U.K. and U.S. However, the mean number of citations per article was significantly higher for those scientists now based in the U.S. than for those now in the U.K. These data suggest that the U.K. government is correct in considering the 'brain drain' of scientists a serious issue." (*Nature*, Sept. 7, 2000, p.13)

BRAINPOWER. Knowledge, creativity.

"New industry brainpower may help. Wal-Mart recently hired an outside consultancy to help tackle its fashion problems, including the George line." (*Wall Street Journal,* July 2, 2004, p. B1)

BRAINSTORMING. Group creative thinking; sharing wild ideas.

"Mr. Mohammed told interrogators that the discussion of U.S. targets began in the early-to-mid-1990s between him and his nephew Ramzi Yousef, architect of the 1993 attack on the World Trade Center. The two 'would think about what drives the U.S. economy when brainstorming about potential targets,' the summary states. Mr. Mohammed 'listed Hollywood, automobiles and wheat as major contributors to the U.S. economy,' the summary states." (*Wall Street Journal,* June 17, 2004, p. A1)

BRAIN TRUST. A group of experts in a discipline who provide guidance to leaders.

BRANDING. The process of creating and reinforcing a brand image that captures the attention and recall of consumers.

BRAND METRIC. Measure of a brand's performance.

BRASS. Management. See also TOP BRASS.

BREAD AND BUTTER. Basic; main component.
"Liberal Party nationalism is hardly original. Sounding the alarm against encroaching foreigners is an old and reliable gimmick to expand the power of the state. It is Fidel Castro's bread and butter." (*Wall Street Journal,* July 16, 2004, p. A13)

BREADWINNER. Family member who brings home cash income. See also BRING HOME THE BACON.
"Integrated Defense, which includes all of Boeing's military and space programs, continued to serve in its role as Boeing's breadwinner, bringing in 12% higher revenue of $7.3 billion." (*Wall Street Journal,* Oct. 30, 2003, p. A3)

BREAK ALL THE RULES. Go against tradition.

BREAK BULK. Shipping term for less-than-container load packages.

BREAK DOWN. Stop suddenly or unexpectedly; to fall apart.
"If the market kicks back into gear, as it did in May, then it can resume its upward climb,' Mr. Hayes says. 'But if you break down here, you could get a new leg to the downside,' he adds." (*Wall Street Journal,* July 25, 2004, p. 1)

BREAKOUT SESSION. A smaller, separate meeting by part of a larger group meeting.

BREAK POINTS. Discount fee schedule for investors as they purchase greater amounts of a brokerage firm's investment products.
"At issue is whether brokers at the Wall Street securities firm who sell mutual funds have in some cases bypassed the use of 'break points,' sliding fee scales under which investors pay lower sales charges for putting more money into Morgan Stanley portfolios." (*Wall Street Journal,* March 5, 2003, p. C1)

BREAK THE ICE. Initiate conversation; make the first sale of the day.
"On Tuesday, he had lunch with a local Presbyterian minister and the two arranged for a joint service at the church next month, followed by a dinner at Mr. Ahmed's mosque. 'Food breaks the ice,' he says." (*Wall Street Journal,* Sept. 14, 2001, p. W1)

BREAKTHROUGH. Dramatically new product or idea.

BREAKUP VALUE. The value of the parts of a business.

BRETTON WOODS. Site of the major international finance conference held in 1944 (New Hampshire). At the Bretton Woods conference, a fixed exchange rate system was agreed upon, and the WORLD BANK and INTERNATIONAL MONETARY FUND were established.

"Under the second Bush administration, the United States has set out to establish itself as a positive force for order in the world, but it has been uninterested in the non-military side of world power, in particular the monetary leadership exercised so successfully by the U.S. during Bretton Woods or Great Britain during the 19th century. A world money would be an extraordinary boon to international stability." (*Wall Street Journal,* June 30, 2003, p. A17)

BRICKS AND MORTAR. A company's physical condition, building. See also, CLICKS AND MORTAR.

BRIDGE LOAN/FUNDING. A short-term loan to facilitate a deal until permanent financing can be arranged.

BRIM BURN. Confusion created by changing job responsibilities (changing hats) too quickly or too often.

BRING HOME THE BACON. Earn income to support one's family.

"His cable strategy has always been risky in economic and technological terms, though he has enjoyed a political honeymoon because he promises to bring competition to local phone markets. But politics won't bring home the bacon for Mr. [Mike] Armstrong's shareholders. The question now is whether he's willing to confront the 'open access' nonsense head-on in order to grab AT&T's real business opportunity." (*Wall Street Journal,* Jan. 26, 2000, p. 23)

BRING THE SYSTEM TO ITS KNEES. To overload a computer so that it crashes or operates extremely slowly.

BRING TO THE TABLE. To offer or provide something to an organization or negotiation.

BRING UP TO SPEED. Inform someone of the most recent events.

BRINK. The edge.

"At that rate, Delta would have a cushion of about $1.5 billion by late October. That is close to the level industry analysts have said could put Delta on the brink of a bankruptcy-court filing." (*Wall Street Journal,* August 10, 2004, p. B3)

BROADBANDING. Promotion and pay structure where employees remain in one large salary range rather than moving from grade to grade.

BROADCAST FOOTPRINT. The geographical area in which broadcast reception is possible.

BROCHUREWARE. A Web site that provides basic information about a company (like a brochure) but does not make use of Internet capability such as hyperlinks, or e-mail.

BROKEN RECORD. Annoying, constant repetition.

BRONX CHEER. Boo. The Bronx is a borough in New York City, whose residents have become famous for voicing their disapproval.

"The move was greeted with a Bronx cheer on Wall Street. Analysts, long ill-disposed to Medco's relationship to Merck, have lately grown even more wary of the combination." (*Wall Street Journal,* July 10, 2002, p. A3)

BROWN-BAG (TO). Bring one's lunch to the office.

"The BYO Power Lunch; Brown-Bagging It Is in Style (Sort of), but Hold the Tuna; Career Savings of $100,000." (*Wall Street Journal,* Oct. 8, 2003, p. D1)

BROWN FIELD. An industrial site that is abandoned and unlikely to be redeveloped due to environmental contamination.

"In 1996, the Clinton administration introduced legislation to clean up brown fields and stimulate redevelopment of former industrial sites in urban areas. Wednesday's theme is the environment, and the president will issue a proposal involving the cleanup of toxic waste sites and so-called brown fields industrial areas." (*Wall Street Journal,* August 26, 1996, p. A12)

BROWNIE POINTS. Positive marks or recognition an employee receives for his or her actions from superiors.

"Nobody is going to rush out in the streets and stage pro-American demonstrations in gratitude for saving Muslims, says John Voll of the Center for Christian Muslim Understanding. You get blamed for specific incidents, but you end up getting Brownie points only incrementally, in the long run." (*Wall Street Journal,* March 26, 1999, p. A16)

BROWN-NOSE (TO). Flatter, kiss up to. See also ASS-KISSER.

"Richard Stengel, a former senior editor at Time magazine, addresses this change in the way we flatter in his thought-provoking new book, '(You're Too Kind) A Brief History of Flattery.' In this loosely constructed study of the apple-polisher and the brown-nose, Mr. Stengel defines flattery as 'strategic praise' and then goes about showing us how it has taken over in our modern society and become our main currency of interaction." (*Wall Street Journal,* June 9, 2000, p. W1)

BUBBA. Uneducated Southerner; among Southerners it is a term of endearment (corruption of "brother"). See also REDNECK. The author once played in a softball game in Charleston, South Carolina, where five of the players were nicknamed Bubba, and four Junior!

"Political analysts say his visits to rural areas are paying off, too, and not only with roadside signs. '... Don't forget the bubba vote,' says David 'Mudcat' Saunders, a builder and developer from Roanoke and a regular at the shad planking in Wakefield. 'Bubba likes this man.' No sooner said than the Bluegrass Brothers band from Salem, posted next to Mr. Warner's beer truck and hired by his campaign, strikes up a country number in praise of the candidate." (*Wall Street Journal,* April 26, 2001, p. A21)

BUBBLE BURST. Sudden decline in stock prices after a rapid increase.

"The percentage for more-mature economies is usually in the teens; even the percentages for South Korea and Thailand didn't reach so high in the lead-up to their financial crises in the late 1990s. Beijing's also is higher than it was when an investment bubble burst in China a decade ago, causing the economy to endure years of deflation." (*Wall Street Journal,* July 19, 2004, p. A9)

BUCK. Dollar; to ignore or oppose authority.

"Through companies' second-quarter earnings reports one can find plenty of instances where revenue was helped along by the swaybacked buck. Procter & Gamble said dollar weakness, which increases the dollar value of the products it sells overseas, added four percentage points to sales growth versus the year-ago quarter." (*Wall Street Journal,* August 18, 2004, p. C1)

BUCKET SHOP. A place where dubious business transactions take place; international travel consolidator.

"In the latest allegations, made in 10 civil lawsuits in federal courts around the country and in three SEC administrative proceedings, the SEC turned its focus from securities brokers to company officials who deceive investors, Mr. (Richard) Walker said. 'We've done things in the past on promoters and bucket-shop brokers,' he said. 'This focuses on those who issue and sell the securities to the public.'" (*Wall Street Journal,* Sept. 15, 1998, p.1)

BUCKLE DOWN. Get to work.

"Hyundai Buckles Down to Reforming—Liabilities Grow Smaller At Korean Powerhouse; Critics Seek More Action" (*Wall Street Journal,* Dec. 28, 1999, p. A15)

BUCK SLIP. An office routing slip listing who is to receive the correspondence.

BUCK STOPS HERE (THE). Take responsibility. A sign on President Harry Truman's desk read "The buck stops here."

"Driving home one night last June, Pete Finazzo chuckled when he came up with what he thought was a great catch phrase for his company's cleaning products: 'The Yuck Stops Here.' But the yuks stopped for Mr. Finazzo when he spied a Kleenex ad in the November issue of Reader's Digest using the same slogan, a play off the classic Harry Truman line, The Buck Stops Here." (*Wall Street Journal,* November 30, 1998, p. B1)

BUCK THE TREND. Act contrary to what others are doing.

"Mr. [David Elliot Cohen] thinks 'America 24/7' could buck the trend, noting that when 'A Day in the Life of America' came out, there was no proven mass market for coffee-table books. 'In a way, that book was like Led Zeppelin—wonderful in itself, but it also spawned a lot of bad heavy metal groups,' he says. 'The quality went down, and the market disappeared. ["America 24/7"] will revive that market.'" (*Wall Street Journal,* Sept. 29, 2003, p. B1)

BUDDHIST ECONOMICS. Economic philosophy that challenges Western assumptions of materialism and motivation. The term and ideas were popularized among Westerners by E.F. Schumacher in his book *Small is Beautiful: Economics As if People Mattered.*

BUDGET BOGEY. Business negotiation term for a strategy in which one side claims its budget does not allow for the proposed solution.

BUFFALO (TO). To confuse or trick someone in order to take advantage of them.

BUG. A weakness or problem in a system; to bother or pester; a secret listening device.

BUILD A FENCE AROUND. Protect.

BUILD/MAKE A BETTER MOUSETRAP. Create a new or better product. Marketers use this phrase to represent firms with a production mentality, who focus on their product rather than the needs of their customers.

"If a man can write a better book, preach a better sermon, or make a better mouse-trap than his neighbor, though he builds his house in the woods the world will make a beaten path to his door." (Attributed to Ralph Waldo Emerson.)

BUILDING SOCIETY. A savings and loan (S&L) institution. During the nineteenth century, S&Ls were created primarily to make home loans to their members. At the time commercial banks were not interested or willing to make these loans, so groups of people organized building societies.

BULIMIC. A short-term stockholder looking to get in and out quickly, from the eating disorder.

BULL. Investor who thinks the stock market will rise; questionable advice; meaningless talk, boastfulness.

"Neither is comfortable with the label 'bull' or 'bear.' Mr. Trennert calls himself 'a bull short-term, and a realist for the long term.' Mr. Levkovich says he is 'neither a bear nor a bull. I am a pragmatist.' Sadly, the two agree that, whatever stocks do this year, they will average only single-digit annual gains for the rest of the decade." (*Wall Street Journal,* August 2, 2004, p. C1)

BULL BY THE HORNS (TO TAKE THE). To take charge of a situation.

BULLETPROOF. Not subject to influence or variation due to outside forces.

BULL MARKET. An upward movement in the stock market.

"'People tend to think they know more than they actually do,' says Terrance Odean, a finance professor at the University of California at Berkeley. Adds John Nersesian, a wealth-management strategist at Nuveen Investments: 'That's not to suggest they shouldn't be well-informed or confident in a strategy they develop,' he says, 'but they shouldn't be lured into a false sense of security. That's why investors overreacted to the bull market,' he says. 'When we get into these bull and bear markets, we think they have a tendency to self-perpetuate, and they don't.'" (*Wall Street Journal,* August 29, 2004, p. 4)

BULL MARKET BABIES. The generation born since 1980 whose experience in the decade of the 1990s was a constantly rising stock market.

BULLPEN. People available to assist or relieve existing workers (baseball); an open work area occupied by many employees.
"After more than two years of increasingly bitter negotiations, Southwest Airlines, Dallas, reached a tentative contract agreement with its flight attendants but only after bringing former Chief Executive Herbert D. Kelleher out of the bullpen." (*Wall Street Journal,* June 28, 2004, p. B4)

BULL'S EYE. A perfect score, match, or outcome.
"You hit a bull's-eye with your Aug. 5 Personal Journal article 'Luxury Home for Sale: 6 Bdrms, Dumpster Vu.' We contracted last week to buy a one-acre home site in Jackson Hole Golf & Tennis Club in Wyoming." (*Wall Street Journal,* August 15, 2004, p. A13)

BUMP (TO). Use seniority to take the job of a younger employee. Bumping is allowed by the NATIONAL LABOR RELATIONS BOARD and the EQUAL EMPLOYMENT OPPORTUNITY BOARD.

BUMP UP. To rapidly push upward.

BUNDLING. The questionable marketing practice of selling a group or package of products rather than selling them individually.

BUNS ON THE SEATS. Sarcastic measurement of sales performance based on the number of people attending a presentation.

BURDEN. The cost; the additional cost of an employee beyond their salary.

BUREAUCRATIC DELAYS. Problems with government or other organizational administration.

BURNED OUT/BURNOUT. Exhausted, tired; exhaustion.

"John Clements was burned out working for a clothing company, but his usual excuses for no-shows were wearing thin. So he woke up early enough one morning to ensure he'd have a naturally scratchy throat when he left a calling-in-sick message for his boss, avoiding, he hoped, any probing questions. But she called him back." (*Wall Street Journal,* June 25, 2003, p. B1)

BURNING A CANDLE AT BOTH ENDS. Working very long hours or doing too many things at one time.

BURNING THE MIDNIGHT OIL. Working very late; performing one's duties at the last minute.

BURN RATE. The rate, usually expressed in dollars per month, that a firm is spending in order to bring a new product to market. Many Internet start-up companies raised millions of dollars and then burned the funds trying to bring their product or service to market.

"As many failed Internet and telecom upstarts with high burn rates have found in recent years, even the prospect of a looming cash squeeze can scare away investors long before the coffers are empty." (*Wall Street Journal,* Sept. 19, 2002, p. C1)

BURN TIME. The time until an option expires. Burn time refers to the decrease in value of an option as it approaches its expiration date.

"Burn time is another way to talk about the effect time has on an option whose stock is range bound. Meaning, intrinsic value is not increasing to compensate for the loss of time value." ("Wall Street Jargon," About.com Web site, Dec. 12, 2002)

BURROWING. The practice of getting one's appointment status with the federal government switched from a political to career civil service position, thus protecting one from being terminated when one's party loses control in Washington.

BUSINESS CASE. Commercial justification. When new product ideas get past the development stage, the next stage is the justification for commercialization or business case.

BUSH LEAGUE. Insignificant; of minor importance (baseball).

"Slobodan Milosevic miscalculated when he didn't take a NATO ultimatum seriously enough and soon had bombs raining down on Serbia. That was because he had been getting by with murder, literally, for years and apparently thought that he could proceed with impunity on a new campaign of ethnic cleansing in Kosovo. His sins were monumental, of course. America's and NATO's sin was in allowing him to believe that they were not up to the task of punishing a bush-league tyrant." (*Wall Street Journal,* August 10, 1999, p. A25)

BUS SPEED. The speed at which data travel among computer components.
"In recent years, computer makers have been increasing the 'bus' speeds, to keep up with advances in the speeds of processors." (*Wall Street Journal,* December 4, 2002, p. D5)

BUTTERFLY RULE. Corporate governance idea that board of directors resign if they change or lose their current job.

BUTT HEADS (TO). Strongly disagree, compete.
"When Mr. [Daniel] Schorr reports that Johnson spent too much money on a 'mindless war' in Vietnam rather than the noble 'war on poverty,' President Johnson phones at midnight to tell Mr. Schorr he's a "prize son of a bitch. Later, Mr. Schorr boasts that his early reporting on [Nixon] 'reflected the generally progressive' policies of the Nixon administration. But when the creator of the EPA and affirmative action showed his 'hostility to social betterment,' Mr. Schorr turned on him. Similarly, Mr. Schorr butts heads with his New York bosses when his edgy reporting on poverty upsets their 'suburban' sensibilities." (*Wall Street Journal,* May 2, 2001, p. A30)

BUTTON DOWN. Address seriously; reach agreement on.
"Just the term market timing 'makes a lot of people very uneasy,' says Bob Bolt, chief investment officer at the University of Texas Investment Management Co., so Mr. [Peter] Bernstein's speech was a surprise to many. 'Peter is viewed as a conservative believer in button-down money management—he's not a wild-eyed bomb thrower,' Mr. Bolt says." (*Wall Street Journal,* August 27, 2003, p. C1)

BUTTON-DOWN AND PINSTRIPES. Corporate dress, suit and tie.

BUTT OUT. Mind your own business (considered rude or impolite).
"No doubt Mr. Grasso will tell us to butt out of his business model. But as he also likes to say, the NYSE is a public trust, at least until it decides to go private as an IPO. Until that day, he is going to need all of his fabled marketing skills to convince the world that a monopoly in trading stocks is the highest form of capitalism." (*Wall Street Journal,* May 2, 2003, p. A14)

BUY DOWN. A cash payment made to a lender in return for a lower interest rate.

BUYER'S REMORSE. Purchaser's post-purchase anxiety.

"Companies once happy to shop for acquisitions with inflated stock market currency are now suffering buyer's remorse and cutting the value of these assets." (*U.S. News & World Report,* May 14, 2001, p. 33)

BUY-IN. Agreement.

BUYING POWER. Income, ability to purchase.

"Home Depot Inc.'s first-quarter profit rose 26% on strong sales gains, but the company won't say how much its retail lumber prices are up. 'Because of our scale and buying power we can minimize the impact of the price increases on consumers, but it's still likely consumers will see some price impact,' David Sandor, a communications director, says." (*Wall Street Journal,* August 11, 2004, p. D1)

BUY ON BAD NEWS. Stock market strategy of purchasing stock after unfavorable news.

BUY THE FARM. Die.

BUZZ. Excitement and interest.

BUZZWORD BINGO. A game played by bored staff members listening to an executive speak. The executive's favorite buzzwords are prearranged in a pattern like a bingo card. The winner is the first person to hear all the buzzwords in a row or column.

BUZZ WORDS. Terms or phrases used by people within a specific group or industry.

BY HOOK OR BY CROOK. Any way it can get done.

"The Friends of the Bayreuth Festival is the most powerful association of opera fans going, mainly because of its lock on ticket allocations. And Bayreuth tickets are hard to get by hook or by crook. At every performance, mendicant opera queens and kings stand out in front, many in evening clothes, holding little signs that say *suche Karte,* I'm looking for a ticket." (*Wall Street Journal,* Sept. 5, 2004, p. A32)

BY THE BOOK/NUMBERS. Following the rules.

C

CAFETERIA PLAN. Benefit package that allows employee choice.

"The U.S. Internal Revenue Service proposed new rules that will make it easier for employees to take advantage of tax-free benefits provided by their employers through arrangements known as cafeteria plans." (*Wall Street Journal,* March 23, 2000, p. 1)

CAKEWALK. Something easy.

"Oops, NBC was supposed to be long gone from the General Electric portfolio. Broadcast TV is no longer a cakewalk: GE must now do a deal with Vivendi for Universal Studios to find a safe harbor for the Peacock network." (*Wall Street Journal,* Sept. 2, 2003, p. B2)

CALIFORNIA PUBLIC EMPLOYEES' RETIREMENT SYSTEM (CALPERS). Large, public retirement fund.

"In its report, the Center for Security Policy in Washington focuses on the investments of 100 public pension funds, including the giant California Public Employees' Retirement System, known as Calpers, which the group says has 20% of its $86 billion in stock assets invested in companies that work with terrorist-sponsoring countries." (*Wall Street Journal,* August 12, 2004, p. C4)

CALL. To challenge someone to justify their actions; a stock market option to buy a stock at a specific price for a period of time.

CALL A BLUFF. To confront or challenge an adversary. In business negotiations, to question or rebuff the opposing person.

CALL CENTER. Centralized communication system.

"As U.S. companies send more work overseas, one often-overlooked economic factor is the plummeting cost of global communications. With companies using India's engineers and call-center operators, the capacity of fiber-optic lines connecting telephone systems into India has increased almost sevenfold, while bringing down prices." (*Wall Street Journal,* March 11, 2004, p.B1)

CALL IN SICK. Take a day off from work.

"Verizon now lets its rivals tap directly into Verizon's computer to place their orders, eliminating the need for humans in many cases. 'It's cheaper to get a machine,' says Mr. Maguire. Machines don't call in sick and are consistent in quality." (*Wall Street Journal,* May 28, 2004, p. A1)

CALL IT QUITS. To close a business or withdraw from something.

CALL ON THE CARPET. Reprimand.

"But some investors still won't buy. 'As a portfolio manager at a big mutual fund, when one of the stocks you own is put on the front page of The Wall Street Journal once a week, and there's all these political attacks, you can be called on the carpet about why you own this thing. So a lot of people just don't want to hear about it,' he says." (*Wall Street Journal,* August 12, 2004, p. C1)

CALL THE SHOTS. Make the decisions.

"The Fed is almost taunting them [the GSEs] a little bit, and letting them know the Fed is going to call the shots, and is not going to bow down or kowtow to the GSEs," said Bert Ely, a banking analyst who is critical of the mortgage giants." (*Wall Street Journal,* Feb. 6, 2004, p. A2)

CAN (TO). Dismiss someone from employment; to terminate.

CANARY INDICATOR. A signal that there is a problem. Miners used canaries to indicate when there was gas present in the air.

"The economy has a flock of canary indicators these days, and half seem to die when put in the mine." (*Wall Street Journal,* August 30, 2002, p. C1)

CANCELABLE WITH NO SHORT RATE. A clause in advertising contracts allowing the advertiser to cancel a campaign at any time, with a refund of the unused budget.

CAN-DO. Capable or positive, as in a can-do attitude.

CANNIBALIZE. Offer a new product that takes sales from another offering in the same product line.

CAN OF WORMS. A complex problem.
"Legal and trade experts said Mr. [John] Kerry's pledge would open a can of worms. Trade rules enforceable in Central America also would apply in the U.S., laying the legal groundwork for possible international challenges to lax U.S. protections for migrant workers—including lack of enforcement of minimum-wage laws and lack of standard benefits given to other U.S. workers, such as Social Security—or the 'right to work' laws in more than a dozen states that protect the right of workers not to join a union." (*Wall Street Journal,* June 1, 2004, p. A6)

CAPITAL FLIGHT. The removal of funds from a country by investors during periods of political and economic turmoil.
"By mid-2002, the real was tumbling, a signal that too many were being printed. Inflation was steady (it lags currency movements), so interest rates went unchanged. Capital flight took hold even though economic growth was adequate. President Cardoso's popularity declined with the currency. The equity market fell sharply, uncertain about the election and inflation." (*Wall Street Journal,* Dec. 5, 2003, p. A13)

CAPITALIZATION. The combination of debt and equity used to finance a company's assets.

CAPITULATION. Stock market technician's term for a big down day that exhausts sellers.

CAPPUCCINO COWBOY. Anyone who regularly stops at Starbucks or other upscale coffee shops on the way to work.

CAPTIVE COMPANY. A company that is created and owned by another company for the purpose of providing goods or services to the parent company. Captive companies are common in finance and insurance.

CARDS ARE STACKED. Situation with a predetermined outcome.

CAREER-LIMITING MOVE (CLM). An action that will adversely affect one's future.
"If at a party you commented that the CEO's spouse had put on a few pounds it would likely be a CLM." (Brian Chilla, Rock-Tenn Company, 1996)

CARNIVORE. The Federal Bureau of Investigation's e-mail surveillance tool, which can retrieve all communication flowing through an Internet service provider.

CARPE DIEM. Seize the day (Latin). The saying, *carpe diem,* was made famous to Americans by actor Robin Williams in the film *Dead Poets Society.*

CARPET BOMB. An e-mail message that goes to everyone in the network.

CARROTS AND STICKS. Positive incentives and negative consequences.

CARRY. Take someone (Southern).

CARRY FORWARDS. Tax losses businesses can apply to offset against future profits for income tax purposes.

CARRYING CHARGE. Fee for purchasing something on credit.

CARRYOVER. Inventory.

CARRY THE BALL. Take charge of a project or situation (football).
"Business investment has been one of the missing ingredients needed for a strong economic recovery. Since late last year, the U.S. economy has been buoyed largely by consumer spending—not business spending. But many economists worry that unless businesses increase investments for plants, technology and other equipment, the U.S. recovery will lose momentum and possibly even dip back into recession. 'The consumer can't carry the ball forever,' Mr. Blinder said." (*Wall Street Journal,* August 21, 2002, p. A2)

CARRY TRADE. Investment strategy using short-term borrowing at lower interest rates to buy long-term debt. The strategy works until interest rates rise, causing short-term costs to increase while the value of long-term debt declines.

"Almost every financial institution has been plying the carry trade in which an investor borrows short-term and buys long-term, making the spread." (*Wall Street Journal,* July 2, 2004, p. C1)

CARRY WEIGHT. Have significant meaning or influence.

"The Council on Bioethics voted 10–7 to recommend the moratorium on human cloning for research and a permanent ban on reproductive cloning. The recommendation doesn't carry much weight because Congress probably won't revisit the issue in the current session and because critics have claimed the panel was biased against cloning." (*Wall Street Journal,* July 12, 2002, p. B6)

CARTE BLANCHE. Full authority to make decisions or commitments.

"One caveat: American politicians should ponder their actions before making Haiti another issue in the American presidential election this year. Certainly John Kerry, the standard bearer of the Democrats, cannot believe that being 'democratically elected' is a carte blanche to undertake mayhem against one's own country." (*Wall Street Journal,* April 6, 2004, p. A16)

CARVE OUT A NICHE. Establish a share of a market or specialty business.

CASH-AND-CARRY. Business that does not offer credit, payments only in cash.

"At a time when a large number of Thai firms are burdened by debt and threatened with insolvency, this cash-and-carry hypermarket operator has almost no debt, a strong market position, and a sound strategy to deal with a collapse in domestic demand, according to analysts." (*Asian Wall Street Journal Weekly*, Feb. 16, 1998, p. 18)

CASH CALL. The offer of shares of stock to existing stockholders before they are offered to the general public.

CASH COW. Business in a slow-growth market that generates surplus revenue.

"Growing Profit Source for Banks: Fees From Riskiest Card Holders Late Payers and Big Borrowers Are Becoming Cash Cows: How Interest Rates Balloon" (*Wall Street Journal,* July 6, 2004, p. A1)

CASHIER'S CHECK. A check issued by a bank with funds provided by the customer. Many businesses require payment in cash or by cashier's check, especially when doing business the first time.

CASH IN ON. Profit from an opportunity.

"An appeals court erased convictions for four men found guilty in a multimillion-dollar plan to cash in on stolen winning tickets in McDonald's Corp. games such as 'Monopoly' and 'Who Wants to be a Millionaire.'" (*Wall Street Journal,* July 21, 2004, p. 1)

CASH ON DELIVERY (COD). A business transaction requiring payment when the goods are delivered.

CASH SURRENDER VALUE (CSV). The value of an insurance policy if canceled by the insured.

CAST IN CONCRETE. Cannot be changed.

CASUAL RULE/BUSINESS CASUAL/CASUAL FRIDAY. Corporate dress policy allowing workers to dress less formally. The policy is often instituted during hot summers. It has also created a new retail clothing segment.

CATCH A FALLING KNIFE. Buy when the stock market is falling.

CATCH-22. An irresolvable contradiction or logic trap. The phrase comes from Joseph Heller's bestselling 1970s novel.

"The steady slackening in the number of people filing for unemployment benefits provides further evidence of the end of the so-called jobless recovery. However, proof that the nation's payrolls are growing again—also seen in the past few months' employment reports—is a Catch-22 for stock investors, who generally favor signs of economic recovery but fear the Federal Reserve rate increases that often accompany those signs." (*Wall Street Journal,* June 11, 2004, p. C1)

CAVEAT EMPTOR. Let the buyer beware (Latin). The seller makes no guarantees.

"Rep. Oxley's advice for corporate executives: 'I would say caveat emptor. You have to sort through what's good and what's not, sort the charlatans from the real folks,' he says. 'That's probably true in any kind of business in any kind of time.'" (*Wall Street Journal,* Oct. 23, 2003, p. R9)

CEILING. Limit.

"Since there is no ceiling on the number of accounts, dollar amounts accumulated, or the number of contributions, conversions, rollovers or beneficiaries, each taxpayer should consider factors which may influence the optimal number of Roth IRAs to be maintained." (*National Public Accountant,* Nov. 1999, p. 26)

CERTIFICATE OF ACCRUAL ON TREASURY SECURITIES (CATS). U.S. Department of Treasury securities that pay no interest and are sold at a deep discount to face value (ZERO COUPON). Holders of CATS are paid full value of the security upon maturity.

CERTIFIED CHECK. A check guaranteed by a bank.

CHAINSAW CONSULTANT. An outside expert brought in to reduce the number of employees without management having to take responsibility. Named after "Chainsaw" Al Dunlap, famous or infamous for cutting workforce numbers wherever he managed.

CHANGE AGENT. Consultant brought in to restructure a company. Also refers to an internal manager or employee who inspires or effects change.

"Behind the wheel is Terry Quan, an In-Q-Tel financial analyst and Ph.D. student at the University of Chicago. In the back seat is Eric Kaufmann, who just joined as business developer after stints at PepsiCo Inc. and Walt Disney Co. They're the type the government finds hard to lure: young and up on the latest trends. Mr. Louie calls them his change agents." (*Wall Street Journal,* April 3, 2000, p. A1)

CHANGE HANDS. Sell; transfer ownership.

"The NYSE said the other two seats that were sold went for $1.3 million and $1.35 million. Before these, the previous NYSE seat to change hands was sold on July 8 for $1.4 million." (*Wall Street Journal,* August 4, 2004, p. A1)

CHANGE POINT. Periods in consumers' lives where they are making major changes.

"Mr. Smith and Ms. Cziglenyi didn't realize it, but they were at a 'change point.' Corporate marketers say certain points in life make consumers especially vulnerable to sales pitches." (*Wall Street Journal,* Jan. 30, 2003, p. B1)

CHANNEL BACK (TO). Return.

CHANNEL MANAGEMENT. Managing distribution channels. Channel management involves placing greater emphasis on communicating with retailers and distributors in markets where end-users rely on the opinions and advice of these people.

"In addition, both Compaq and IBM now let major corporate customers buy directly from them, further adding to the unrest. 'We're just giving customers the opportunity to be better satisfied,' insists Ronald Schneider, Compaq's director of channel management." (*Wall Street Journal,* Aug. 26, 1994, p. B4)

CHAPTER 11. Bankruptcy laws allowing the debtor to maintain control of the business and to have latitude in negotiating new payment terms.

"Mr. Grinstein's moves came as Delta accelerated its efforts to avoid filing for Chapter 11 bankruptcy–court protection by asking holders of debt backed by its aircraft to give it more flexibility to restructure its debt." (*Wall Street Journal,* August 19, 2004, p. B6)

CHAPTER 7. Bankruptcy proceeding where a court-appointed trustee oversees company activities, protects a company from creditors, and usually manages liquidation of the company's assets.

"Since at least one senator, Democrat Russ Feingold of Wisconsin, has vowed to filibuster the legislation, 60 votes would be needed to gain passage in the Senate. He and allies in the labor and consumer movement believe the bill unfairly benefits credit-card companies and banks at the expense of debt-ridden consumers. The bill would clamp down on filings by individuals under Chapter 7 of the bankruptcy code, which wipes out all debts once filers liquidate their assets." (*Wall Street Journal,* Nov. 18, 2002, p. A4)

CHAPTER 22. Humorous way of describing a company that has gone into CHAPTER 11 bankruptcy more than once.

CHARM SCHOOL. A mocking term for training courses for newly appointed managers and other employees who now are in the PUBLIC EYE.

"Career Journal: Chinese Charm School; Seminars Help Businessmen Conform to Western Manners; Tip: Always Answer E-Mail." (*Wall Street Journal,* Jan. 13, 2004, p. B1)

CHARM THE PANTS OFF. Flatter.

CHARTISTS. Stock market analysts who graph movements of market statistics. See ELVES.

"You can teach school on this chart, he asserts, pointing out a price formation known as a 'reverse head and shoulders'—a very

BULLISH omen to the chartists." (*Wall Street Journal,* July 16, 1994, p. T2)

CHASING DOWN SMOKESTACKS. Making sales calls to industrial customers. See also COLD CALLS.

CHASING THE MARKET. Buying securities as prices rise or selling as prices decline. Investors who FOLLOW THE HERD often chase the market.

CHECK IS IN THE MAIL. A stalling tactic when confronted for payment.

CHECK THE PULSE. Evaluate the current condition.

CHECKOFF. System where the employer withholds union dues from workers' paychecks.

CHECKOUT. Sales desk; to pay for one's purchases.

CHERRY-PICKING. Choosing only the best or most profitable of the choices available.

CHEW OUT. Verbally reprimand; harshly criticize.
   "Other factors may also be at work. The typical discretionary account owner is older and richer than nondiscretionary account holders, and is more likely to have weathered a downturn before. There also is the opaque nature of discretionary account performance: It is harder to track on a daily basis, and so investors aren't gaping at stock tables every morning, then reaching for the phone to chew out their adviser." (*Wall Street Journal,* Jan. 22, 2001, p. B11)

CHICAGO BOYS. Monetary economists; University of Chicago economists.

CHICKEN FEED. Small sums of money.
   "Although owning 50 stocks may strike the average investor as too many to track successfully, it is chicken feed to two professors from the University of Nevada at Las Vegas. Gerald Newbould and Percy Poon posited in a 1996 study that investors needed to hold more than 100 small-cap or large-cap stocks to remain within 5% of average risk, which they define as the average volatility of the 40,000 simulated portfolios created for the study." (*Wall Street Journal,* Jan. 29, 2001, p. R16)

CHINESE WALL. Rules and safeguards to prevent improper disclosure of information within an organization.

"At Merrill Lynch & Co., to gain access to instant messaging, workers must register on an internal Web page, and certain employees are prohibited from registering. Other Merrill Lynch workers can only send messages internally, and certain groups of workers are barred by the system from communicating with certain other groups; Merrill won't say which. 'We have very strict Chinese walls in place,' says Wilson D'Souza, Merrill's vice president of e-mail and collaboration services." (*Wall Street Journal,* June 16, 2003, p. R8)

CHIPS AND SALSA. Computer chips and software.

CHITCHAT. Casual conversation.

"Not only did the woman dressed as the Mattel doll make chitchat with John Snow last week, but she also escorted him through part of his tour of Toys "R" Us Inc. megastore in New York's Times Square, where he weighed in on how affordable toys have become." (*Wall Street Journal,* Dec.17, 2003, p. B4b)

CHUMMING. Illegal investment market practice of creating false transactions on one exchange in order to drive up the price on another exchange.

CHURN/CHURNER. Turn over; improper stockbroker action of generating commissions by unauthorized buying and selling; deceptive insurance practice.

"'Allowing customers to keep their old wireless phone numbers when switching carriers hasn't increased "churn" in the wireless industry,' a top Federal Communications Commission official said. 'The overwhelming conclusion is that churn has stayed relatively flat,' said John Muleta, head of the agency's Wireless Telecommunications Bureau, in response to a question from FCC Chairman Michael Powell at a commission meeting. He added that there 'have been shifts in market share' between the different carriers." (*Wall Street Journal,* May 14, 2004, p. 14)

CIRCUIT BREAKERS. Rules created by the major stock exchanges and the SEC to halt trading temporarily during periods of severe price fluctuations. These rules were created in response to BLACK MONDAY (1987), when the DJIA fell over five hundred points in one day.

"Circuit-Breaker Levels for Fourth-Quarter 2003 The New York Stock Exchange resets its trading curbs each quarter based on the Dow Jones Industrial Average's level. As announced yesterday by the NYSE, new trading halt triggers (which shut trading for specific lengths depending on time of day) are: In the event of a 950-point decline in the DJIA (10%), up from the previous 900-point level, this would happen: Before 2 P.M. 1-hour halt 2 P.M. 2:30 P.M. 30-minute halt After 2:30 P.M." (*Wall Street Journal,* Oct. 1, 2003, p. C17)

CLASS ACTION. A legal action filed by a group of people all with the same complaint against an individual or group. Class action lawsuits have become frequent and expensive for businesses in the United States.

"Mr. Bondi's filings are being closely watched by class-action attorneys in the U.S. representing investors from around the world who either bought shares in Parmalat or debt securities issued by the company. In an initial filing earlier this year in federal court in the Southern District of New York, those class-action suits also target Citigroup, Deutsche Bank and Parmalat's former auditors." (*Wall Street Journal,* August 20, 2004, p. A6)

CLAWBACK. Refunds venture capital firms make to investors.

"VCs can be required to pay clawbacks when they take their 20% share on a fund's early investment gains—a common practice—and later deals lose money." (*Wall Street Journal,* Dec. 10, 2002, p. C1)

CLEANING HIS/HER CLOCK. A total victory over an opponent (boxing).

CLEAN SHEET/SLATE. Fresh start; putting aside past errors.

"'Bark for [Wesley] Clark' reads the sign on Jim Barrett's golden retriever, Miles. 'He's not a political insider yet,' Mr. Barrett says of the candidate, whom he describes as 'a fresh start, a clean slate.' After listening to Mr. Clark at a Concord stop, Reginald Comeau, a 69-year-old educator who has followed Mr. [Howard] Dean 'pretty much' for months, counts himself a convert too." (*Wall Street Journal,* Jan. 14, 2004, p. A4)

CLEAR-CUT. Obvious, well-defined.

"They found that seven, or 1.7% of the patients with the disease had a mutation in the fibulin 5 gene, compared with none in the control group. Results from the other four fibulin genes turned up no clear-cut results, though there were enough mutations to lead Dr. Stone to conclude that the fibulin family may account for 7% or 8% of AMD cases." (*Wall Street Journal,* July 22, 2004, p. D3)

CLEARING HOUSE. An organization that provides for settlement of bank or stock market transactions; centralized source of services.

"European bankers recently formed a pan-European automatic clearing house, known as Peach, to speed cross-border clearing. 'One day, and we can't say when, it will be exactly the same process for domestic as it is for international payments in the euro zone,' said Patrick Poncelet, senior adviser to the European Banking Federation in Brussels." (*Wall Street Journal,* August 22, 2003, p. B3C)

CLEAR SAILING. No obstacles.

"'Business spending is about to turn up,' predicts William Miller, the superstar mutual-fund manager at Legg Mason Inc. 'The next 12 months seem to be clear sailing for equities.'" (*Wall Street Journal,* Jan. 2, 2004, p. R2)

CLEAR THE AIR (TO). Put aside past differences; clarify an issue.

"So what the lower court incorrectly characterized as an issue of 'candor' in FBI affidavits and certifications was in reality the result of confusion brought on by the tortured interpretation of the statute by the original FISA court. Of course, any real issue of an FBI agent's candor in an affidavit should properly remain under investigation by the Department of Justice. But it was a constructive exercise for these judges to 'clear the air' on this issue for which the FBI has been unfairly criticized." (*Wall Street Journal,* Nov. 26, 2002, p. A24)

CLICK-THROUGH RATE. How often Internet users respond to an ad by clicking on it and going to the advertiser's Web site. Click-throughs are measured by the click rate.

CLICKS AND MORTAR. A business that has both an Internet presence and a physical location.

CLIENT/SERVER. The computer architecture consisting of personal computers sharing resources stored on more powerful server computers.

CLIMB TO THE TOP. Become successful.

"It's a philosophy that has helped Ms. Estes, 40 years old, climb to the top of the male-dominated bond world. She has just been elevated from co-chief to sole chief of government-bond trading at Morgan Stanley Dean Witter & Co., where her group generates an estimated 5% of the firm's trading revenue and where she earns, by head-hunters' estimates, more than $1.5 million a year." (*Wall Street Journal,* Nov. 26, 1999, p. A1)

CLINCH (TO). Come to an agreement, close a deal.

"OAO Yukos won more time to clinch a lifesaving deal with the state on a $3.4 billion back-tax claim after a court said Friday it needed two more weeks to make a ruling. Yukos has said a prompt demand by the court to pay taxes immediately would sink the company, whose assets are frozen." (*Wall Street Journal,* June 28, 2004, p. B45)

CLINCHER. Deciding element.

CLIP JOINT. A business that regularly overcharges customers.

CLONE. Make copies of; a very close imitation.

"'The Governing Council is not going to appoint itself, it's not going to clone itself,' spokesman Ahmad Fawzi said yesterday." (*Wall Street Journal,* June 1, 2004, p. A15)

CLOSE. The end of the business day.

CLOSE A POSITION. Eliminate a security from one's portfolio.

CLOSE, BUT NO CIGAR. Not quite correct.

"Close, But No Cigar: In the pressure cooker of pro-sports coaching, winning used to be the best defense. However, no fewer than six coaches or managers were recently fired despite having taken their teams to championship contention." (*Wall Street Journal,* Feb. 27, 2004, p. W7)

CLOSED-END INVESTMENT COMPANY. A mutual fund that issues a limited and fixed number of shares and does not redeem the shares. Once issued, the closed-end shares trade like common stock, with share values varying with the value of the price of the stocks held in the fund.

CLOSED SHOP. A firm in which union membership is a precondition for employment. The Taft-Hartley Act (1947) outlawed closed shops, but de facto closed shops exist in situations where union halls are used to match employer needs with worker qualifications.

"So outrageous were union actions during the war that citizens pressured Congress to amend federal law in order to rein in abuse. Passed in 1947 over President Truman's veto, the Taft-Hartley Act allowed prosecution of unfair labor practices committed by unions and banned the closed shop, where union membership was required before an employee could be hired. But Taft-Hartley did not eliminate compulsory unionism, the root of union arrogance and abuse. Instead, it sought to regulate its ill effects." (*Wall Street Journal,* Oct. 9, 2002, p. A18)

CLOSELY HELD. A company with only a few stockholders.

"Fiji Water LLC, the closely held Basalt, Colo., company that bottles and markets the up-and-coming water, insists that its main selling point is an ultra-clean taste and pristine source gushingly described on its label as a 'virgin ecosystem far from acid rain, herbicides, pesticides, and other pollutants.'" (*Wall Street Journal,* August 20, 2004, p. B1)

CLOSER. Salesperson whose job is to finish the deal.

CLOSE THE LOOP. Come full circle with a deal or transaction.

CLOSE TO ONE'S VEST (TO KEEP). Guard against others finding something out. In the card game of poker, players keep their cards close to their vest to prevent anyone from seeing them.

"'People like that drive you nuts,' Mr. Thomas Ward says. 'They play the most common pieces of information so close to the vest.'" (*Wall Street Journal,* August 5, 2003, p. B6)

CLOSING COSTS. The variety of ancillary expenses involved in purchasing real estate.

CLOSING TICK. The number of stocks whose last trading price of the day was higher than the previous trade, minus the number of stocks whose last selling price was lower. A positive closing tick is considered BULLISH, and a negative closing tick is BEARISH.

CLOUD ON A TITLE. Any legal issue that questions or makes unclear the ownership of property. Clouds on a title usually must be removed before a business transaction takes place.

"For New Yorkers, however, this is no time for self-congratulation. Manhattan's perennial district attorney, Robert M. Morgenthau, who will soon be celebrating his millennium in the job, has shanghaied two paintings by Egon Schiele (1890–1918) on loan from a state-financed Austrian foundation to the Museum of Modern Art. Mr. Morgenthau, having read in the New York Times that there might be clouds on the title to these works by the Austrian master of erotic anguish, moved to impound them." (*Wall Street Journal,* July 9, 1998, p. 1)

CLOUT. Influence.

"A breakdown in the WTO talks would deliver the stiffest blow to poorer countries because few have the clout to cut separate deals with the big trade powers on terms that would aid poorer nations. The newest trade juggernauts—China, India and Brazil—also have a huge stake in the continued success of the WTO talks. Developing nations are trying to use newfound clout at the negotiating table to rebalance the world's agricultural trade." (*Wall Street Journal,* August 2, 2004, p. A2)

CLUB (TO). In venture-capital markets, to form a partnership with other private-equity firms to bid for target businesses.

"While venture-capital firms have long 'clubbed' together to minimize risk, the trend has now extended to the other part of the private-equity business—leverage buyout firms." (*Wall Street Journal,* October 15, 2002, p. C1)

CLUSTER FUNK. A situation in which multiple problems occur on a computer system at the same time.

CNN EFFECT. The negative effect on the economy caused by people staying home to watch CNN or some other news source during a crisis such as an attack or war. One of the reports after 9/11 was what consumers bought at Wal-Mart that day. In the morning sales slumped. In the early afternoon sales of water, ammunition, and other survival goods flourished, and by evening American flags were sold out.

"Amid the current price wars, burger wars and other so-called warfare among rival foodservice forces looms the threat of a real-war, which would be led by the US against the nation of Iraq. Foodservice operators should remember the 'CNN effect' of the last Gulf War. Rather than congregate leisurely at mealtime in dinnerhouses and diners, masses of Americans stayed glued to their home televisions for war-news updates, often opting for drive-thru fare, home delivery and takeout, but sometimes only if it was speedy and convenient." (*Nation's Restaurant News,* Feb. 17, 2003, p. 2)

COALS TO NEWCASTLE (TO BRING). Not needed; to do something unnecessary. Newcastle is a seaport in the coal-producing region of Great Britain.

"Eating Their Lunch: Coals to Newcastle, Ice to Eskimos; Now, Noodles to the Chinese—How Brothers From Taiwan Suddenly Seized Share In a Very Basic Industry—Dare to Try, and Move Fast" (*Wall Street Journal,* Nov. 17, 1997, p. A1)

COATTAIL INVESTING. Engaging in trading practices similar to those of successful investors. Many investors make their investment decisions based on what Warren Buffett, a leading value investor, does.

COCKROACH PROBLEM. A problem that is bigger than it initially appears.

"Well, Terry, Procter & Gamble has a cockroach problem, and, you know, we know what that means; in other words, you've got one little piece of bad news, and there is always more, just like those little bugs." ("In the Money," *CNN,* June 8, 2000)

COFFEE BREAK. Rest time in a workday.

COIN A PHRASE. Make up words to describe something.

COLD CALL. Sales call to new potential customers without prior communication.

"Edward Stern, the scion of a wealthy New York family, seemed to be the perfect client. While many wealthy clients come from hard-earned referrals, Theodore Sihpol III, who reported to Charles Bryceland, landed Mr. Stern with a cold call." (*Wall Street Journal,* Sept. 12, 2003, p. C1)

COLD CASH. Currency, not a check.

COLD FEET. Fear about a decision or choice.

COLD WAR. Post–World War II political and diplomatic conflict between the United States and the Soviet Union.

"Mr. Kerry tells us that he understood both the importance of winning the Cold War and the difference between freedom and oppression from his time as a child in Berlin. This makes his passionate opposition to resisting communist expansion in Southeast Asia harder to understand." (*Wall Street Journal,* August 2, 2004, p. A10)

COLLAR. Parts of an agreement that limit investment capital required.

COLLATERAL DAMAGE. Side effects or unintended consequences of an action.

"The NFIB supports alternatives such as tax credits for heads of households as opposed to raising the minimum wage, which it says will 'shrink job opportunities' for low-wage workers and place undue 'collateral damage' on small businesses." (*Wall Street Journal,* July 27, 2004, p. B3)

COLLECTIVE BARGAINING. Negotiations between management and representatives from employees' unions.

COME IN LOW. Make a low bid on a contract. See LOW-BALL.

COME-ON. A deceptive act; seduction.

COME OUT OF LEFT FIELD. Surprise; suddenly become visible or important (baseball).

COME BACK AND BITE US LATER. Become a problem in the future.
"We realized we needed to dig deeper and see whether there were things that were going to come back and bite us later." (*Wall Street Journal,* July 6, 2004, p. R1)

COMER. Someone or something with recognized potential.
"Meanwhile, Wall Street firms continue to aggressively chase hedge-fund business. Newer entrants are particularly focused on serving start-up hedge funds—as illustrated by UBS's acquisition last year of the prime-brokerage business of ABN Amro, which had relationships with small but growing hedge funds. And wealthy and institutional investors are fielding increasing invitations from prime brokers to meet the up and comers." (*Wall Street Journal,* July 22, 2004, p. A1)

COMMERCIAL CREEP. The process of commercial real estate encroaching into residential areas.

COMMERCIAL PAPER. Short-term borrowing instruments used by U.S. businesses.
"The average maturity of the investments in taxable funds, including commercial paper and Treasury bills, fell to 56 days from 57 days." (*Wall Street Journal,* April 29, 2004, p. 1)

COMMODIFICATION. A market situation in which the products offered by competitors become very similar, like commodities. Some analysts describe the personal computer market as having become commodified.

COMMUNITY PROPERTY. Assets of a married couple belonging to both people. Divorce laws vary in the United States, with some states being community property states.
"Real-estate lawyers say that Texas real-estate law is unique and borrowers are likely to get improperly prepared documents

if lawyers aren't involved. Diane Gleason, a Houston real-estate lawyer, says she has seen out-of-state lenders and out-of-state lawyers cloud a property title by not understanding Texas laws on homestead liens, community property and power of attorney." (*Wall Street Journal,* August 9, 2000, p. T2)

COMP. Free or complimentary.

COMPARABLE WORTH. Antidiscrimination argument that people doing the same job or having the same level of responsibility should be paid the same regardless of race or gender.

"'Comparable worth' is a concept being pushed by a Gore ally, Democratic Sen. Tom Harkin of Iowa. Essentially, the goal is to raise the compensation of entire professions dominated by women, such as nurses, teachers and secretaries, and require those workers to be paid comparably to those in similar, male-dominated job categories." (*Wall Street Journal,* August 28, 2000, p. A20)

COMPARISON SHOPPER. Consumer who evaluates alternatives before making purchase decisions; researcher used to investigate marketing practices of competitors. See also SECRET SHOPPER.

"With online car-booking soaring (Budget says 23% of reservations are booked online, up from 12% in 2001), some travelers suspect the warnings are just an attempt to discourage comparison shoppers from making duplicate reservations." (*Wall Street Journal,* Jan. 24, 2003, p. W4)

COMPETITIVE EDGE. Advantage.

COMP TIME. Compensatory time; time off for past extra work.

"Mr. Smith's boss, Chairman John Boehner (R., Ohio), is pushing a bill that would implement the 'comp time' change sought by Mr. Bush, but not the 'flex time' proposal, which is more controversial." (*Wall Street Journal,* August 3, 2004, p. A2)

CONDOR. An option trading strategy based on buying both puts and calls at different strike prices. The payoff diagram looks like a bird, hence the name condor.

CONFIDENCE GAME. Conspiracy where criminals gain the trust of an individual (PIGEON) and then cheat the person out of money.

"In the aptly if flatly titled 'Confidence,' Ed Burns plays a cocksure con man named Jake Vig. A confidence game, Jake says, 'is like putting on a play where everyone knows their part—everyone, that is, except the mark.'" (*Wall Street Journal,* April 25, 2003, p. W1)

CONFORMING LOANS. Mortgage loans that meet the requirements of FANNIE MAE or FREDDIE MAC, the two major lending intermediaries. Loans that conform to their requirements are packaged and sold to investors.

CONNECT THE DOTS (TO). To assess or consider all the information leading to the solution or problem.

CONSTANT DOLLARS. Statistical adjustment used to eliminate the effect of inflation when comparing dollar amounts in two or more time periods.

CONSUMER CONFIDENCE. Consumers' feelings about the future of the economy and their economic well-being. The University of Michigan Survey of Consumer Confidence is the most widely reported and respected measure of consumer confidence.

CONSUMER DURABLES. Consumer goods that have a use-life of more than one year, including automobiles, appliances, and furniture. "Consumer durables" is a category in GDP accounting. Changes in consumer durables expenditures are an indicator of consumer confidence.
"Tata Steel Chairman Ratan Tata said the reduction was aimed at checking India's rising inflation, as steel is the main input for most industries. 'Steel-price increases have a cascading effect on the prices of most domestic manufactured products in the engineering, consumer durables, and automobile segments,' Mr. Tata said." (*Wall Street Journal,* August 24, 2004, p. B3)

CONSUMER PROFILING. The marketing practice of developing a database with information about consumers' purchasing practices and demographics.

CONTAGION. The influence of actions in one market on other markets. Negative conditions in one market often spread to other markets.

CONTINGENCY ALLOWANCE. Allowance made for unforeseen delays or costs.

CONTRACT MOD. Contract modification; change order.

CONTRARIAN. Investor whose ideas are often opposite those of the majority of investors.
"Since being launched in July 2003, the 'Benjamin Graham' portfolio is up 48%, William O'Neil is up 26%, Kenneth Fisher is

up 32% and contrarian investor David Dreman is up 44%." (*Wall Street Journal,* July 25, 2004, p. 4)

CONVENIENCE GOODS. Goods consumers routinely purchase without comparison. These goods are usually brand-name, low-priced items and can be divided into three subcategories: staples, impulse items, and emergency items. Widespread distribution is critical to success in marketing convenience goods.

CONVERGENCE. The combining of television, telephone, and computer into one interactive communication medium.

CONVERSION RATE. The percentage of prospects who become customers.

CONVERTIBLES. Corporate debt securities that can be exchanged for shares of stock.

COOKIE. A small data file created by a Web server that is stored on the user's computer either temporarily for that session only or permanently on the hard disk. Cookies provide a way for the Web site to identify users and keep track of the user's preferences. Because personal data resides in the cookie files in your computer, this storehouse of private information is sometimes the object of attack.

"Most cookies are harmless, but some that record Web surfing habits and personal information are considered spyware." (*Wall Street Journal,* April 26, 2004, p. R6)

COOKIE CUTTER. Mass-produced, as if stamped out with a cookie-cutter.

COOKIE JAR ACCOUNTING. The practice of building up reserves and underreporting revenue during good periods and drawing from them in poor periods to boost results.

"Cookie jar reserves. It has nothing to do with stealing money from the company till. Rather, this is one of the accounting games some companies play to make themselves look more profitable than they really are." (*Charleston News & Courier,* Nov. 24, 2002, p. 13)

COOK THE BOOKS. Falsify records.

"The former chief accountant at Vivendi Universal SA agreed to settle fraud charges brought by the Securities and Exchange Commission. John Luczycki, who was Vivendi's chief accounting officer and controller, settled without admitting or denying the

SEC's claims that he helped cook the books at the international media company." (*Wall Street Journal,* April 25, 2004, p. A1)

COOLING-OFF PERIOD. Government-imposed period, usually sixty days, during which a union is restricted from striking and employers are restricted from locking out employees; any government-imposed restriction or delay.

"They differ in detail. The two stock markets, for instance, define "independent director" differently. Nasdaq proposes a three-year 'cooling off' period during which a person, such as a former executive, can be considered independent; the NYSE calls for five years." (*Wall Street Journal,* July 7, 2003, p. C7)

COPPOCK CURVE. An investment tool used in technical stock market analysis for predicting market lows. The technique was invented by Edwin Coppock in 1962.

"The curve is constructed by making time weighted moving averages of between 11 and 14 months. An upturn from levels below zero generate buy signals. These have proved highly successful, but corresponding sell signals do not work so well. A modified version of the Coppock indicator is a component in our technical investment model for foreign currency, government bond and stock markets worldwide." ("Stock Market Investment Jargon," Investors RouteMap Web site, www.stock-market-investment.com, Dec. 12, 2002)

COPY. Words in an advertisement.

COPYCAT. Anyone in the copy industry; a product made to resemble an existing popular product.

CORE BUSINESS. Basic activities.

"This term almost always includes an announcement by the straight-faced president, CEO* or chairman of the board, 'We are pleased to announce that the company is returning to its core business.'... Actually, core business means that the company is bordering on insolvency as a result of ego-driven forays into a series of unrelated enterprises for which it had no knowledge or expertise then failed." (*Supervision,* Jan. 1994, p. 3)

CORE COMPETENCY. What a company does best.

"Market pressures and consumer requirements eventually forced many auto manufacturers to begin outsourcing to remain profitable. By outsourcing I mean subcontracting. They realized that some parts of their products were not critical to their competitive advantage and did not need to be produced in-house. Subcontracting freed these companies to focus on their core competency." (*Wall Street Journal,* Feb. 4, 2004, p. B2)

CORNER OFFICE. Strategically-located office or position, not necessarily a corner room.

"An account of the unhappy experiences in the work force of Robert T. Stokes, who was kept on for a year after the computer service company he headed was sold, then let go in October 1996, ending a 26-year association in which he worked his way up from customer service to the corner office." (*Wall Street Journal*, April 20, 1999, p. B1)

CORNERSTONE. Foundation; indispensable part.

"But you can't end 'separate but equal' without ending compulsory assignment to a public school. From the vantage point of Brown we can now see that vouchers have become the cornerstone for a fundamental civil right." (*Wall Street Journal,* May 17, 2004, p. A20)

CORNER THE MARKET (TO). Gain controlling interest in a company, product, or market.

CORPORADO. A corporate executive with little concern for the environment. A play on the word desperado.

CORPORATE ANOREXIA. The problems that arise after a company has dramatically reduced its workforce; the company no longer functions as well or is as healthy as it was.

CORPORATE ELITE. Top executives.

"This week, however, he's taking the stage in Switzerland, where world leaders and the corporate elite are set to gather in Davos for the World Economic Forum." (*Wall Street Journal,* Jan. 22, 2004, p. B4)

CORPORATE LADDER. Business hierarchy. Managers are encouraged to climb the corporate ladder.

"By his own admission, Mr. Parker was never the hard-charging type who set out to climb the corporate ladder. For years, he was known as Southwest's 'Mr. Fix-It,' tapped for big projects like leading Southwest's successful opposition to a high-speed rail project in Texas." (*Wall Street Journal,* July 16, 2004, p. A1)

CORPORATE PILOT FISH. Former employees who start a new business based primarily on contacts and contracts with their old company.

"Now consider the corporate pilot fish, a departed employee of a giant corporation who still swims with his former employer for sustenance and protection." (*Wall Street Journal,* April 9, 1996, p. B1)

CORPORATE RAIDER. Individual or group trying to take control of another company.

"Whether 'corporate' is the right word for his presidential agenda is debatable. His policies favored the entrepreneurial sector. Mr. Reagan's 'decade of greed,' after all, was dominated by corporate raiders and junk-bond financed start-ups that upset the status quo in industry after industry." (*Wall Street Journal,* June 16, 2004, p. A15)

CORPORATE TAKEOVER. One company buying another.

CORPORATE WELFARE. Government efforts that subsidize corporations.

CORRECTION. Downward movement of stock market prices.

CORRIDOR CRUISER. A worker who spends a lot of time walking through office hallways, usually en route from one meeting to another.

"The emerging Tablet PC user will be the 'corridor cruiser' and not necessarily someone in a small business, he said. 'The target market for Microsoft is clearly the enterprise user—from desktop to boardroom and back,' Smith said." (Heather Clancy, "Take 2 Tablets ...," *Computer Reseller News,* June 10, 2002)

CO-SOURCING. Provision of a service that was previously performed solely within the company by an outsourcer.

COST OF CARRY. Expenses associated with an investment position. Margin interest charges and transaction fees are typical carrying costs.

COST PER CLICK (CPC). Internet pricing where advertisers pay based on the number of people who click through an advertisement and go to their Web site.

COST PER POINT (CPP). The cost per rating point of a radio or television station's coverage area. CPP is used to compare same-medium broadcast vehicles in the same market.

COST-PLUS CONTRACT. Contract with payment based on costs plus a fee.

"Halliburton's KBR unit has done about $6 billion of work in Iraq under cost-plus contracts that range from supplying troops to repairing oil fields. Other U.S. contractors have received about half that amount combined." (*Wall Street Journal,* Feb. 13, 2004, p. A2)

COST-PUSH INFLATION. Inflation caused by rising labor and material costs.

"If the money stock is accommodating, the result is the well-documented case of cost-push inflation. As a net consequence of innovation or technological change, the marginal revenue product of personal services rises, and thus the ability and willingness to pay higher wages." (*Business Perspectives,* Spring 2004, p. 44)

COUCH POTATO. Lazy person; inveterate television watcher.

"The theory has always been that readers are more engaged than tube-staring couch potatoes. 'Your brain on print—when you are reading and interacting—there are a lot more synapses firing,' says Andrew Swinand, a senior vice president at Publicis Groupe SA's Starcom Worldwide." (*Wall Street Journal,* July 22, 2004, p. B1)

COULD NOT HACK IT. Quit; could not take the pressure.

COUNTER (TO). Make a competing offer.

COUNTER-PARTY. The other person or firm in an exchange. For example, for every sale in the stock market, there has to be a counter-party buyer.

COUNTERTRADE. International barter. Countertrade is often used by developing countries lacking sufficient foreign currency to obtain goods and services from industrialized countries.

"A countertrade commitment included in an international sales contract can be beneficial to all parties involved. Countertrade can generate the needed hard currency to pay for products or repatriation of blocked funds. In addition, countertrade can give a competitive advantage, improve customer relationships and create goodwill with the importing country's government. This goodwill can result in the reduction of import tariffs and restrictions. With this in mind, always remember the countertrade golden rule: Do not quote prices until the countertrade situation is clear." (*Business Credit,* April 2002, p. 48)

COUNTERVAILING DUTY. Import tax intended to protect a domestic industry.

"The study shows that the tariffs created supply shortages by deterring imports and gave U.S. steel producers massive pricing power. This subsidy for inefficiency is precisely why the U.S. steelmakers lobbied for the tariffs, as well as for a spate of anti-dumping and countervailing duty levies that also whacked consumers at the end of 2001." (*Wall Street Journal,* Feb. 25, 2003, p. A14)

COUNTERVAILING POWER. Union power to counterbalance the power of major companies. The term is attributed to economist John Kenneth Gailbraith.

COVERED CALL. The sale of a call option against shares of stock owned by the seller. Covered calls provide income in exchange for forgoing capital gains if the stock price rises.

COVER FOR SOMEONE (TO). Temporarily take on another worker's responsibilities.

COVER LETTER. Letter sent with a document or resume introducing it or adding further explanation to the reader.

COVER-UP. An act to conceal a wrongdoing.
"The complaint had alleged Swatch, of Biel, Switzerland, used its British Virgin Islands subsidiary, Swatch Group Asia Inc., to evade taxes and customs duties in several countries, including the U.S. It also alleged Swatch's senior management tried to cover up the purported tax-evasion activities in April after the two former employees complained about the practice." (*Wall Street Journal,* August 16, 2004, p. B3)

COVER YOUR ASS (CYA). Protect yourself from criticism or blame should a project fail.

COWBOY. An unmanageable person.
"All of which shows that Mr. Kerry and his party aren't running on ideology. They have been running mainly on character and the Senator's biography as the anti-Bush. He won three purple hearts in Vietnam while Mr. Bush stayed home in the National Guard. He's smart and sees the nuances of issues that the uncurious and witless Mr. Bush doesn't. He'd get the Europeans to love us again, while Mr. Bush the cowboy cannot." (*Wall Street Journal,* July 26, 2004, p. A14)

CRACK-BACKED. Getting surprised by something you did not see coming, from football, where a crack-back block is an illegal, dangerous block from behind.

CRACKPOT. Someone with unorthodox ideas; crazy person.

"Unlike throwing more money at Brazil. That nation's problem isn't 'contagion' from Argentina's collapse; investors have been bailing out because they see two left-wing populists leading in the polls for Brazil's October presidential election. Front-runner Luiz Inacio Lula da Silva spent much of his career as a crackpot Marxist, before recently moderating his rhetoric." (*Wall Street Journal,* August 7, 2002, p. A14)

CRADLE TO GRAVE. From birth to death; socialism.

"Mr. Beito's 'From Mutual Aid to the Welfare State' shows how fraternal societies in 19th-century America provided a network of services and institutions for their members that, taken together, resemble virtually every aspect of today's welfare state, including health insurance, hospitals, orphanages and retirement homes. Fraternal societies, in short, sustained needy citizens from cradle to grave." (*Wall Street Journal,* July 10, 2000, p. A30)

CRAMDOWN. A bankruptcy court decision for reorganization that may not be favored by some creditors.

CRASH. Dramatic drop or fall.

"Alan Greenspan nicely teed up the 'ownership society,' presumed theme of George Bush's convention speech Thursday night. Mr. Bush will rightly emphasize the positive, but he'll be offering a way to deal with the pending crash of the welfare state, topic of the Fed chairman's widely noted talk last Friday." (*Wall Street Journal,* Sept. 1, 2004, p. A13)

CRASH AND BURN. To fail miserably.

CRAWLING PEG. An exchange rate system that automatically devalues the country's currency a set percentage per time period.

CREATIVE ACCOUNTING. Falsification of financial records.

"To be sure, broad interpretation of the capitalization rules isn't necessarily contrary to generally accepted accounting principles. In their 2002 book, 'The Financial Numbers Game: Detecting Creative Accounting Practices,' Georgia Institute of Technology accounting Profs. Charles Mulford and Eugene Comiskey devote a 30-page chapter to Aggressive Capitalization and Extended Amortization Policies." (*Wall Street Journal,* August 18, 2004, p. C3)

CREATIVE BOUTIQUE. A specialty advertising agency that works for clients or other advertising agencies.

CREATIVE DESTRUCTION. The constant replacement of existing products and technology with new and improved choices. The term was coined by Austrian economist, Joseph Schumpeter.

CREDIT CRUNCH. A situation in which financing is scarce. Interest rates tend to rise when funds for lending are in short supply.

CREDIT ENHANCEMENT. The use of financial guarantees purchased from insurance companies to increase the rating of debt securities, thereby lowering the cost of borrowing.

CREDIT SCORING. Computerized method of rating a consumer's credit worthiness based on income, past credit experience, and debt.

"In its filing with the Supreme Court, the company denied the allegations. It said credit-scoring is commonly used by insurance companies to establish risk and, hence, rates. The company said it takes into account such things as where the insured person lives, what kind of house the person lives in, and what kind of auto the person drives, when setting rates." (*Wall Street Journal,* April 27, 2004, p. A2)

CREDIT SQUEEZE. Government anti-inflation policy where raising interest rates reduces consumer and business borrowing.

CREDIT WATCH. Announcement by credit rating agencies that a company is under review, usually indicating a possible lowering of the company's credit rating.

CREEPING FEATURISM. The tendency for computer programmers to add marginally beneficial features to software products, thinking added features improve the value to users. Often this process leads to confusing and slow-operating software.

CREEPING INCREMENTALISM. Motions toward progress without results.

CRITICAL LIST, CRITICAL TRADE VENDOR. A priority list of a bankrupt company's vendors. Critical vendors are more likely to be paid what they are owed.

"To be classified as 'critical' by a Chapter 11 debtor company is about the best present a trade creditor can hope for because it means it will get paid at least a portion of whatever the debtor owed it before filing for bankruptcy protection." (*Wall Street Journal,* Dec. 30, 2002, p. B2)

CRITICAL MASS. Sufficient size to survive and be self-sustaining. The term comes from nuclear physics, where critical mass is the amount of fissionable material it takes to sustain a chain reaction.

"In short, U.S. oil companies will be trading access to their network of gasoline stations in order to secure adequate oil supplies at a stable price. Under this scenario, joint-venture strategic alliances could benefit U.S. oil companies by allowing some to achieve 'critical mass'—an industry commanding height whereby a firm attains global reach, scale and scope while retaining a measure of market-agility." (*Wall Street Journal,* August 18, 2004, p. A10)

CRITICAL-PATH ANALYSIS. Management analysis of the most important sequence of an operation.

CRONYISM. Favoritism to people one knows. See also OLD BOYS CLUB.

CROSS-FERTILIZATION. Mixing of ideas.

"This exhibition explores the ways in which the Mongol trading world of Genghis Khan led to a cross-fertilization of artistic ideas in Asia and parts of Europe." (*Wall Street Journal,* April 18, 2003, p. W2)

CROSSOVER POINT. The point at which income from a tax shelter investment exceeds deductions, resulting in taxable income.

CROSS SABERS (TO). Disagree or have a conflict with.

"Because pricing decisions are made by the sales service division, we often cross sabers with them." (Brian Chilla, Rock-Tenn Company, 1995)

CROSS-SELL (TO). To sell other companies' products in addition to one's own.

CROWDING OUT. Economic theory that government borrowing in financial markets increases interest rates and reduces private-sector borrowing and investment.

CROWN JEWELS. Most successful products or divisions of a company.

"He may need his ties to the boss as much as anything else to shake up Mercedes, where he is scheduled to take the helm on Oct. 1. With its high profile and thick margins, the luxury-car maker is the crown jewel in Mr. Schrempp's strategy of turning

DaimlerChrysler into a globally integrated auto maker." (*Wall Street Journal,* July 30, 2004, p. A8)

CRUNCH THE NUMBERS. Calculate the cost, price, value.
"Instead, you would file as 'married filing jointly' or, possibly, 'married filing separately.' But 'married filing separately' rarely will save you money. When in doubt, crunch the numbers both ways. Don't forget to factor in any state-income-tax considerations." (*Wall Street Journal,* March 21, 2004, p. 4)

CUBE FARM. An office arranged into cubicles.

CULL. Reject the lowest-quality items.
"Auto makers, wounded by brutal price wars and foreign competition, are making a more-concerted effort to cull capacity. In the last contract signed with the United Auto Workers union, Ford Motor Co., General Motors Corp. and DaimlerChrysler AG's Chrysler Group generally agreed not to close any plants." (*Wall Street Journal,* Sept. 8, 2003, p. A1)

CULTURAL DIVERSITY. Recognizing various ethnic groups and their contribution to the workplace.
"That's a model that workplaces might do well to emulate, says Prof. Nisbett: The more cultural diversity and, hence, thinking styles in a workforce, the likelier it is to see problems clearly and solve them." (*Wall Street Journal,* March 28, 2003, p. B1)

CUME. Cumulative ratings (advertising).

CURRENT ACCOUNT. A measure of a country's international trade derived by the sum of the value of merchandise, services, investment income, and unilateral transfers from exports and imports. The current account is part of a country's balance of payments.

CURVE BALL. A trick or deception or surprise (baseball).
"The Jeb Bush campaign attempted to throw another legal curve ball into the contest proceeding before Judge N. Sanders Sauls. If Mr. Gore's requests for recounts of Democratic-leaning South Florida counties are granted, the Republican lawyers said, Mr. Bush wants the court to order recounts of votes in several other counties, including some overseas military ballots that Republicans think will increase Mr. Bush's lead over Mr. Gore." (*Wall Street Journal,* Dec. 1, 2000, p. A16)

CUSHION. Financial resources available to help a company survive a downturn.

CUSH-JOB. Easy job.

CUSIP NUMBER. The number given to a security to distinguish it from other stocks and bonds. Most securities exist only as a CUSIP number.

CUT AND RUN. Stop and leave, often without finishing a job (nautical).

CUT ONE'S LOSSES. Concede defeat. See also BAILOUT.

CUT THE CAKE. Complete a business deal; divide the profits or benefits.
"United States: Time to cut the cake a different way?; Latinos and blacks" (*The Economist,* Dec. 8, 2001, p. 46)

CUT THE MELON. To share profits among owners and employees.

CUT THE MUSTARD. Able to meet the standard, effective.
"With travel advertisers back on board, the successful broadcasters can prove they can still cut the mustard." (*Campaign,* May 30, 2003, p. S5)

CUTTHROAT COMPETITION. Tough competition.
"Alitalia, which is 62% owned by the Italian government, is struggling to stay aloft amid cutthroat competition from discount carriers and consolidation among the big players. The carrier is trying to reach a restructuring plan and secure a 400 million euro ($481 million) government-backed loan by Sept. 15." (*Wall Street Journal,* August 30, 2004, p. A10)

CUTTING EDGE. Newest, most advanced technology.
"Many pancreatic-cancer patients are diagnosed at very advanced stages of the disease, when it is harder to get into clinical trials. With such detailed information on researchers, the map offers the ability to track down cutting-edge research that may not be listed on Web sites yet." (*Wall Street Journal,* July 27, 2004, p. D1)

CYBER HUSTLER. Marketers who buy the rights to Internet domain names that are not renewed. Cyber hustlers then sell space to advertisers, much like a billboard, which is then viewed by

Internet users searching for information from the previous owner of the domain name.

"Cyber hustlers are marketers who legally purchase rights to domain names that are not renewed." (*Encyclopedia of American Business,* pp. 257–258)

CYBERNATE (TO). Control by computer.

CYCLE BILLING. System distributing billing activities over a time period.

D

DAISY CHAIN. Collusion among buyers who bid up the price of a stock and then sell to unsuspecting investors; linking together a series of equipment.

"Some PC makers defend the skimpy number of USB ports on the grounds that you can supposedly 'daisy-chain' a large number of USB devices, by hooking up only one to the PC's USB port and then linking the devices to each other. But almost none of the USB peripherals I've seen support this feature." (*Wall Street Journal,* April 13, 2000, p. B9)

DAMAGE CONTROL. Corporate efforts to minimize the impact of negative publicity.

DANGLER. A sign hanging down from a shelf designed to catch the attention of shoppers.

DARWINISM. See ECONOMIC DARWINISM.

DATA MINING. Reviewing and analyzing information in the company's database for marketing insights and ideas.

DATING. Extending credit beyond the usual agreement.

DAWN RAID. The purchase of all the available shares of a company being targeted for hostile takeover.

DAY ORDER. A stock market order directing execution that day or otherwise canceling the order.

DAY TRADER. Stock market speculator who buys and sells in the same day. With the advent of Internet trading and reduced trading fees, day traders are an increasing presence in U.S. stock markets.

D-COMMERCE (DIGITAL COMMERCE). Electronic commerce involving the sale of news, subscriptions, or documents delivered over the Internet. D-commerce companies act as a wholesaler, taking orders and distributing information from multiple sources.

DEAD CATS BOUNCE. See EVEN DEAD CATS BOUNCE.

DEAD HAND. Clauses in corporate director contracts that authorize only the existing board of directors to remove a company's "poison pill." Thus, the old board of directors, even if removed by a takeover, still have power over the company.

DEAD IN THE WATER. Unable to move, stuck (nautical).
   "Yet even as Mr. Ron Wyden is telling Oregon voters he's saved them from 'catastrophic fires,' the Senate Democratic leadership has been refusing to grant unanimous consent to hold a House-Senate conference on the bill. Until it does, Healthy Forests is dead in the water." (*Wall Street Journal,* Nov. 13, 2003, p. A18)

DEAD ON ARRIVAL (DOA). Not viable. Frequently, the president's budget plan is declared "dead on arrival" by the opposition party in Congress. In medicine, "dead on arrival" refers to a patient's condition when reaching the hospital.
   "Under any other set of circumstances, a program such as this might have been dead on arrival because trial lawyers would have howled that it was a form of 'tort reform.' Ironically, the Fund may ultimately serve as a prime example of a compensation program far superior to the traditional tort system." (*Wall Street Journal,* Dec. 16, 2003, p. A16)

DEAD PRESIDENTS. Money. Most U.S. currency has pictures of past presidents.

DEAD TIME. Time not working. When an assembly line is temporarily halted, workers have dead time.

DEAD-TREE VERSION. A paper copy of a document. See also TREEWARE.

DEAD WOOD. People who are part of an organization but no longer contribute to the firm's output. Before DOWNSIZING in corporate America, people who were considered dead wood were often PUSHED UPSTAIRS.

"Tenure guarantees employment for life at the lowest common denominator. There is no incentive to produce once you are tenured and, hence, the 'dead wood.' Given a university's limited financial resources, tenure does so at the expense of hiring new faculty (be they young, middle-aged or elderly)." (*Wall Street Journal,* Jan. 18, 2002, p. A11)

DEALER LOADER. A valuable premium given to a retailer in exchange for a larger or specialty item order.

DECERTIFICATION. Cancellation of union representation by employees.

DECISION TREE. Flow chart to facilitate analysis of a complex problem.

"Described as business school-style 'decision trees,' the charts reflect legal and political constraints facing the administration." (*Wall Street Journal,* March 5, 2002, p. A18)

DECRUITMENT. Termination from employment. The opposite of recruitment.

DEEP-DISCOUNT BOND. A bond sold at a price well below face value.

DEEP DIVE (TO). To research a subject in-depth.

DEEP IN/OUT OF THE MONEY. A call option with an exercise price significantly higher than the current market price is considered deep out of the money.

DEEP POCKETS. Companies or investors with a lot of money.

"Such blame-shifting is useful to Ms. Nappier and Mr. Blumenthal, who have ambitions for higher office. Ms. Nappier would not want a telecom fiasco on her resume if she runs for governor on a fiscal responsibility platform. So shout 'fraud,' throw up a lot of legal smoke, and hope that a jury of financial amateurs is fooled enough to go along with raiding someone else's deep pocket." (*Wall Street Journal,* July 6, 2004, p. A22)

DEEP SIX (TO). Dispose of. A military term referring to discarding something at sea, where it will not be found.

DE FACTO. In fact (Latin). A situation where customary practices have become the accepted standard without rules or regulation.

"Hong Kong's de facto flagship air carrier, Cathay Pacific, rose 4.2% to HK$13.80 as oil prices softened." (*Wall Street Journal,* August 25, 2004, p. C16)

DEFERRED DATING. Scheduling the payment of a bill to a manufacturer or wholesaler at a later date to allow the buyer time to sell the product.

DEFRAG. Defragmentation. A procedure used to optimize a computer hard drive by eliminating unused memory capacity.

DE JURE. By law (Latin).

DELI. Delicatessen; meat, cheese, and sandwich store.

DELINQUENCY. When loan payments are overdue.

DELIVERABLES. Parts of a project available for delivery to the customer. Many consulting projects have a schedule of deliverables.

DELIVER THE GOODS. Perform, come through, succeed.

"'It's the same as in politics: A political party can go only so far on a patriotic platform. Ultimately, if they don't deliver the goods, voters give them the boot,' says Mickey Chak, planning director of DDB Worldwide Communications Group Inc. China." (*Wall Street Journal,* Jan. 21, 2004, p. B4)

DELLIONAIRE. An affluent person whose wealth is based on owning stock in Dell Computer Corporation.

"That simple scheme made millionaires of many of Mr. Dell's early employees, even secretaries and clerks, and it made billionaires of some.... Soon all of Austin was gossiping about the new Dellionaires." (R.W. Apple Jr., "Booming in Size and Brio," *New York Times,* April 28, 2000)

DELPHI TECHNIQUE. Business forecasting and decision-making method where each panel member submits a recommendation that is shared with the other panel members. Revisions are made until a consensus is reached.

DEMAND-PULL INFLATION. Inflation caused by excessive demand, usually brought on by overly stimulative fiscal or monetary policies.

DEMAND WENT SOFT. People no longer wanted the product.

DE-MARKETING. Rationing limited quantities of a good, thereby restricting demand.

DE NOVO. Anew (Latin). Ignoring past problems or performance.
   "If a judge chooses not to follow those guidelines for whatever reason, their rulings would be subject to de novo review by appellate courts, without any of the messy questions of deference often accorded jury determinations." (*Wall Street Journal,* Oct. 31, 2002, p. A18)

DEPARTMENT OF HOUSING AND URBAN DEVELOPMENT (HUD). Federal agency that provides incentives and financing for housing programs in the United States.

DEPARTMENT OF LABOR (DOL). Federal agency that oversees labor laws and programs. Usually considered a lesser White House Cabinet appointment, first-term Clinton administration Secretary of Labor, Robert Reich, became a leading spokesperson of social policy.

DEPOSITORY INSTITUTIONS DEREGULATION AND MONETARY CONTROL ACT (DIDMCA). 1980 federal legislation that drastically changed banking rules, including gradual elimination of interest-rate ceilings and restrictions on stock brokerage firms offering checking accounts. Among bankers it is referred to as the "1980 Act" or DIDMCA.

DERAIL. Wreck, throw off course.
   "Australian Prime Minister John Howard warned that the Labor Party's 'unnecessary' and 'heavy-handed' changes to the agreement could derail the accord." (*Wall Street Journal,* August 13, 2004, p. A13)

DESCENDING TOPS. A stock price pattern where each successive peak price is lower than the preceding peak.

DESK JOCKEY. Office worker.

"He clearly chafed at authority and believed that he could do things better. He wasn't a 'subservient desk jockey,' as he puts it, and his bosses didn't appreciate it. He needed to be an entrepreneur." (*Wall Street Journal,* May 14, 2001, p. R15)

DEUTSCHE MARK (DM). The unit of German currency.

DEVIL IN THE DETAILS. What at first glance looks promising may not look that attractive when all the information is analyzed.

DEVIL'S ADVOCATE (PLAY). Ponder or predict criticism of a project as a means to improve the quality of the proposal.

"Mr. Monti's handling of the Microsoft decision reflects his response to the court's criticisms. The former Italian economics professor introduced new checks and balances in antitrust reviews. For example, Mr. Monti subjected an early draft of the commission's decision to an internal 'devil's advocate' panel of officials who weren't part of the Microsoft-case team." (*Wall Street Journal,* March 25, 2004, p. A2)

DEVOLUTION. Delegation of power by a central government to local governments. Often power and responsibility is transferred without sufficient funds to maintain the programs.

"Hardly anyone today, Democrat or Republican, is calling for an immediate withdrawal from Iraq. But as the monetary and human costs of the occupation mount, there will be increasing demands for an 'exit strategy.' In a sense, this debate has already begun, in the form of sparring between the U.S. and France at the U.N. over the speed with which authority should be devolved to a new Iraqi government. President Bush himself in his speech last week to the U.N. General Assembly rejected a quick devolution and insisted on a more deliberate timetable for the turnover of power." (*Wall Street Journal,* Oct. 1, 2003, p. A18)

DIALING AND SMILING. Telephone solicitation of new customers. See also COLD CALL.

DIALOGUE MARKETING. Marketing programs designed to build a relationship with the customer. See also RELATIONSHIP MARKETING.

DIAMONDS. Dow Jones Industrial Average Tracking Stock.

DICKER (TO). Negotiate.

DIE OR MOVE AWAY (DOMA). A customer-oriented company wants to lose customers only if they DOMA.

DIFFERENT BREED. Different type; unusual.

"Japan's car-campers are a different breed from recreational-vehicle owners in the U.S. For one thing, U.S.-style RVs are just too big for narrow Japanese roads." (*Wall Street Journal,* April 5, 2004, p. A1)

DIFFERENTIALLY ABLED. POLITICALLY CORRECT manner of describing a person with handicaps.

DIGERATI. Computer experts; a pun on the word "literati" (lovers of literature).

"It's amusing: 99% of the digerati who rave about Google couldn't distinguish Google results from those of Yahoo or Ask Jeeves if presented with them blindly, a la the Pepsi Challenge. Googlephiles may think they are exhibiting technical sophistication by their loyalty, but what they are really proving is the extent to which they have been conditioned to respond to logos and brands, just like street kids with their sneakers." (*Wall Street Journal,* May 3, 2004, p. B1)

DIGITAL JEWELRY. Electronic devices people wear, including cell phones, pagers, and personal digital assistants.

DILBERT/DILBERT PRINCIPLE. Referring to a popular 1990s cartoon by Scott Adams that finds humor in corporate absurdities.

"The Dilbert Principle is adapted from the PETER PRINCIPLE, a popular management aphorism of a few years ago. Mr. Adams observes that the most ineffective workers are systematically moved to the place where they can do the least damage: management." (*Wall Street Journal,* May 30, 1996, p. A11)

DIME A DOZEN. Very cheap.

DIME STORE. Business selling low-priced goods.

"Which is why Sam Greenblatt, a Computer Associates senior vice president, wore a giant penguin suit at the software maker's recent annual confab in Las Vegas. 'Anything I can do to get the user groups interested,' says Mr. Greenblatt, who greeted attendees with waving flippers. The suit wasn't just any dime-store Halloween penguin costume, but custom-made for Computer Associates, Mr. Greenblatt says." (*Wall Street Journal,* August 14, 2003, p. B4)

DINGBAT. A dumb person. The term was frequently used by ARCHIE BUNKER to describe his wife on the 1970s situation comedy *All in the Family.* It is considered crude and sexist language.

DINGER. A success (baseball).

DINOSAURS. Large companies that have not changed with the times.
"The PRI's chairman, Roberto Madrazo, a leader of the so-called dinosaur wing of the old PRI machine, selected Mr. Hank for the Tijuana race, on which, many Mexican political analysts say, Mr. Madrazo is tying his hopes of consolidating the PRI's presidential nomination two years from now." (*Wall Street Journal,* July 30, 2004, p. A9)

DIRECT PLACEMENT. The sale of securities by a company to large institutional investors such as insurance companies or pension funds without the use of an intermediary.

DIRT BAG. A sleazy, disreputable person.

DIRTY LAUNDRY. Questionable or scandalous past activities. See also SKELETONS IN THE CLOSET.
"'Prices of asset-management companies have not come down in relation with the problems the industry has,' he said. 'We would hardly want to take on somebody's dirty laundry at this time.'" (*Wall Street Journal,* April 23, 2004, p. B4)

DIRTY TRICKS/POOL. Dishonest or underhanded practices (referring to the game of billiards).
"Also, don't give out the names of references indiscriminately or prematurely. One of the oldest dirty tricks in the search business is for a recruiter to feign interest in a candidate simply to gather references as future leads, says Daniel Parrillo, president of Strategi LLC, a small high-tech recruiting firm in Stockton, Calif." (*Wall Street Journal,* Sept. 17, 2002, p. B8)

DISCONNECT. A conflict or inconsistency.
"There's 'a disconnect between landlords and tenants,' says Mr. DeMeola. The results make clear that 'before landlords put a waterfall in the building, they should be putting in extra security' measures and 'upgrading life-safety systems and emergency lighting,' he says." (*Wall Street Journal,* July 7, 2004, p. B4)

DISCONTINUOUS CHANGE. Completely rethinking the way things are done in an organization.

"Discontinuous change threatens authority because it's the idea that the best way to go about doing something may not be the way it's currently done." (*Across the Board,* Nov./Dec. 1993, p. 51)

DISCOUNT (TO). Lower the price.

DISCOUNT WINDOW. Federal Reserve short-term loans to banks.

"Under the old system, the Fed lent through its 'discount window' to banks that had exhausted other sources of funds, but banks became reluctant to use it for fear it would suggest they were in trouble. Many days, there is less than $100 million in discount-window loans outstanding. That leapt to almost $46 billion after the Sept. 11, 2001, terrorist attacks on the U.S. disrupted the money markets." (*Wall Street Journal,* Jan. 7, 2003, p. A2)

DISINTERMEDIATION. The removal of intermediaries from the manufacturing to consumer process.

"That is where the media-disintermediation business comes in. Disintermediation means getting rid of the middleman, and right now, cable and satellite companies are middlemen because TV is whatever they say it is." (*Wall Street Journal,* May 10, 2004, p. B1)

DISMAL SCIENCE, DISMAL SCIENTISTS. The study of economics, economists. Economists are often accused of finding the negative in any situation. One popular saying is economists have predicted nine out of the last five recessions!

"Dismal scientists expect that the preliminary September reading will tick down to 87.0, compared with a final reading of 87.6 in August." (*Wall Street Journal,* September 13, 2002, p. C1)

DIVERSIFICATION. Increasing the variety of investments or products, usually as a way to reduce risk.

DIVERSITY. Variety of minorities and ethnic groups.

DIVVY UP. To divide among the participants.

DOCTOR (TO)/DOCTORING. Altering records (implies illegal or unethical activity).

"Wall Street circulated that memo yesterday morning after the second-largest buyer of U.S. mortgages, Freddie Mac, got rid of its three top executives. Freddie even attacked one executive for apparently doctoring personal business records he furnished the audit committee's counsel." (*Wall Street Journal,* June 10, 2003, p. C1)

DODGE REPORTS. F.W. Dodge monthly report of new construction activity in the United States.

DOG. Unsuccessful product; a low-growth product with a low market share.
"'Of course,' he says with a smile, 'a company may be debt-free for two reasons. If it's a dog, it's because no one will lend them money.'" (*Wall Street Journal,* May 28, 1996, p. R18)

DOG-AND-PONY SHOW. Simple, planned presentation; too often dog-and-pony shows insult the intelligence of their audience. See also MUSHROOM JOB.
"K-Mart hasn't yet held an analyst or investor day to discuss its strategy and has no plans to hold one soon. It hasn't attended investor conferences or put up a tent at any dog-and-pony shows. Unlike the vast majority of retailers, it doesn't issue weekly or monthly sales updates." (*Wall Street Journal,* June 1, 2004, p. C1)

DOG-EAT-DOG. Highly competitive.
"Indeed, meeting wave after wave of Iraqi exiles, he has keen insights into the dog-eat-dog psychology of survival for ordinary Iraqis. 'I eat, drink and sleep Iraq. I even force myself to watch Iraqi satellite TV,' he says." (*Wall Street Journal,* August 5, 2002, p. A11)

DOGS OF THE DOW. The lowest performing stocks in the Dow Jones Industrial Average. One stock market strategy advocates buying the dogs of the Dow each year on the assumption that the worst performing stocks will do better in the upcoming year.

DOLLAR DRAIN. The impact on the United States of continually running a trade deficit, causing dollars to leave the country.

DOLLARIZE. For a country to abandon its national currency, replacing it with the U.S. dollar.
"Mr. Canto would like to see the DR dollarize, not on the grounds that it would solve problems like the alleged criminal behavior at Banco Intercontinental, but because it would end the wealth and income destruction caused by inflation and devaluation. 'It's important to note that even if the country had been dollarized, the Baninter crisis would have caused a fiscal problem,' Mr. Canto told me. 'But the benefits of dollarization would be that

Dominican inflation would not have taken off and purchasing power of workers would not have deteriorated.' The best corollary to look at, notes Mr. Canto, is Panama, where dollarization has not solved all economic problems but has removed inflation and problems associated with balance of payments." (*Wall Street Journal,* Oct. 31, 2003, p. A13)

DO LUNCH. Have lunch together.

DOMAIN NAME. Internet address.

DOMINO EFFECT. One action causing a series of subsequent effects.

"In 2002, Bethlehem Steel off-loaded $3.6 billion in unfunded pensions on the PBGC in the biggest hit to the agency so far. A United Airlines dump would be almost double that. If that's not bad enough, the PBGC itself had a deficit of more than $11 billion last year. Since the government stands behind the PBGC to make up the difference, if United caused a domino effect in the rest of the industry, the result could be tens of billions of dollars in a bailout underwritten by taxpayers." (*Wall Street Journal,* August 11, 2004, p. A10)

DONE DEAL. An agreement even though a contract has not been signed; FAIT ACCOMPLI; a certainty.

"The Bendix transfer to Federal-Mogul isn't a done deal. In July, Honeywell Chief Executive Dave Cote said the transfer was 'very iffy.' Federal-Mogul has said that the Honeywell transaction would be completed only if Honeywell received an injunction from the federal bankruptcy court shielding it from these liabilities." (*Wall Street Journal,* Sept. 26, 2003, p. B6)

DON'T FIGHT THE TAPE. Do not try to go against the direction of the market.

DON'T HOLD YOUR BREATH. Do not expect anything to happen quickly.

DON'T STEP ON MY AIRHOSE. Do not interfere with what I am doing. Employees often fear managers will step on their airhose, making it more difficult to do their job.

DON'T TAKE ANY WOODEN NICKELS. Be careful, take care of yourself. The phrase was a fad in the 1920s.

DOTTED LINE. Place for signature on a form or contract. Sometimes "signing on the dotted line" is an implied consent or agreement rather than an actual signature on paper.

"Indeed, all most investors can hope for is the future—and that is squarely where Mr. Immelt's eyes were as he repeatedly signed on the dotted line last week." (*Wall Street Journal,* October 13, 2003, p. C1)

DOUBLE BOTTOM. Stock market chart with two declines followed by a recovery.

DOUBLE-DIPPING. Practice of retiring, collecting a pension, and then starting a second career.

DOUBLE INCOME, NO KIDS (DINK). Working couples who do not have children.

"DENKS—Dual Employed, No Kids—are childless working couples, and media attention has ballyhooed them and their almost identical twins—the DINKS—as the wave of the future. (DINKS stands for Double Income, No Kids.) But a new Census Bureau report reveals that the great growth over the past decade has been in DEWKS (pronounced dukes)—Dual Employed, With Kids." (*Wall Street Journal,* July 21, 1988, p. 1)

DOUBLESPEAK. The intentional use of language to confuse or mislead. The term comes from George Orwell's book *1984.*

DOUBLE-TIME. Quickly (military).

DOUBLE WHAMMY. Two consecutive negative events compounding the problem.

DOUBLE WITCHING DAY. When two related option contracts expire on the same day, often creating added trading in the contracts.

DOUGH. Money.

DOVETAIL. Link together neatly, coincide.

"The rule's progress could dovetail with an Oct. 1 deadline for the SEC to report its progress on fund-disclosure issues set by Reps. Michael G. Oxley (R., Ohio) and Richard H. Baker (R., La.) in a July 30 letter to SEC Chairman William H. Donaldson." (*Wall Street Journal,* August 18, 2003, p. D7)

DOW JONES INDUSTRIAL AVERAGE (DJIA). Weighted average of the prices of thirty stocks considered representative of the U.S. economy. The DJIA is the most frequently quoted measure of the U.S. stock market. As the economy has moved away from manufacturing to service industries, the DJIA has been reconfigured to reflect the changing economy.

DOWN. Not working.

DOWN AND DIRTY. Hastily written first draft.

DOWN AND OUT. Broke (having no money).

DOWN IN THE DUMPS. Depressed.

DOWNLINE. Sellers in a MULTILEVEL MARKETING chain whose sales generate commissions.

DOWNSIDE. Negative.
"'The downside of a [permanent] two-tier wage system is that it creates, in essence, two separate work forces,' says Jim Micali, chairman and president of Michelin North America Inc., of Greenville, S.C., which is part of France's Michelin SA." (*Wall Street Journal,* Sept. 1, 2004, p. A2)

DOWNSIZE. Reduce the size of a company.
"Aside from tax measures, Ms. Arroyo asked Congress to pass legislation that would arm her with the power to 'downsize' the government and provide a safety net for public-sector workers who may be displaced by the 're-engineering' process." (*Wall Street Journal,* July 27, 2004, p. A14)

DOWN THE DRAIN/TUBE. Lost, wasted.
"'I understand that in a country like India there has to be shock and awe,' he says. 'But I think of the potential it holds for something to go wrong. All the good work that Kartick is doing could go down the drain in a moment of madness.'" (*Wall Street Journal,* July 15, 2003, p. A1)

DOWN THE ROAD. In the future.

DOWNTICKS. When a stock sells at a lower price than the previous trading price.
"The curbs prohibit certain types of program trades on 'downticks,' while the market is still falling, and thus put a brake on the decline." (*Wall Street Journal,* July 24, 2002, p. C1)

DOWN TIME. Any period when workers or machines are idle.

"Mr. Keker, who often chewed on one arm of his red-framed reading glasses in court, spent the down time during deliberations reading books in a back corner of the courtroom, including 'Elizabeth Costello,' by Nobel laureate J.M. Coetzee." (*Wall Street Journal,* October 28, 2003, p. C9)

DOWN TO BRASS TACKS. Dealing with essentials.

DOWN TO THE WIRE. Last-minute, completed just before the deadline (horse racing).

"The race between the two went down to the wire and depended heavily on where yields on short-term Treasury bills closed at the end of trading Wednesday, which was the final day of the first half of 2004." (*Wall Street Journal,* July 2, 2004, p. A2)

DOWNWARDLY MOBILE (DOMO). A young person who gives up a high-paying, high-pressure job to pursue a more satisfying lifestyle is sometimes labeled a DOMO.

DO YOU READ ME? Do you understand?

DO YOUR HOMEWORK. Prepare.

"On the Road: How to conduct a long-distance job search:—Do your homework before moving to an expensive city. Learn about the local job market by reading area newspapers and joining professional associations." (*Wall Street Journal,* July 6, 2004, p. A18)

DRAG ONE'S FEET. Delay, deliberately complete a task slowly.

DRAW. Payment against commission; receiving part of a loan.

DRAW A LINE IN THE SAND. To make a final offer or decision.

DRAW A PICTURE. Explain in detail.

"Dozens of refugees in both Macedonia and Montenegro interviewed in recent days draw a picture of Serbian forces using extreme brutality—including mass murder, beatings, extortion and looting—to empty Kosovo of its ethnic Albanian population." (*Wall Street Journal,* April 6, 1999, p. 1)

DRAWBACK. Repayment of a customs duty when goods are exported again; problem.

"Site also provides tips on using pedometers. Comment: One drawback: Pedometer was hard to open—and sometimes we popped its back off instead, exposing the electronic works inside." (*Wall Street Journal,* June 25, 2004, p. W9C)

DRAW DOWN (TO)/DRAWDOWN. Reduce; amount that has been borrowed under a loan agreement.

"Borrowers who don't draw down their lines may face a 'non-usage' fee, typically $50. Homeowners who pay off the line within the first three years may also be hit with an early termination fee of $250 to $600." (*Wall Street Journal,* Dec. 14, 2003, p. 4)

DRAYAGE. The charge by a trucking company for pick up and delivery of an ocean shipping container.

DRESSING UP A PORTFOLIO. Practice by mutual fund managers of selling stocks about which there has been bad news, or buying stocks that have received positive news, so that the quarterly report will look good.

DRILL BIT STOCK. A stock that has a price under one dollar. Like drill bits, which come in fraction of an inch sizes.

"Heard the latest lingo on the Street? It's 'drill bit stocks,' as in stocks trading in the drill-bit range (3/64, 5/16, etc.)." (Andy Serwer, "Loose Change," *Fortune,* April 30, 2001)

DRINK FROM A FIRE HOSE. To be overwhelmed with information.

DRIVE HOME. Emphasize.

"'The basic message that the administration drives home is that Americans can compete with anybody if given a chance,' Mr. Zoellick says. 'It's to our advantage through trade agreements to level the playing field.'" (*Wall Street Journal,* August 29, 2004, p. 1)

DRIVER. An important factor influencing the outcome of a situation.

DROP A BUNDLE. Lose or spend a lot of money.

"Attracted at least partly by the promise of globalization, a lot of wealthy organizations want to get into the action and are willing and able to drop a bundle to get in." (*Forbes,* Nov. 21, 1994, p. 244)

DROP-DEAD DATE/DAY. The absolute deadline.

"It obviously has surprised E*Trade and Telebanc. After announcing the merger June 1, E*Trade, Menlo Park, Calif., filed its application to become a thrift holding company with the OTS on June 28—and set the drop-dead date of Dec. 31." (*Wall Street Journal,* Dec. 14, 1999, p. C1)

DROP THE BALL. Fail to do what one said one would.

DRUM ROLL. The signal that an announcement is about to be made.

DRUM UP. To secure or find.

DUAL BANKING. Regulatory system in the United States whereby some banks, called national banks, are chartered and regulated by federal agencies and others are regulated by state banking authorities. The rules differ, which creates incentives for new banks to do regulatory shopping.

DUAL-CAREER MARRIAGE. Husband and wife both work (especially, both professionally).

DUAL TRACKING. In business finance, the simultaneous consideration of buyout offers while proceeding with an initial public offering.
   "Advertsing.com used a strategy that is increasingly common among startups. Investment bankers call it 'dual tracking,' or entertaining an acquisition offer at the same time as preparing for a public offering." (*Wall Street Journal,* July 24, 2002, p. C1)

DUB. To copy; label; a copy of an audio or video recording.
   "He plans to dub foreign-language shows, adding a humorous touch." (*Wall Street Journal,* April 28, 2003, p. B5)

DUBYA. Nickname for President George W. Bush used to distinguish him (by his middle initial) from his father, President George H.W. Bush. Dubya is not considered a kind reference to the president.

DUCKS IN A ROW (TO GET ONE'S). To get organized, prepare.
   "Last Friday's resignation of Ambassador Jack Pritchard for 'personal reasons' suggests that the Bush administration may finally be getting its ducks in a row for discussions of the North Korean nuclear menace in Beijing tomorrow." (*Wall Street Journal,* August 26, 2003, p. A13)

DUE DILIGENCE. Thoroughly investigated (legal).

"Says Charley Polachi, a Sherborn, Mass., headhunter, 'There's a lot more due diligence' by prospective candidates about job offers because 'near-term history has got a lot of wreckage.'" (*Wall Street Journal,* August 31, 2004, p. B1)

DUMMY. A mock-up showing the actual size, with details of advertising brochures, products, or displays.

DUMP. Sell in foreign markets at prices below domestic market prices. Dumping is a controversial practice in international trade; many accusations are made, but they are difficult to prove.

DUMP BIN. Display box holding products loosely dumped inside.

DUN (TO). Exert pressure for payment of past-due accounts.

DUN & BRADSTREET (D&B). Established credit evaluation company. Creditors and potential investors will often ask for a company's D&B report.

DUPE. Duplicate; deceive.

DURATION GAP. The difference between the weighted average maturity of assets versus liabilities. Financial institutions with a significant duration gap are at risk if interest rates change rapidly.
"The letter came after Fannie Mae said in a monthly financial disclosure that its so-called durations gap, which measures its success in matching its assets and liabilities, swung from negative nine months in July to negative 14 months in August, due to low interest rates and heavy refinancing activity." (*Wall Street Journal,* September 15, 2002, p. A2)

DUTCH AUCTION. Pricing method in the U.S. government securities market whereby the lowest price bid necessary to sell the entire amount of securities offered becomes the price at which all are sold.
"That's the question that launches a thousand news stories on IPO day and causes the breath of CNBC anchors to become labored and irregular. Google's goal, by adopting a 'Dutch auction,' was to eliminate a good deal of suspense from the process. Its stock would be introduced at a real market price rather than a blind man's approximation. No pop, no instant wealth, no opportunity for lucrative favoritism." (*Wall Street Journal,* August 25, 2004, p. A11)

DUVET DAY. A company-approved day off that employees can take if they feel too stressed or tired to work.

"'Duvet days were introduced because we realized that everyone has those days when they just cannot face work,' explains Katherine Nicholls, HR manager at August One. 'In the past, these may have been days when people would have called in sick or they may have had to be pre-planned as holiday. The beauty of duvet days is that they are not pre-planned and people do not have to pretend or feel guilty about calling in.'" (Roisin Woolnough, "Don't Let Stress Make You Sick of Working," *Computer Weekly,* Feb. 1, 2001)

DWEEB. An Internet "citizen" often found in chat rooms, usually male, with a tendency to expound on any and all subjects with apparent authority.

DYNAMIC SCORING. Political/economic forecasting technique that assumes that budget reductions stimulate economic activity, thereby further reducing budget deficits.

"Advocates of dynamic scoring have tried to make the most of these tepid results, calling the report a good first step. 'You've got to crawl before you can walk, and you've got to walk before you can run,' says economist Bruce Bartlett, a senior fellow at the National Center for Policy Analysis and former Reagan administration Treasury Department economist who pushed Mr. Douglas Holtz-Eakin for the CBO post." (*Wall Street Journal,* April 1, 2003, p. A4)

E

EAGER-BEAVER. Very energetic.

"On Jan. 7, NBC launched a 'reality show' it called 'groundbreaking,' presumably because it is the first one to feature Donald Trump. 'The Apprentice,' (Wed., from 8–9 p.m.) started out with 16 eager-beaver contestants, divided into two all-male and all-female teams." (*Wall Street Journal,* Jan. 23, 2004, p. W2)

EAR CANDY. Flattery. Compliments designed for a specific audience.

EARL SCHEIB. A quick and cheap job (reference to well-known car-painting firm).

EARLY BIRD. Person or object that arrives before the regular time.

"When rates rise, he says, he will look for a long ocean cruise instead of less-expensive gambling cruises he has recently gone on. He also will expand his restaurant selection beyond early-bird specials and 'free lunch' investment seminars." (*Wall Street Journal,* June 29, 2004, p. C1)

EARMARK. Set aside for a specific purpose.

"Precisely how much investors earmark for index funds and for active management depends on their investment horizon and risk tolerance." (*Money,* Aug. 1995, p. 68)

EARNED INCOME. Internal Revenue Service definition of wage, salary, and tips compensation.

EARNEST MONEY. Deposit made when entering into a contract.

EARNINGS PER SHARE (EPS). Total profit for a period divided by the number of shares of stock outstanding.

EARN ONE'S STRIPES. Put in time with an organization, thereby earning one's position or promotion (military).

EASTER EGGING. Replacing unrelated parts of a computer or other machine in the hope that it will solve the problem.

EASY AS ABC. Very simple.

EASYGOING. Mild-mannered.

EASY MARK. Someone or something easily cheated.

"Attracted by comparatively weak laws governing their activities, mobsters in the past decade have made Canada 'one of the most important bases for the globalization of organized crime,' says Antonio Nicaso, a Canadian authority on global crime. Adds Jack Ramsay, a member of the Canadian Parliament: 'The laws say to the professional criminal that Canada is an easy mark.'" (*Wall Street Journal,* July 6, 1998, p. 1)

EAT SOMEONE'S LUNCH. Overwhelm the competition. To eat the lunch of a competitor implies blatantly taking bread (sales) from it.

ECHO BUBBLE. A sharp but temporary rise in stock prices following the collapse of a recent stock market bubble.

"Given where tech stocks are at the moment—wheezing at a red light after a 17-month romp—where will they go from here? Will the Nasdaq hitch up its socks and dash to 2500 or maybe 3000? Or is the 'echo bubble' starting to leak? And will this pull Nasdaq down to 1500?" (Rich Karlgaard, "Tech Stocks at a Crossroads," *Forbes,* March 1, 2004)

ECONOMIC DARWINISM. Survival of the strongest in the marketplace.

"Competition yields efficiency and efficiency benefits society. However, competitive societies live in fear; deadlines, sales quotas, profit margins, making the cut, or getting the job are all part of competitive market pressures. Competitive markets have been called 'economic Darwinism.'" (*Understanding NAFTA and Its International Business Implications,* 1996, p. 244)

ECONOMIC GIANT. Corporate or business leader.

ECONOMIC MELTDOWN. A severe downturn in the economy (nuclear reactors).

"Even as the Turkish stock market has tumbled on war uncertainty, investors and brokerage trading desks have been buying Turkish debt, gambling that the U.S. and institutions like the International Monetary Fund will bail Turkey out before any government default. They figure the U.S. can't risk allowing a Turkish economic meltdown at a time when America is touting Turkey as the model of a democratic, secular Muslim state—and when it desperately needs access to Turkish military bases for a war in Iraq." (*Wall Street Journal,* March 7, 2003, p. C1)

ECONOMIC TIDES. Shifts in economic conditions.

ECO-PORN. Corporate advertisement that extols the company's environmental policies or record.

"We're all used to eco-porn by now; those beautiful television ads featuring some natural jewel, during which an announcer with a four-balls voice tells us how much Exxon or some other gross polluter is doing to keep our precious earth green." (Molly Ivins, "Think eco-porn's bad? Check out pharma-porn," *Seattle Times,* May 14, 2001)

EDGAR REPORTS. Securities and Exchange Commission–required financial reports.

EDSEL. A failure. Ford Motor Company introduced the Edsel with great fanfare in the 1950s. The car, which was based on out-of-date research and contained gimmicks rather than added value for consumers, was a dismal failure.

EFFICIENT MARKETS THEORY. Stock market theory that investors correctly incorporate all information known about a company, resulting in fully valued prices and no bargains.

E.G. (EXEMPLI GRATIA). For example (Latin).

EGGS IN ONE BASKET. All one's money in one investment.

"I asked one of my assistants to find for me the Japanese equivalent of the proverb, 'Don't put all your eggs in one basket,' he says, acknowledging a tough road ahead. 'Not only couldn't he find one, he found two Japanese proverbs that suggested, in fact, it was best to put them all in one basket.'" (*Wall Street Journal,* July 19, 2004, p. C1)

EGO TRIP. Self-centeredness.

EIGHT-HUNDRED-POUND GORILLA. Powerful, important person or group.
"Fidelity, the 800-pound gorilla of brokerage-house clients, wants electronic access to the models used by the firms' analysts to estimate earnings of the companies they follow." (*Wall Street Journal,* August 30, 1996, p. C1)

EIGHTY-SIX (TO). Throw away.

EIGHTY-TWENTY RULE. The concept that a few items or customers (20 percent) generate most (80 percent) of a company's sales.

ELECTRONIC COMMUNICATIONS NETWORK (ECN). An electronic trading system that eliminates stock brokers as intermediaries.

ELECTRONIC DATA GATHERING ANALYSIS AND RETRIEVAL SYSTEM (EDGAR). The electronic database used by the Securities and Exchange Commission for the filings of public corporations.

ELECTRONIC DATA INTERCHANGE (EDI). The exchange of digital information, particularly business sales transactions between buyers and sellers.

ELECTRONIC FUNDS TRANSFER SYSTEM (EFTS). Bank processing system that allows payments to be made without having to write a check.

ELEPHANT HUNT. Trying to find a major corporation to move into one's community, stimulating economic development. When South Carolina snared BMW Corp. and Alabama lured Mercedes Benz to their states, they had carried out successful elephant hunts.

ELEPHANTS. Large institutional investors who tend to have a herd instinct, moving together as a group.

ELEVATOR PITCH. A quick, short sales presentation.

ELEVENTH HOUR. Very last minute.

"Indeed, last month, in a move that took investors by surprise, Vodafone Group PLC, the world's biggest wireless carrier, made a serious run to acquire AT&T Wireless Services Inc., the third-largest U.S. wireless carrier, only to lose out at the eleventh hour to U.S. bidder Cingular Wireless, a joint venture of BellSouth Corp. and SBC Communications Inc." (*Wall Street Journal,* March 4, 2004, p. C1)

EL JEFE. The boss (Spanish), a term of respect.

ELVES. Stock market technical analysts. Elves chart the movement of statistical measures of the stock market, including volume, short sales, ODD-LOT sales, and others. Elves make financial recommendations based on these statistics, as opposed to changes in the FUNDAMENTALS of a company or industry. See also CHARTISTS.

EMINENT DOMAIN. The power of government to seize private property for a public purpose.

EMOTIONAL LABOR. Job where employees are required to express false or exaggerated emotions; the effort of expressing those emotions.

"Erickson wants to look at what she calls 'emotional labor'—or what nurses face in creating or suppressing their own feelings to make others feel OK. Nurses, for example, might have to hide their feeling of frustration and act happy with patients even when they're extremely overworked. This stress can contribute to burnout." (Cheryl Powell, "Nurses have area expert on their side," *Akron Beacon Journal,* April 24, 2002)

EMPLOYEE STOCK OWNERSHIP PLAN (ESOP). A company program fostering employee purchases of stock. ESOPs have sometimes been used by management to divest a company of unwanted divisions, selling them to the employees, using their retirement funds.

EMPLOYER IDENTIFICATION NUMBER (EIN). The Internal Revenue Service requires all employers to have an EIN.

EMPOWERMENT. To allow greater employee decision-making.

"Management's definition [of empowerment]: Work harder with fewer people, don't rock the boat and don't complain." (*Supervision,* Jan. 1994, p. 3)

EMPTY NEST. A family whose children have grown up and left home.

"Maybe a place for the in-laws or children to live, an increasingly common add-on for the nation's big home builders. A recent survey by Pulte Homes of Dallas found that more than half of empty-nest home buyers could foresee their children or grandchildren living with them during their retirement, more than double the number two years ago." (*Wall Street Journal,* Dec. 20, 2002, p. W1)

EMPTY SUITS. Robot-like middle management executives.

ENCRYPTION. The conversion of plain text into code so that unauthorized people cannot easily read it.

ENDANGERED SPECIES. Nearing extinction.

ENDLESS CHAIN METHOD. A sales technique where salespeople ask prospects and customers for names of other potential customers.

END-USER. Ultimate user of a product or service.

ENERGIZING VISION. New idea. See also PARADIGM SHIFT.

"Inspiring leadership, of the heart, engages with people, giving them an energizing vision. All managers must exercise strategic and supervisory leadership of the head and hands. However, good managers go further and inspire people with the heart—rendering their leadership transforming." (*Leadership Organizational Development Journal,* June 1994, p. 8)

ENRONESQUE. Secretive, illegal business activities, a reference to Enron Corporation.

"A final version of the new guidelines, expected to be issued as early as this month, reveals that the effort to restrict the use of Enronesque off-the-books partnerships has become mired in the kind of detail that only an accountant can wallow in." (*Wall Street Journal,* Jan. 13, 2003, p. C1)

ENRONOMICS. A fiscal policy or business strategy that relies on dubious accounting practices, overly optimistic economic forecasts, and unsustainably high levels of spending.

"Democratic National Committee staffers urge candidates to run against 'Enronomics,' an albatross even worse than recession that they hope to hang around Republican necks." (Martin Kaplan, "How Enron stole center stage," *USA Today,* Jan. 23, 2002)

ENTERPRISE ZONE. An area, usually an economically depressed area, offering tax incentives for companies to relocate to.

ENTREPRENEURIAL SPIRIT. Eagerness to take business risks.

ENVIRONMENTAL IMPACT STATEMENT (EIS). Government document evaluating the environmental impact of a proposed project or policy. Environmentalists have often insisted that government agencies produce a full EIS as a way to stall a program or project that they oppose.

ENVIRONMENTAL MOVEMENT. Groups that encourage the preservation and protection of the Earth.
"The fervor with which LBJ's speeches describe the Great Society's legislative crusade matched and even exceeded Ronald Wilson Reagan's. His 1964 State of the Union Speech was astonishing in its list of "we must" goals: 'All this and more can and must be done.' He committed the government to 'unconditional war on poverty.' The next year he was giving speeches on the signing of historic bills for civil rights, Medicare, education, even highway beautification, which seeded the environmental movement." (*Wall Street Journal,* June 11, 2004, p. A8)

ENVIRONMENTAL PROTECTION AGENCY (EPA). Government environmental policy and enforcement agency created in 1970.

E PLURIBUS UNUM. "One among many" (Latin). The motto printed on the U.S. dollar bill.

EQUAL EMPLOYMENT OPPORTUNITY COMMISSION (EEOC). Government-created commission (1964) empowered to enforce equal opportunity laws in the United States.

EQUITIZE/EQUITIZATION. To reduce corporate debt in favor of equity.
"Those low rates mean holding even a small portion of its portfolio as cash can produce a drag on the fund's investment performance. So managers unable to find specific securities to purchase may choose to 'equitize' their available cash by buying shares of an ETF that tracks the fund's benchmark, such as the iShares Russell 2000 ETF or the SPDR Trust, the ETF known as the "Spider" and which tracks the Standard & Poor's 500-stock index." (*Wall Street Journal,* July 7, 2003, p. R9)

EQUITY RISK PREMIUM. The expected additional return on investment in equities (stocks) over the return on risk-free assets. Investors often compare the added expected return on an investment to the return on U.S. Treasury bonds, considered a risk-free investment, to determine whether the potential reward is worth the additional risk.

ERROR RATE. Number of faulty products expressed as a percentage of total output.

ESCALATOR CLAUSE. Part a contract providing for future increases in payments, taxes, wages, etc.

ESQUIRE (ESQ.). Professional title sometimes used by attorneys.

ET AL. And others (Latin, abbreviated).

EULA. End-uses license agreement. Contracts that accompany most software programs and dictate the terms of use of the software.

EUROBOND. A bond sold outside the United States but denominated in U.S. dollars.

EUROPEAN UNION (EU). Agreement among Western European countries creating access to each other's markets and allowing a flow of workers within the Union.

EVEN BREAK. A fair and equal chance.

EVEN DEAD CATS BOUNCE. Even stocks or bonds that were once considered worthless can rise in price.

EVEN KEEL. Balanced, steady.
"If the Clinton administration had even considered adopting one of these policies, China would likely have reacted angrily. Yet today Mr. Jiang Zemin and his colleagues are forgoing petulant protests in favor of keeping the U.S.-China relationship on an even keel." (*Wall Street Journal,* Oct. 21, 2002, p. A14)

EVIL TWINS. Wi-Fi sites created by criminals to capture Internet users' personal information.
"Evil twins are wireless networks that pretend to offer trusty Wi-Fi connections to the Internet like those available at some coffee shops, hotels and conferences." (*Wall Street Journal*, May 17, 2005, p. B1)

EX-DIVIDEND. Shares of stock being traded without the right to receive a dividend that has been announced but not yet distributed to shareholders.

EXECUTIVE SUITE. Top management position.

EXERCISE PRICE. The price at which an option holder has the right to buy or sell the underlying shares of stock represented by the option.

EXIT INTERVIEW. Personnel office interview of someone who is leaving the company.
    "In an exit interview Tuesday with the *New York Times,* Mr. [Michel] Camdessus said, 'We created the conditions that obliged President Suharto to leave his job,' then said he flew to Moscow to tell Boris Yeltsin the same forces were headed his way." (*Wall Street Journal,* Nov. 11, 1999, p. A26)

EXIT MEMO. A message to the employees of a company, written by a person about to leave the company.
    "Against the clear advice of career counselors to hold one's tongue and not send anything but contact information, many people are unable to resist waxing sentimental, self-indulgent or bitter, especially in the case of a layoff. This holiday season, typically a time of departures as executives collect year-end bonuses and move on, the sputtering economy seems to have created a thicker-than-usual stream of exit memos." (Katherine Rosman, "They Got Mail: Not-So-Fond Farewells," *New York Times,* December 1, 2002)

EXIT STRATEGY. Business strategy designed to get out of an existing situation or market.

EXPLODING OFFER. Business offer that has a specific deadline, after which it is no longer available.
    "The MGM tactic, known as an 'exploding offer' in merger parlance, is risky and usually used as a last resort when a buyer feels that the seller is being unreasonable. The maneuver could very well backfire as Vivendi could call MGM's bluff. Should MGM then walk away, it hurts its standing on future deals as it could reinforce the skepticism with which merger partners view Mr. Kirk Kerkorian." (*Wall Street Journal,* July 15, 2003, p. A3)

EXPONENTIAL SMOOTHING. Market forecasting method weighting past results.

EX POST FACTO. From a thing done afterwards (Latin), subsequently.

EXPOSURE. In finance, exposure is financial risk; in marketing, exposure refers to visibility.

EXTERNALITIES. Costs or benefits not included in market prices.

EYEBALL (TO). Check by quickly viewing.

EYEBALLS. Internet viewers. See STICKINESS.
"It seeks to lay out guidelines for corporations to create Web sites that abet conversations and relationships with customers, rather than the sort of sites now prevalent, which are devoted to capturing as many eyeballs as possible." (*Wall Street Journal*, April 9, 1999, p. B1)

EYEBALL-TO-EYEBALL. Direct communication. See also FACE-TO-FACE.
"A Garcia victory would lengthen a growing list of hard-line populists coming to power in the region over the past few years. Brazil's Luiz Inacio Lula da Silva, Venezuela's Hugo Chavez and Argentina's Nestor Kirchner all won elections threatening to go eyeball-to-eyeball with international bondholders, but, once in power, none have been as strident as they were on the campaign trail." (*Wall Street Journal,* April 5, 2004, p. A17)

EYE-TO-EYE. In agreement.
"At the same time, Mr. Parsons doesn't let disputes fester. He acted quickly in pushing Turner cable networks to work with Warner Bros. on programming for preschoolers when the two sides weren't seeing eye to eye (see accompanying article). 'We are trying to run the company to maximize the value of the whole company,' says Mr. Parsons." (*Wall Street Journal,* Dec. 11, 2003, p. B1)

E-ZINE. Electronic magazine.

F

FACE-OFF. Confrontation, argument (hockey).

FACE THE MUSIC. Accept the consequences.
"'The dealers blame the factory and the factory blames the dealer body, and nobody wants to take ownership,' said John Hiebert, general manager at Jack Wolf Chrysler-Jeep in Belvidere, Ill. 'It seems now that both sides are getting off their butts to face the music.'" (*Wall Street Journal,* Nov. 12, 2003, p. B2)

FACE TIME. Visibility in the office.
"A hybrid schedule of mixing face time at school with online classes, live Internet chats with professors, and e-mail is used by 80% of ALU's students. The other 20% of ALU's students learn solely via the Internet; one student is a U.S. soldier in Kosovo." (*Wall Street Journal,* August 17, 2004, p. B3)

FACE-TO-FACE. In person.
"Coalition forces were waiting on an order from Allawi to pull out. Renegade Sadr agreed to the plan in a face-to-face meeting

with leading Shiite cleric Sistani."(*Wall Street Journal,* August 27, 2004, p. A1)

FACE VALUE. On a bond, the amount originally borrowed and to be paid at maturity.

FACTOID. A small piece of information, frequently quoted by others.

FACTORING. The practice of selling accounts receivable in order to receive cash before payment is due.

FAIRNESS DOCTRINE/EQUAL TIME. Principle that U.S. media must provide time for opposing views on important social issues.
"The Fairness Doctrine refers to a former policy of the Federal Communications Commission (FCC) wherein a broadcast station which presented one viewpoint on a controversial public issue had to afford the opposing viewpoint an opportunity to be heard." (*Federal Communications Law Journal,* Sept. 1994, p. 51)

FAIT ACCOMPLI. Accomplished fact (French); something already taken place.
"The mistake is to think it's anything new. From a distance of 60 years it's not hard to toast our strong wartime alliance. In truth, however, de Gaulle was kept in the dark about D-Day until two days before the attack. So enraged was he that at first he refused to deliver a radio address after Eisenhower (the 'after' was but one sticking point) to ask the French to rally to their own liberation. And in point of fact we didn't even recognize de Gaulle and his Free French as the legitimate authority in France until months later, after he'd more or less made it a fait accompli." (*Wall Street Journal,* June 7, 2004, p. A21)

FALLBACK POSITION. Alternative plan (military).

FALL BY THE WAYSIDE. Discontinue; fail.
"'The outlook for this year's earnings is quite good and that should help stocks in 2004,' said Bob Davidson, co-manager of Touchstone Small-Cap Growth Fund. 'But there is no question earnings will slow and especially the weaker competitors could fall by the wayside in 2005.'" (*Wall Street Journal,* May 17, 2004, p. C4)

FALL DOWN ON THE JOB. Fail at one's responsibilities.

FALLEN ANGELS. Stocks or bonds that were originally considered of high quality but subsequently have become risky.

"All told, 374 stocks moved in, including those that became too small to stay in the Russell 1000 Index of large stocks. The fallen angels include Reader's Digest, Krispy Kreme Doughnuts, Ethan Allen Interiors and Delta Air Lines, which all are small stocks that trade on the New York Stock Exchange." (*Wall Street Journal,* June 28, 2004, p. C4)

FALL GUY. Person blamed for a bad decision.
"The two announcements raise the prospect that Mr. Richard P. Scalzo, a 46-year-old partner in the accounting firm's Boston office, could wind up being the fall guy for PricewaterhouseCoopers as it tries to avoid regulatory sanctions over its audits for Tyco." (*Wall Street Journal,* August 14, 2003, p. C1)

FALL ON THE SWORD. To take the blame or responsibility for something. In ancient Rome, falling on one's sword was considered the honorable way to commit suicide.

FALLOUT. Repercussions, side effects of a decision (reference to nuclear weapons).
"Though Mr. Sharon quietly supports the changes, he is allowing Mr. Netanyahu to take the lead—and bear the brunt of the political fallout. But amid signs the economy is bouncing back—growth in the first half of this year reached 4.1%, the government said recently—Mr. Netanyahu hopes a successful campaign could bolster his standing and pave the way for his eventual return to the prime minister's office." (*Wall Street Journal,* August 18, 2004, p. A9)

FAMILY LEAVE. Time off from work to take care of family members.
"Some 30% of big companies now offer domestic-partner benefits, she estimates, compared with 22% in a 2000 Hewitt survey of 570 companies. 'We're seeing an increase in employers who say, Let's provide family leave and other work-life benefits for whatever definition of family our employees have,' Ms. Sladek says." (*Wall Street Journal,* March 18, 2004, p. D1)

FAMILY VALUES. Values associated with traditional home life in America. See also OZZIE AND HARRIET. In the 1990s the term became associated with anti-abortion and anti-homosexual political groups.

FAM TOUR. Familiarization tour offered to travel agents and convention organizers by tourism industry operators.

FANNIE MAE. See FEDERAL NATIONAL MORTGAGE ASSOCIATION.

FAQ. Frequently Asked Question, especially with reference to the Internet.

"The site has an easy-to-use order form, though there is no separate help or FAQ page that explains store policies." (*Wall Street Journal,* June 10, 2002, p. R8)

FARM OUT (TO). Subcontract; delegate.

"NEC Corp. said it plans to farm out more software-development work to companies in China in a move to cut costs and strengthen ties with the companies." (*Wall Street Journal,* May 17, 2004, p. 1)

FAR OUT. Weird, out-of-the-ordinary (1960s slang).

"*People* magazine has gone online, with an electronic version of CompuServe. The online edition is typical of the magazine itself— trendy, but not too far out." (*Information,* March 1995, p. 17)

FAST AND LOOSE. Irresponsible; deceitful.

"On the historical inaccuracy, the scholars note that the four gospels were written decades after Christ died and 'we're only getting highlights,' observes Professor Kimball. Then the movie picks and chooses from them, with John the dominant one. 'Mel Gibson plays fast and loose with the gospels,' says Prof. Mary Foskett." (*Wall Street Journal,* March 25, 2004, p. A17)

FAST BUCK. Quickly earned money.

"The SEC is worried that customers are being suckered into signing up with companies that are less interested in making an honest living than in making a fast buck on the back of the Internet bubble." (*Wall Street Journal,* August 16, 1999, p. C1)

FAST-TALKING. Persuading with deceitful statements.

FAST-TRACK. The way to rapid promotion or success.

"That's bad news for foreign investors pursuing stakes in China's smaller banks as a relatively safe means to gain fast-track access to the financial industry." (*Wall Street Journal,* June 8, 2004, p. A13)

FAT CAT. Tycoon; wealthy person.

"That would be almost as crazy as the current effort by some Bush backers to focus attention on John Kerry's Vietnam War record and subsequent protests. This is being significantly funded and directed by Texas fat cats and political operatives who have more than a passing relationship with Bush political guru Karl Rove." (*Wall Street Journal,* August 5, 2004, p. A11)

FAUX PAS. Mistake ("false step," French).

FEATHERBEDDING. The practice of retaining unnecessary union jobs.
"YPFB simply can't do it. Like other state-owned enterprises in Bolivia, its record is besmirched with repeated episodes of corruption, featherbedding and sheer inefficiency. Even raiding Bolivia's pension funds won't provide sufficient capital." (*Wall Street Journal,* July 9, 2004, p. A11)

FEATURE CREEP. Adding new features or options to old, user-unfriendly products, making the product even more cumbersome.

FEATURE DUMP. Salesperson or sales promotion that talks about only the product features.

FED. See FEDERAL RESERVE BOARD.

FEDERAL DEPOSIT INSURANCE CORPORATION (FDIC). A quasi-government organization created during the Depression to insure depositor's funds in commercial banks after nearly ten thousand banks failed in two years.

FEDERAL FUNDS. Deposits made by commercial banks in their Federal Reserve Banks to meet reserve requirements.

FEDERAL HOME LOAN BANK (FHLB). Government system created to provide credit to the savings and loan industry. In 1989 the FHLB was replaced by the Federal Housing Lending Board.

FEDERAL HOME LOAN MORTGAGE CORPORATION (FHLMC), "FREDDIE MAC." Publicly held corporation that packages and resells mortgages to institutional investors.

FEDERAL INSURANCE CONTRIBUTION ACT (FICA). Federal law requiring employers and employees to contribute a percentage of their wage income to Social Security and Medicare programs.

FEDERAL NATIONAL MORTGAGE ASSOCIATION (FNMA), "FANNIE MAE." Originally a government agency (1938), this mortgage market intermediary buys federally insured mortgages from lenders, thereby releasing funds so that lenders can make more loans, and then packages the loans for resale to investors.

FEDERAL RESERVE BOARD (FRB), "FED". Semi-autonomous group responsible for monetary policy in the United States. The Open Market Committee of the Fed meets monthly, in secrecy, to review the performance of the economy and consider changes in discount rates, reserve requirements, or funds available in the lending markets.

FEDERAL SAVINGS AND LOAN INSURANCE CORPO-RATION (FSLIC). A quasi-government organization created during the Depression to insure depositor's funds in savings and loans. FSLIC went bankrupt in the 1980s. Bankrupt S&Ls* were taken over by the RTC*, and solvent S&Ls became members of the FDIC*.

FEDERAL TRADE COMMISSION (FTC). Created in 1914, the FTC's goal is to stop unfair trade practices, including monopolies, price discrimination, and false advertising.

FEEDBACK. Response; especially, evaluation of performance.

FEEDER. A source of materials or supplies for a manufacturer.

FEEDING FRENZY. Impulsive buyer activity.
"In the early 1990s, soon after it was privatized, British Airways joined the rest of the airline industry in a feeding frenzy, grabbing for all the passengers it could and trying to win market share by flying lots of big planes." (*Wall Street Journal,* May 22, 2003, p. A1)

FEELERS. Initial discussions, often casual, without formal negotiations.

FEEL-FELT-FOUND METHOD. Sales technique where the salesperson responds to a customer's objections by stating, "I know how you feel. Other customers have felt the same and found our product helped them."

FEEL THE STING. Incur the cost or burden.
"New Way to Curb Medical Costs: Make Employees Feel the Sting." (*Wall Street Journal,* June 23, 2004, p. A1)

FENCED IN. Cannot get out.

FENCE-MENDING. Apologizing or attempting to repair a broken relationship.

F2F. Face-to-face.

FIAT MONEY. Currency that has no intrinsic value. Fiat money is money because government declares it to be "legal tender." The danger with fiat money is that a government may decide to create too much of it, the most famous case being in Germany between World War I and World War II.

FICTOMERCIAL. A book, television show, or other work in which a company pays the writer to incorporate the company's products into the story.
   "British writer Fay Weldon opened up a whole new financial can of worms with her novel 'The Bulgari Connection,' sponsored by the Italian jewelry company Bulgari in return for a few mentions in the plot. Some critics wailed about the new field of fictomercial, but most accepted the book for what it is: a harmless little experiment by a talented novelist." ("Whew! What a year," *Atlanta Journal and Constitution,* Dec. 15, 2001)

FIGHTING BRAND. Branded product introduced to compete with a competitor's product and protect the company's leading brand.
   "British Airways (BA) is jeopardizing long-standing relationships with travel agents by launching World Offer, its first ever price-fighting brand. World Offer is an umbrella brand for discounted economy class tickets to destinations identified as having spare capacity." (*Marketing,* March 31, 1994, p. 5)

FILE THIRTEEN. Trash basket.

FILE TRANSFER PROTOCAL (FTP). A standard method for transferring files across the Internet.

FILL. Execute an order in the stock market.

FILLING THE GAPS. Technical stock market term for an asset that has quickly risen in price, faster than would be expected by technical (chart) analysis. Chartists, also called "elves" by Louis Rukeyser, predict that the asset will decline, to fill in the gaps on their charts.
   "This is a trading term used to describe trading in an asset that has moved higher too quickly, and has 'leapfrogged' over some points on a chart, which then has to go back (trade lower) and 'fill

in the missing gaps.'" (*Review & Focus,* EverBank World Market report, April 1, 2004, p. 1)

FILL OR KILL. A stock purchase order. Either complete the order or cancel it.

FILTER OUT. Remove.

FINANCIAL PORNOGRAPHY. Books, newsletters, and articles that glorify investment bankers, venture capitalists, and money managers and the deals they make.
"In *The Four Pillars of Wisdom,* author William Berstein devotes a well-deserved chapter to the financial press and its weakness for financial pornography lurid coverage of star money managers." (Scott Burns, "Reboot your portfolio," *Seattle Times,* August 4, 2002)

FINDER'S FEE. Fee charged by an intermediary in a business transaction.

FINE PRINT. Details of a contract.
"United Policyholders, a 12-year-old advocacy group that represents consumers and commercial-insurance buyers, maintains the boilerplate disclosures brokers provide aren't enough, given a broker's role as a buyer's representative. 'If you're going to tell me I've got to read the fine print, that's not what people are paying for,' said Amy Bach, executive director of the San Francisco group." (*Wall Street Journal,* August 11, 2004, p. C3)

FINGER CHECK. A typing error on a computer.

FIRE (TO). Dismiss from a job. See also CAN.
"In exchange for money to recruit, train and pay raises to teachers, he wants to make it easier for schools to fire those who are incompetent. Mr. Kerry calls for tougher teacher-certification tests—someone with about a 10th-grade education could pass them now—and for 'rewards' for teachers who show 'more skill or better results.'" (*Wall Street Journal,* July 28, 2004, p. A6)

FIRE AWAY (TO). Begin asking questions whenever ready.

FIREPOWER. The potential resources or capacity for action (military).

FIREWALL. Specialty software designed to prevent unauthorized access to a computer by outsiders.

FIREWIRE, 1394, i.Link. A fast connector on personal computers.

"Apple, which helped invent the technology and has marketing in its bones, calls this connector 'FireWire.' Then Windows PC makers use the geeky term '1394.' To make matters worse and a little more confusing, Sony calls the same connection 'i.Link.'" (*Wall Street Journal,* Dec. 4, 2002, p. D5)

FIRST CLASS. Best available.

FIRSTHAND. Directly.

FIRST IN, FIRST OUT (FIFO). Accounting method that assigns cost to the ending inventory by assuming that the cost of the units in the ending inventory is also that of the most recent units purchased.

FIRST OUT OF THE GATE. Initial leader; fast starter (horse racing).

"The Risk Assessment bill will be first out of the gate to relate directly to the 9 major environmental statutes." (*Environment Today,* Jan./Feb. 1995, p. 22)

FIRST STRING. Best individual(s) (sports).

FIRST TIME QUALITY. Zero defects.

FIRST WORLD. The industrialized countries of the world.

FISCAL DRAG. The time between when a government spending policy is approved and when it affects the economy.

"Mexican fiscal policy affects growth at the margin. High taxes hold down growth not only through fiscal drag, but also by using up President Fox's political capital and attention." (*Wall Street Journal,* Jan. 11, 2002, p. A11)

FISCAL YEAR. Year for accounting purposes, not necessarily beginning in January. The U.S. government's fiscal year runs from October 1 through September 30.

FISHBOWL. In the public eye.

FISHING EXPEDITION. An enquiry into an issue without a developed plan.

"Susanne Martinez, public policy vice president for Planned Parenthood Federation of America, called Mr. Ashcroft's effort to subpoena 900 medical records at six Planned Parenthood affiliates 'a calculated fishing expedition' and an 'attempted sweeping invasion of medical privacy.' In one of the trials, a federal judge in California ruled last month that Mr. Ashcroft couldn't view the records." (*Wall Street Journal,* April 23, 2004, p. A4)

FISH OR CUT BAIT. Forceful request to make a decision or take decisive action.
"The White House fears a bill won't pass, and a senior official blames Senate Majority Leader Daschle. Bush, GOP House Speaker Hastert and Senate GOP leader Lott will give him a 'fish-or-cut-bait' message at the leaders' White House breakfast." (*Wall Street Journal,* Nov. 23, 2001, p. A1)

FISHYBACK. Transportation system using both trucks and ships.

FIT AND FINISH. Quality of execution of details; to complete the final details.
"The five brands that slipped in rank: BMW, Jaguar, Porsche, Land Rover and Mercedes-Benz. Power's U.S. surveys show that Mercedes is suffering from complaints about features and controls, fit and finish, and sound systems." (*Wall Street Journal,* Nov. 12, 2002, p. D3)

FIVE AND DIME/TEN. A variety store selling cheap items; low-priced merchandise.
"Typically, we end up buying whatever oversize basket we can find at our local five-and-dime. But after suffering one too many baskets filled with waxy chocolate, stale jelly beans and enough artificial grass to cover an indoor baseball stadium, this year we went searching catalogs and Internet sites for the definitive word on Easter goodies." (*Wall Street Journal,* March 31, 2001, p. W15C)

FIVE NINES. 99.999 percent accurate.

FLAG (TO). Call attention to; stop production of.

FLAGSHIP. The most important product, division, office of a company.

FLAGSHIP BRAND. Leading brand.
"In 1912, Chinese statesman Sun Yat-sen took his first ride in an automobile—a Buick. The last emperor of China bought two of them in 1924, the first cars to enter Peking's Forbidden City. In the 1930s, GM's flagship brand in China was fashionable among Shanghai's rich factory bosses, and the Buick became a symbol for

an era of great wealth amid great poverty." (*Wall Street Journal,* July 22, 2004, p. B1)

FLAK. Abuse or criticism (World War II, German; or "flack").

"'Yes, we took some flak from the decision, to pay cash dividends,' said Eric Wintemute, chief executive of American Vanguard, an American Stock Exchange–traded maker of crop-protection chemicals." (*Wall Street Journal,* July 26, 2004, p. C4)

FLAME (TO). Send nasty messages on the Internet.

FLASH IN THE PAN. A person, idea, or business that starts with much fanfare but quickly fades or fails.

FLAT. Empty; completely sold out. In bond trading, "flat" means without any accrued interest.

FLAT CHARGE. Fixed price.

FLAT ORGANIZATION. An organization in which formal layers of management have been eliminated, ostensibly to promote more flexible decision-making, collaboration, and project management.

FLAVOR OF THE MONTH. The current fad.

FLESHMEET. A face-to-face meeting, especially one composed of people who usually or only converse online.

"The Opera Forum is a closely knit group. With 40 or so active participants scattered across at least a dozen states and three continents, and many more lurkers, members have organized two official group 'fleshmeets,' and several members have attended the opera together in various cities." (Amy Harmon, "In an Online Colloquy, an Absent Voice," *New York Times,* Oct. 4, 2001)

FLESH OUT (TO). Fill in the details of an agreement or procedure. After business or political leaders decide on a plan of action, staff members are often directed to flesh out the details.

FLEXTIME/FLEXITIME. Policy allowing workers to define their own working hours.

FLIGHT RISK. The probability that an employee will leave the company.

FLIGHT TO QUALITY/VALUE. Movement of capital to the safest investments.

FLIP. Buy and then quickly sell shares of stock purchased in an INITIAL PUBLIC OFFERING.

FLIP-FLOP. Change back and forth.

"It's a bigger story he has to tell. It's a 35-year commitment to trying to make things better. He didn't flip-flop. He kept at it, and it was a major foreign-policy accomplishment." (*Wall Street Journal,* Sept. 2, 2004, p. A6)

FLIP SIDE. Counter-argument or -idea.

FLOAT. Initiate; the time between when a check is written and when an account is debited.

"Your checks will soon clear much faster, and that means no more 'playing the float.'" (*Wall Street Journal,* August 1, 2004, p. 4)

FLOAT A LOAN. Borrow money.

FLOOD (TO). Overwhelm with details; supply large quantities.

"The first noise you ever hear comes from the employees, who began to flood his clients' employee-benefits departments with complaints about unpaid Cigna medical claims." (*Wall Street Journal,* Nov. 4, 2002, p. B6)

FLOOD OF ORDERS. A sudden increase in demand.

"In anticipation of a flood of orders for the Alpha chip, DEC built semiconductor foundries." (*Computer Technology Review,* Spring/ Summer 1994, p. 8)

FLOOR. A lower limit, usually imposed by government on prices or wages.

FLOOR PLANNING. Financing for inventory, usually associated with automobile dealerships, where dealers use manufacturers' credit to finance the new cars in their showrooms.

FLOP. Failure or to fail.

FLUB. Mistake or to make a mistake.

"In interviews, the president echoed senior aides' denials of post-war flubs and assertions that things are better than the media has painted." (*Wall Street Journal,* Oct. 14, 2003, p. A1)

FLUFF IT AND FLY IT. Make it look good and then sell it.

FLUNKY. Low-level employee. See also GOFER.

FLUSH. Having plenty of money.

FLY-BY-NIGHT. Temporary; of questionable ethics.

"The rhetorical smearing depicts an important financial center as a shady, disreputable offshore haven that attracts capital with fly-by-night tax schemes that don't pass muster. 'The talk of closing down the Bermuda loophole,' is just such an example, he says." (*Wall Street Journal,* May 7, 2004, p. A17)

FLYING CIRCUS. A fly-in and inspect tour by corporate executives. Such executives are likely to receive TRAVEL DAZZLE.

FLYING OUT THE WINDOW. Being discarded.

"Now, many of the assumptions built into those systems are flying out the window as changes in travel spur one of the biggest overhauls in pricing since deregulation." (*Wall Street Journal,* August 17, 2004, p. B1)

FOCUS GROUP. A small group of potential consumers brought together to discuss a product or idea. Focus groups are used to get in-depth information from select groups of customers or potential consumers.

"Republicans had hoped Medicare legislation would be a political boon. But for that to happen, said Bill McInturff, a Republican pollster who moderated the foundation's focus groups, 'there would have to be a very, very substantial change.'" (*Wall Street Journal,* June 4, 2004, p. B3)

FOLD (TO). Close, quit; merge.

"The takeover agreement calls for UFJ, Japan's fourth-largest bank, to fold its operations into No. 2 bank Mitsubishi Tokyo by Oct. 1, 2005. The new bank, to be called Mitsubishi UFJ Holdings Inc., will be the world's largest, with 189 trillion yen, or $1.7 trillion, in assets—surpassing Citigroup Inc.'s $1.3 trillion." (*Wall Street Journal,* August 13, 2004, p. A13)

FOLLOW-ON OFFERING. New shares of stock sold to investors after an initial public offering.

FOLLOW THE HERD. To invest in what other investors are buying.

FOLLOW THROUGH. Finish, complete a task.

FOLLOW-UP. Response to an inquiry; to check on status.

"If customers didn't follow through on their aftermarket indications, Morgan encouraged its sales force to follow up, the SEC said." (*Wall Street Journal,* June 22, 2004, p. C1)

FOOD AND DRUG ADMINISTRATION (FDA). Federal agency responsible for food, drug, and medical safety in the United States. The FDA was created in 1906 by Theodore Roosevelt's administration, in part because of his experience with contaminated food during the Spanish-American War.

FOOD CHAIN. The organizational hierarchy.

FOOD FOR PEACE. International food giveaway program (Public Law 480).

FOOTHOLD. A beginning, a start.

FOOT IN THE DOOR (TO GET ONE'S). Establish an initial contact.
"'I'm qualified enough to get my foot in the door,' he says, 'but there's a vast pool of candidates out there with strong resumes. When I applied to b-school, I certainly had not anticipated a recession that wouldn't go away.'" (*Wall Street Journal,* Sept. 17, 2003, p. R5)

FOOTPRINT. A firm's or product's presence or recognition in a market.

FOR A SONG. Inexpensively.

FORCE IN NUMBERS. Power resulting from the presence of a large group.

FORCE MAJEURE. External contingencies that unavoidably affect performance of a contract (French).
"The arbitration ruling in February 2003 by the Delta Pilots System Board of Adjustment turned back a challenge from the union over Delta's use of 'force majeure' to justify laying off pilots. Force majeure is a legal concept under which parties to a contract are released from liability if unforeseeable circumstances prevent them from fulfilling their obligations under the agreement." (*Wall Street Journal,* April 29, 2004, p. A3)

FORCE THE NUMBERS. Make up numbers; manipulate statistics.

FOREIGN/FREE TRADE ZONE (FTZ). A special government program or location where firms can import materials and not pay duties until products made from the materials leave the FTZ. Products that are exported are exempt from import duty.

FOREX, FX. Abbreviations for foreign exchange.

FORMICA PARACHUTE. Unemployment compensation. When U.S. corporations DOWNSIZE, executives often receive GOLDEN PARACHUTES, while rank-and-file employees receive only minimal unemployment compensation.

FOR THE BIRDS. Unreal or ridiculous.

FORTRESS EUROPE. Protectionist policies of European countries (World War II).
"Economic Slowdown Enters Fortress Europe" (*Wall Street Journal,* March 26, 2001, p. A1)

FORTUNE 500. *Fortune* magazine's list of the five hundred largest manufacturing companies in the United States. In 1995 *Fortune* developed a separate list of the five hundred largest service companies.

FORUM SHOPPING. Efforts by lawyers to shop for the most favorable court to hear a case.
"Forum shopping, in which attorneys maneuver to find the court most sympathetic to their case, is a common complaint among defense attorneys in the massive asbestos-litigation arena." (*Wall Street Journal,* Nov. 18, 2002, p. B3)

FOR YOUR INFORMATION (FYI). For your consideration, usually not requiring a response.

FOULED UP BEYOND ALL RECOGNITION (FUBAR). A mess.
"With its myriad of programs the welfare system in the U.S. is FUBAR." (Professor Martin McMahon, University of Kentucky, 1996)

FOUR-FIFTHS RULE. Used by the EEOC*. If an employment practice results in minorities being hired at a rate less than 80 percent of white applicants, the EEOC may rule that the minority group has been adversely affected by the practice.

419 SCAM. A fraud, particularly one originating in Nigeria, soliciting money to help secure the release of, and so earn a percentage of, a much larger sum. 419 refers to the section of the Nigerian laws making these scams illegal.
"The classic 419 scam asks the victim to help some hapless relative of a deposed despot get millions of dollars out of the con artist's

country. The con artist offers the victim a percentage of this illusive pot of gold, hoping to suck the victim into paying all sorts of fees to get trunks of money out of Nigeria, Sierra Leone, the Philippines or whatever exotic locale the con artist chooses. In the end, the money is never sent, but the victims are often out thousands of dollars." (Kathy M. Kristof, "Nigerian Money Con Targets Small Firms," *Los Angeles Times,* Sept. 7, 2003)

FOUR Ps. A firm's marketing mix: product, price, promotion, and place.

FOUR TENS (4 10s). Four ten-hour workdays.

FOUR TIGERS. Taiwan, Singapore, Hong Kong, and Korea.
   "Most Americans know that Taiwan is one of Asia's 'Four Tigers,' but few are aware of the spectacular statistics behind the country's achievements." (*Forbes,* Jan. 16, 1995, p. 35)

FREDDIE MAC. See FEDERAL HOME LOAN MORTGAGE CORPORATION.

FREEBIE. A free sample used to stimulate interest among customers.

FREEDOM OF INFORMATION ACT (FOIA). Federal law requiring open access to government information.

FREE-FALL. A rapid decline in the market.

FREE-FLOWING. Loose.

FREE LUNCH. Something for nothing—proverbially, there is no such thing as a free lunch. In business, this means that everything has a cost.

FREE ON BOARD (FOB). Invoicing term meaning that the buyer pays shipping costs.

FREE RIDERS. Those who do not pay but enjoy the benefits.

FREESTANDING INSERT (FSI). Advertisements inserted into newspapers.

FREE-WHEELING. Creative; ignoring rules or laws.

"Still, he worries that Mr. Kerry is too hesitant to engage people in the kind of free-wheeling style that was so much a part of Dr. Dean's big moment." (*Wall Street Journal,* July 28, 2004, p. D10)

FRICTION-FREE CAPITALISM. A very efficient market in which buyers and sellers can find each other easily, can interact directly, and can perform transactions with only minimal overhead costs.

"We have waited a long time for broad-based electronic commerce, and it looks like 1997 will be the year that the market gains legitimacy," says Bill Gurley, an analyst with Deutsche Morgan Grenfell, an investment bank. "No wonder industry titans such as Bill Gates, the boss of Microsoft, regale the world's leaders with the promise of friction-free capitalism: the idea that ubiquitous and equal access to information will create the closest thing yet to Adam Smith's perfect market." ("In search of the perfect market," *The Economist,* May 10, 1997)

FRIENDS-AND-FAMILY SHARES. Shares of stock given to friends and family members prior to an initial public offering.

"The phenomenon is growing so rapidly that friends-and-family shares are becoming a new currency in the Bay Area. Some new employees even negotiate friends-and-family shares as part of their employment contracts." (Kathleen Pender, "Be Cautious When Business Associates Offer Access to IPO Shares," *San Francisco Chronicle,* April 7, 2000)

FRINGE BENEFITS. Non-wage compensation that comes with a job. Fringe benefits may include health insurance, travel and clothing allowances, retirement plans, and other PERKS.

FROBNICATE/FROB. Manipulate or adjust.

"If someone is turning a knob on an oscilloscope, then if he's carefully adjusting it he is probably tweaking; if he is just turning it but looking at the screen he is probably twiddling it; but if he is just doing it because turning a knob is fun, he's frobbing it." (Professor Julianne Morgan, USCA, 1996)

FROM SCRATCH/THE GROUND UP/THE WORD "GO." From the beginning.

"In these days of ownership CHURN and affiliation switches, many stations face having to start a newscast from the ground up." (*Broadcasting & Cable,* Sept. 4, 1995, p. 31)

FRONT BURNER. Of immediate importance or attention.

"AOL's talks with Disney about merging CNN and ABC are back on the front burner amid concerns about costs and advertising." (*Wall Street Journal,* September 25, 2002, p. A1)

FRONT END. The part of a business that deals directly with customers.

FRONT-LINE. The first people customers interact with.
"A deadly discrepancy exists between the available medical knowledge about aortic aneurysms and the ignorance of many front-line physicians." (*Wall Street Journal*, Nov. 4, 2003, p. A1)

FRONT LOADING / FRONT-END LOAD. Loan fee or sales commission paid from the initial funds borrowed.

FRONT MONEY. The initial amount needed to start a project.

FRONT OFFICE. The central office, office that deals with customers.

FROWN UPON. Disapprove of.

FROZEN ASSETS. Assets that cannot be bought or sold because of a legal dispute.

FRUG (TO). To solicit donations and attempt other forms of fundraising while pretending to conduct market research. Frug is an acronym meaning fundraising under the guise of.
"Other protests come from the advertising research industry, which is furious about a venerable direct mail gimmick: cloaking a pitch as a survey, pretending that the purpose of a letter is to seek opinions rather than sell a product or raise funds. ... 'What drives me crazy is sometimes these are organizations I'm a member of and believe in,' he added, referring to the fundraisers that sell under the guise of research. The foundation even has a name for such trickery, frugging." (Stuart Elliott, "You've Got Mail, Indeed," *New York Times,* October 25, 1999)

FRUITS OF ONE'S LABOR. Money or assets one worked to acquire.

FUBAR. See FOULED UP BEYOND ALL RECOGNITION.

FUDGE FACTOR. A margin of error in an estimate.

FUDGE THE FIGURES. Cheat with numbers. See also CREATIVE ACCOUNTING.

"Richard Grace, a Shawnee, Okla., appraiser, says he and other appraisers are frequently encouraged to fudge the numbers. A case in point came earlier this year when he was asked to determine the value of a two-bedroom log house in rural Oklahoma. The buyer was willing to pay about $87,000 for the home, but Mr. Grace appraised it at $68,200, the value of comparable homes in the area." (*Wall Street Journal,* August 13, 2001, p. A1)

FULFILLMENT. Filling orders from mail-order marketing.

"WalMart.com, the retailer's Internet unit, based in Brisbane, Calif., is teaming with Geneva Media, which in January purchased Liquid Audio's digital-music fulfillment business. Geneva is an affiliate company of Anderson News Co., which distributes books and magazines to Wal-Mart's retail outlets. Another Anderson affiliate supplies compact discs to the retailer." (*Wall Street Journal,* Nov. 13, 2003, p. B3)

FULL COURT PRESS. Maximum pressure, all-out effort (basketball).

"Given his druthers, Mr. George W. Bush likely would have avoided his diplomatic full-court press to get U.N. Security Council approval to oust Saddam Hussein, and instead gone with an ad hoc coalition from the outset." (*Wall Street Journal,* March 10, 2004, p. A4)

FULL DISCLOSURE. Laws requiring sellers to provide all information relevant to the business transaction.

FULL FAITH AND CREDIT. The promise that accompanies government debt issues.

"The bonds carry a repayment pledge of the state's full faith and credit, as well as backing from a slice of a state sales tax." (*Wall Street Journal,* May 6, 2004, p. C6)

FULL-SERVICE AGENCY. A large firm that can provide anything a client wants.

"Jack Myers, president of Myers Communications, said that the trend away from independents is less a function of them losing the business than full-service agencies responding to these changes and winning it." (*Advertising Age,* April 10, 1995, p. 1)

FUMBLE. Make a mistake, error (football).

"And lately the president has talked up telecom and the need to clear away 'the regulatory underbrush.' But such talk has been a long time coming. Indeed, next to the steel-tariffs fumble, Mr. Bush's neglect of information technology—a sector responsible for almost two-thirds of the rise in labor productivity in the late 1990s—might be his most serious economic misstep." (*Wall Street Journal,* July 21, 2004, p. A11)

FUME DATE. The date on which a company runs out or is expected to run out of cash. See BURN RATE.

"Was it a success? The WebTaggers guys say they will not know until the wire transfer date, Aug. 15, when WebTaggers anticipates that funds from investors will have traded hands. After that? Jan. 1, 2001, the fume date, which no one really wants to think about—the point at which, if no venture capital is coming in, the partners must admit defeat." (Courtney Barry, "10 Months, 10 Minutes, $10 Million," *New York Times,* June 7, 2000)

FUNDAMENTALS. Basic operations or activities of a business. In the 1990s many American businesses returned to their fundamentals. See also CORE BUSINESS.

FUN MONEY. Uncommitted funds. Consumers often shop with fun money.

FUNNY MONEY. Securities that are not well-known and of questionable value.

FUZZWORD. Business jargon.

"In effect, a fuzzword carries with it an aura of a new, more exciting reality, but one that has no basis in the real world." (*Marketing News,* May 10, 1993, p. 4)

FUZZY LOGIC. A logic system used in expert systems and artificial intelligence that generates probabilities that a proposition is true or false.

G

GAINSHARING. Management program where workers' pay is related to various performance goals.

"A special bulletin released by the Department of Health and Human Services' inspector general states that while hospitals have a legitimate interest in trying to reduce costs, they can't apply the practice known as 'gainsharing' to fee-for-service Medicare and Medicaid patients. Under gainsharing, physicians receive a percentage of the hospitals' savings when they make treatment choices that save money." (*Wall Street Journal,* July 9, 1999, p.1)

GALLEY. Preliminary layout for a print publication.

GAME PLAN. Marketing strategy (football).

"During last year's soccer playoffs, one visiting team found a video camera and a microphone hidden in its locker room. That team's coach claimed the equipment had been installed by Mr. Ahumada's side to steal his game-plan. Another opposing coach alleged that Mr. Ahumada's team had tear gas sprayed in his team's hotel." (*Wall Street Journal,* June 23, 2004, p. A1)

GAME THEORY. Management planning technique based on anticipating competitors' actions and reactions.

GAMMA STAGE. The expansion stage of a new enterprise when initial financial results are available.

GARAGE SALE. Sale of unwanted items at extremely low prices.
"Ms. Gilbert, a co-worker of Mr. Brian Ellin's at software firm Janrain Inc., also uses RSS to scan the Web for job listings for her unemployed husband, and for garage sales in the family's Portland neighborhood." (*Wall Street Journal,* May 24, 2004, p. R12)

GARBAGE IN, GARBAGE OUT (GIGO). Output can be no better than the quality of the inputs.
"Dr. Temple's view was, 'Garbage in, garbage out,' he says in an interview. If the data were unreliable, so was the conclusion." (*Wall Street Journal,* May 25, 2004, p. A1)

_____ **GATE.** A scandal.
"Since Watergate, the 1970s political scandal that ended the Nixon presidency, visible unethical activities in the U.S. are commonly referred to as '_____ gates.'" (Robert Botsch, professor of political science, USCA, 1996)

GATEKEEPER. Person who controls access to managers. Gatekeepers are important members of organizational buying centers. They control the flow of information to be reviewed by the group making purchase decisions.

GAZUMP (TO). Raise the price after initially agreeing to a lower one (real estate).
"Gazumping may sound like a polite response to a sneeze, or perhaps a sneeze itself.... 'It's become slang for when a seller disappoints an intended purchaser by raising the price after accepting his or her offer.'" (*Wall Street Journal,* June 6, 1996, p. B10)

GEAR DOWN (TO). To reduce the size of an operation.

GEAR UP (TO). Get ready.
"IPOs often begin trading with a measure of disorder, as investors gear up to trade and market makers try to figure out where a stock should open, and Google's had its share of problems." (*Wall Street Journal,* August 20, 2004, p. C1)

GEEK. A computer technology expert.

GENERAL ACCOUNTING OFFICE (GAO). Congressional accounting agency monitoring fiscal activities of the government. The GAO and its executive branch counterpart the OMB*, often differ in budget estimates and assumptions.

GENERAL AGREEMENT ON TARIFFS AND TRADE (GATT). 1940s United Nations–sponsored agreement to reduce and eliminate trade barriers. The GATT was incorporated in the WORLD TRADE ORGANIZATION in 1994.

GENERALLY ACCEPTED ACCOUNTING PRINCIPLES (GAAP). Standardized rules and procedures for accounting.

"These officials 'ought to have been aware that the establishment and/or release to income of such accruals and provisions were not in accordance with applicable generally accepted accounting principles,' a Nortel statement said. Further, the improper use of accruals and provisions 'misstated the company's financial statements,' Nortel said." (*Wall Street Journal,* August 20, 2004, p. A3)

GENERAL OBLIGATION BOND (GO BOND). A municipal bond (tax-free for federal income) that is backed by the municipality issuing it. GO bonds are considered less risky than revenue bonds, which are issued by municipalities, tax-free, but are backed only by the revenue from the investment made with the funds from the sale of the bonds.

GENERAL SERVICE (GS) RATING. Most federal government service jobs in the United States have a GS rating that determines the pay scale for the position.

GENERATION X. Used to describe the generation of people born in the 1960s and 1970s, after the BABY BOOMERS. Originally thought to be slackers and lacking identity.

"Generation X-ers are known for being cynical and risk-averse, but home buying might signal a new optimism. 'They were told the sky was falling down and they wouldn't do as well as their parents,' says Bernard Carl Rosen, a Cornell University sociologist who published a book about Generation X." (*Wall Street Journal,* July 18, 2003, p. B1)

GENERATION Y. Term often used for the generation of people born after GENERATION X.

GET A JUMP ON. A head start; to get started before your competitors.

"Attempting to get a jump on their judicial colleagues, or to placate 'feeder' professors, these judges pushed the application/interview date to a full year before their now-proposed solution." (*Wall Street Journal,* August 19, 2002, p. A12)

GET A KICK OUT OF. Enjoy.
"Robert Canepa, owner of the Mill Valley Market, Mill Valley, Calif., says employees get a kick out of decorating, and shoppers appreciate the effort, so there are ghosts in the deli, goblins in the meat department and pumpkins all over." (*Wall Street Journal,* Oct. 26, 2000, p. A1)

GET AWAY WITH. Do something wrong without getting caught.

GET BEHIND. To support.

GET BOUNCED. Be forced out, fired.

GET HAMMERED. To suffer severe setbacks.

GET IN BED WITH. To work closely with.

GET IN ON THE GROUND FLOOR. To become involved in the beginning of an enterprise.

GET IT TOGETHER. Become organized.
"At a news conference last week at the Securities Industry Conference in Boca Raton, Fla., Sanford I. Weill, Citigroup's co-chairman, defended the management shake-up, arguing that the integration of the corporate banking businesses wasn't coming together. 'We had to do something to get it together,' Mr. Weill said at the conference." (*Wall Street Journal,* Nov. 9, 1998, p. 1)

GET IT WHILE THE GETTING'S GOOD. Take the opportunity while it is there.

GET LOST. Go away (impolite command).
"Brand franchise mergers and acquisitions are on a roll, and will continue to be on a roll because consumers and retailers have forced marketers into that 'get out front or get lost' mentality that led to the Quaker, Grand Metropolitan and Campbell moves late last year and in early 1995." (*Brandweek,* June 26, 1995, p. 16)

GET MILEAGE OUT OF. Exploit; to benefit from.

GET ONE'S DUCKS IN A ROW. Get organized.

GET-RICH SCHEME. Way to make money fast (often risky or fraudulent).

"Despite the potential of INFOMERCIALS, by 1994 this exciting, promising uniquely sales-intensive medium has remained a ghetto for gadgets, get-rich schemes and gaudy promises of fantasies fulfilled." (*Advertising Age,* April 11, 1995, p. S8)

GET SIDETRACKED. Become distracted.

GET THE AX. Be dismissed, eliminated.

"Still, with a limited number of young viewers to go around, analysts expect an unusually large number of shows to get the ax early on. DeWitt Media, a New York-based ad-buying firm, forecasts that only seven of the new shows will still be afloat by Christmas, including 'Ally' and the new 'Law and Order.'" (*Wall Street Journal,* August 13, 1999, p. W1)

GET THE BALL ROLLING. Get things started.

GET/GIVE THE BOOT. Be dismissed.

"Indeed, Mr. Adams wasn't the only stock-fund manager to get the boot last week. On the same day that Berger, a unit of Kansas City Southern Industries Inc., announced a reorganization including Mr. Adams's plan 'to pursue other interests,' Liberty Financial Cos.' Stein Roe funds unit announced the departure of two managers." (*Wall Street Journal,* May 12, 1999, p. C1)

GET THE BUSINESS. Be treated roughly.

GET THE DRIFT/HANG OF IT. Understand.

GET THE INK. Get the customer to sign the contract.

GET TO WHERE THE ACTION IS. Find where decisions are made or opportunities can be found.

GETTING AT (WHAT ONE IS). The point or essence of what one is saying.

GETTING ONE'S FEET WET. Beginning to learn about a new market or product.

GHOSTING. Writing for someone else who will claim it as his or her own work. Books by celebrities are often written by professional writers who are not acknowledged in the book.

GHOST RIDER. Person who falsely claims to have been in a vehicle involved in an accident in an effort to collect for alleged injuries.

GHOST WORK. To do the work of people who have been terminated, in addition to one's regular job.

"The result is no one gets the training needed to do this 'ghost work,' or the jobs of departed colleagues." (*Wall Street Journal,* Oct. 22, 2002, p. B1)

GIFFEN GOODS. Goods that do not obey the law of demand, in that quantity demanded decreases as price decreases (from British economist Robert Giffen).

GIG. A job, often a temporary position.

GIGABYTE. A measure of memory or computer disk capacity equal to 1 billion bytes.

GILT-EDGE. Of high quality and reliability.

"Gilt-edged bonds are marketable bonds denominated in sterling that are issued by the Bank of England on behalf of the treasury." (*Euromoney,* August 1995, p. 68)

GIMMICK. A special item practice or feature of a product designed to gain customer interest.

"The plush ducks remained on the show's set for the entire segment—an accolade in itself: 'Live' gets sent thousands of promotional gimmicks a year but 99.9% of them don't get on the air. 'Unless it's really clever it won't make it,' says Michael Gellman, executive producer of 'Live.'" (*Wall Street Journal,* July 30, 2004, p. B1)

GINNIE MAE. Nickname for GOVERNMENT NATIONAL MORTGAGE ASSOCIATION.

GIVE A LITTLE. Compromise.

GIVE AWAY THE FARM. Sell at a very low price.

GIVE-BACKS. The surrender by unions of previously agreed upon benefits.

"The bankers also concluded that the labor savings that US Airways is seeking aren't out of line, and 'only on such basis would such a [turnaround] plan be potentially workable.' They said the company seems to have taken full advantage of its first bankruptcy to reduce costs, and said they didn't see other significant opportunities for expense cutting, save for further employee givebacks, terminating other unions' pension plans or throttling back capital expenditures. The pilots plan was terminated in last year's Chapter 11." (*Wall Street Journal,* August 13, 2004, p. A3)

GIVE IT THE ONCE-OVER. Check something but not spend a lot of time carefully reviewing it.

GIVE SOMEONE PAPER. Place an order.

GIVE THE NOD. Give approval to a plan; perceive as having an advantage.
"For this year, the top analysts expect the leisure category to rebound ahead of most other business sectors. They're counting on an army of well-to-do baby boomers entering the biggest-spending years of their lives. Mr. Conder says he likes Brunswick Corp., the boat maker; Mr. Joe Havorka gives the nod to Polaris, the fishing and hunting vehicle maker; and Mr. Bob Simonson is going with Royal Caribbean." (*Wall Street Journal,* May 12, 2003, p. R7)

GIZMO. A tool or gadget.

GLAD-HANDING. Shaking hands with everyone present. See also SCHMOOZING.

GLAMOUR STOCK. A stock that is widely followed. In the 1990s many technology companies were glamour stocks.

GLASNOST. Openness. From the Russian term for the new openness to discuss differences with the West, initiated by Soviet President Gorbachev in 1990.

GLASS CEILING. Invisible barrier (discrimination) to career advancement for women and minorities.
"They cited examples of women at the firms complaining about the memberships, along with allegations of harassment, unequal pay and glass ceilings culled from media reports and other sources. Mr. Mehri called Wall Street 'Fallujah, Iraq, for women.' Dr. Burk compared Augusta's members to Georgia's late segregationist governor, Lester Maddox." (*Wall Street Journal,* April 9, 2004, p. C4)

GLASS-STEAGALL (ACT OF 1933). Depression-era banking reforms that prohibited commercial banks from offering stock brokerage and insurance services. Banking reforms in the 1980s and 1990s have gradually removed many of the barriers among these service industries.

GLIMMER OF HOPE. A slight chance of success.
"At Dean rallies, and on his Web site, there are still glimmers of hope and signs of devotion to the candidate." (*Wall Street Journal,* Feb. 6, 2004, p. A4)

GLITCH. A small problem or temporary setback.
"The news threatens to cast another cloud over an Intel conference next week for technology developers, in addition to a series of technical glitches and AMD innovations that have tarnished Intel's image as the industry's pace-setter." (*Wall Street Journal,* Sept. 3, 2004, p. A3)

GLITZ/GLITZY. Flashiness/bright, showy.
"Something uneasy has entered into the contract of illusion between us and celebrities. A sharp change occurred in the immediate aftermath of 9/11, when most citizens felt a twinge of nausea at the sight of an Entertainment Weekly cover. This acute aversion to hollow glitz lasted awhile, and seemed to fade, but has now revived due to the unelected tub thumping of Robert Redford, Susan Sarandon and their ilk." (*Wall Street Journal,* Feb. 19, 2003, p. D16)

GLOBAL ARENA. World marketplace.

GLOBALITY. Functioning on a global basis.

GLOBAL PACE OF CHANGE. Speed of business worldwide.

GLOBASM. A company or executive who becomes obsessed with expanding globally is said to be experiencing globasm.

GLOCAL. Combined global and local.
"Refuting the argument that globalization is a homogeneous process, this study found that a glocal strategy, as opposed to a standardized global strategy, was being practiced in cyberspace by many of the companies with top brands." (*Public Relations Review,* Sept., 2004, p. 285)

GOBBLEDYGOOK. Unnecessary details, jargon, or clutter.

GO BELLY UP. Fail; go bankrupt.

GO BOND. See GENERAL OBLIGATION BOND.

GOFER. Low-ranking employee; errand boy (from "go-for").
"Ms. Lenore Lillie, 26 at the time, started as little more than a gofer. But with only one other person left in the purchasing department, she soon found herself sorting out those suppliers willing to give the company some financial leeway, and finding replacements for those who wouldn't." (*Wall Street Journal,* Feb. 12, 2002, p. B1)

GO FOR IT. Take the risk or chance.

GO-GO FUND. Risky, aggressive mutual fund. These funds tend to do well in BULL markets but poorly in declining markets.

GOING CONCERN. Existing business.

GOING GREAT GUNS. Working or producing at full capacity.

GOING LONG. Purchasing a stock or other investment.

GOING SHORT. Selling a stock without owning the shares. When going short an investor sells shares borrowed from the brokerage firm, expecting the price of the stock to decline. See also SHORT SQUEEZE.

GOING THE EXTRA MILE. Paying attention to detail; providing quality service, usually above and beyond what is expected.
"As colleagues of Danny Pearl, we certainly appreciate (and admire) the risks that journalists are sometimes obliged to take. But that argues all the more for going the extra mile to make clear that journalists are non-combatants." (*Wall Street Journal,* April 17, 2003, p. A12)

GOLDBRICKER. Employee who tries to do the least amount of work without getting fired, lazy worker. The author's father told the story of a framing carpenter who, when he heard the four o'clock whistle ending the workday, had a nail halfway into the piece of wood. When asked why he pulled the nail out of the wood rather than nailing it in, the goldbricker replied, "I don't get paid for overtime." (Ex Rel. Morris Folsom, 1970)

GOLDBUG. Investor in gold or gold stocks. Goldbugs perceive the commodity to be a safe investment during periods of depression or hyperinflation.

GOLD COASTER. Someone who is doing very little work as they approach retirement.

GOLDEN BOOT. Incentives offered to older employees to get them to retire.

GOLDEN FLEECE AWARD. Symbol of exorbitant prices (from ancient Greek mythology). For years former U.S. Senator William Proxmire made symbolic Golden Fleece Awards bringing public attention to inflated prices charged by businesses for products sold to the government.

GOLDEN GOOSE. The prize; valuable asset. The golden goose is used in many fairy tales as a magical source of wealth.
  "One can build a case that the summer of 2000 was the turning point for United. UAL managers were desperately trying to win approval from labor and government to acquire US Airways Group Inc., and were willing to buy pilot approval. Rick Dubinsky, the former head of United's pilot's union, famously said pilots didn't want to kill the golden goose, 'We just want to choke it by the neck until it gives us every last egg.'" (*Wall Street Journal,* Dec. 5, 2002, p. D5)

GOLDEN HANDCUFFS. Attractive financial incentive designed to keep executives from leaving a company.
  "Sotheby's Holdings Inc. reported wider fourth-quarter and annual losses, chiefly due to the payment of 'golden handcuffs' packages to top executives and settlements related to a price-fixing inquiry." (*Wall Street Journal,* March 18, 2003, p. D5)

GOLDEN PARACHUTE. Special retirement benefits for executives.
  "Tom Glocer, the first American to run London-based Reuters, drew angry press attention for extracting a promise of a golden parachute of more than $3.5 million if he was fired." (*Wall Street Journal,* May 25, 2004, p. B1)

GOLDEN SHARES. Special shares of stock, often retained by European governments in companies that were privatized. The special shares give the government power to overrule corporate board of directors' decisions.
  "EU governments put golden-share arrangements in place in the 1980s, when they began privatizing strategic state-owned companies." (*Wall Street Journal,* June 5, 2002, p. A12)

GOLD MINE. A very profitable opportunity.

"At one point UC's Mr. David Russ even faced the danger that he would lose some of the Google gold mine. The university has investments in two funds that own Google stakes." (*Wall Street Journal,* May 11, 2004, p. A1)

GO NAKED. Stock market action of selling a call option without owning the stock.

GOOD-FAITH LOAN. Credit provided to a borrower based on his or her character and past payment history, without collateral. Also called a signature loan.

GOOD-FAITH MONEY. A deposit made as a commitment to a transaction. Also called EARNEST MONEY.

GOOD-OLD-BOY CLUB/SYSTEM/NETWORK. See OLD-BOY CLUB/NETWORK.

GOOD SCRUB. To review a business plan.

GOOD-TILL-CANCELED ORDER (GTC). Stock market buy or sell order with no time restriction. Most stock orders are either day-orders or GTC.

GOODWILL. The amount by which the purchase price for a business exceeds the value of its real assets.
"Givaudan SA, a producer of flavors and fragrances, reported a steep rise in first-half net profit, mainly due to a change in its accounting rules that freed it from goodwill charges. Givaudan, of Geneva, said net profit jumped 70% to 220 million Swiss francs ($175.5 million) from 130 million francs a year ago." (*Wall Street Journal,* August 11, 2004, p. 1)

GO POSTAL. To become extremely violent.

GO PUBLIC. Sell shares of stock in a company that was previously privately owned.
"The average IPO is down 1.2% from its offering price this year, compared with a 26% average gain in 2003. Seventy-six, or 51%, of the 148 companies to go public this year now trade below their offering prices, according to Thomson Financial." (*Wall Street Journal,* August 23, 2004, p. C1)

GORDON GEKKO AWARD. Noteworthy greed (from the film *Wall Street* character who espoused, "greed is good").

"The hands-down winner of the Gordon Gekko Award, however, appears to be former Tyco boss Dennis Kozlowski." (*Wall Street Journal,* August 8, 2002, p. A12)

GO THROUGH THE RANKS. Start at the bottom of an organization and be promoted upward.

GO THROUGH THE ROOF. To become extremely upset.

GO TO BAT FOR. Support (baseball).
"Two Ex-Attorneys General To Go to Bat for Microsoft" (*Wall Street Journal,* Jan. 31, 2000, p. 1)

GO TO THE MAT. Argue forcefully in favor of a project or idea (wrestling).

GO TO THE WALL. Do everything possible to make something successful.

GOVERNMENT NATIONAL MORTGAGE ASSOCIATION "GINNIE MAE" (GNMA). Government corporation that guarantees payment on mortgage-backed securities.

GRAB YOUR WALLET. Be careful with your money.

GRACE PERIOD. Period of time until a bill becomes due.
"Some consolidators will require a certain loan amount in consolidation for you to benefit. Others won't give you the discounts if you consolidate during your grace period, which is often the best time to do it, said Mr. Thibeault." (*Wall Street Journal,* June 2, 2004, p. D2)

GRAIN OF SALT (WITH A). Less than certitude.
"'The first thing I'd say is to take each posting with a grain of salt,' says Bobbi Moss, a vice president at Management Recruiters International, a Philadelphia search firm. 'It's also very typical for an employer to list every idealistic trait, so you should try to figure out what is the overall objective in the ad.'" (*Wall Street Journal,* Dec. 16, 2003, p. B8)

GRANDFATHER CLAUSE. A provision in a law exempting existing individuals or businesses from the requirements of a new law.
"But if the changes are approved, a few dozen other states are expected to follow suit. And when rules governing Medicaid planning

change, there's no grandfather clause. That means that even if you gave away your assets years ago, you still would have to follow the rules in effect when you apply for the program." (*Wall Street Journal,* Feb. 23, 2004, p. R4)

GRAPEVINE. Informal communication network; gossip.
"Don't count on it, Mr. Newt Gingrich warns. In fact, he predicts, the details of the Medicare overhaul will flash through the senior-center grapevine as fast as gossip on the teenage instant-message circuit." (*Wall Street Journal,* August 27, 2003, p. A4)

GRASS STAIN. Slight damage or signs of strenuous effort. In baseball, the players who have played usually have dirty uniforms, including grass stains, while those who sat on the bench have clean uniforms.
"Because we PLAYED BALL, we came through with a few grass stains but no serious injuries." (*Wall Street Journal,* June 17, 1996, p. A14)

GRAVE INSULT. Serious affront.

GRAVEYARD SHIFT. Work shift that starts around midnight.

GRAY MARKET. Legal but unauthorized (by the producer) distribution channel. Many U.S. manufacturers license their technology and brands abroad. Licensees agree not to sell their output in the United States, but their distributors are not bound by this arrangement.

GREASE (TO). Make happen by the payment of a bribe.

GREASY SPOON. A small, cheap restaurant.
"Today's diners must overcome an image, often incorrect, of a greasy spoon." (*Nation's Restaurant News,* Jan. 16, 1995, p. 7)

GREAT DEAL OF. A lot of.

GREATER FOOL THEORY. The idea that there is always someone willing to pay a higher price.
"'As borrowing costs went down, people were willing to pay more for buildings,' said Lloyd Lynford, Reis's chief executive. 'Buyers are beginning to look at the performance of a building and say, My goodness. Maybe I shouldn't subscribe to the greater-fool theory that somebody will buy it at an ever-greater cost.'" (*Wall Street Journal,* August 26, 2003, p. B5)

GREAT SOCIETY PROGRAMS. Social programs initiated during the Lyndon Johnson administration, 1964–1968.

"I think the underlying problem goes back to a great mistake that America made in the late '60s. We decided to give resources and preferential treatment more to victims of racism than to people who simply suffer cultural and economic deprivations. Even President Johnson's Great Society programs used poverty largely as a proxy for racial oppression." (*Wall Street Journal,* March 29, 2002, p. A12)

GREENBACK. The American dollar.

GREEN CARD. Immigration permit allowing a person to work in the United States.

"The U.S. will require foreigners with work visas to reapply at embassies outside the U.S. when the visas expire. An item in the World-Wide column in some editions yesterday incorrectly stated that the new procedure applied to those with green cards." (*Wall Street Journal,* June 24, 2004, p. A1)

GREENFIELD. New and innovative.

GREEN LIGHT. Signal to proceed.

"The SEC said the executives concluded a deal was pending when they were given the go-ahead to publicize within 48 hours a previously secret contract with Dean Foods. Armed with a green light from Dean Foods, the dairy executives bought stock and options in Dean Foods." (*Wall Street Journal,* August 5, 2004, p. 1)

GREENMAIL. Payment made to a CORPORATE RAIDER to stop buying up shares of the company. A company buys back shares of its stock for more than the original market price before the corporate raider bought up shares.

GREEN MARKETING. The real or symbolic use of environmentally friendly products, ingredients, or technology in order to satisfy consumers' concerns about the environment.

GREENPEACE. International organization that advocates for environmental issues via visible symbolic efforts, including protests at nuclear test sites and intervention in the whaling industry.

GREEN REVOLUTION. The hoped-for increase in output from the use of Western technology in agricultural production in the developing world.

"Environmentalist Paul Ehrlich has proved himself to be a stupendously bad prophet. In 1968 he declared: 'The battle to feed all of humanity is over. In the 1970s, the world will undergo famines—hundreds of millions of people are going to starve to death.' They didn't. Indeed, a 'green revolution' nearly tripled the world's food supply." (*Wall Street Journal,* May 20, 2004, p. D10)

GREEN SHOE. When an underwriter of an INITIAL PUBLIC OFFERING has the option to sell extra shares.

"The sale would increase in size to 5.7 billion euros if investors exercised the green-shoe overallotment option, and it would eventually cut the state's stake in Finmeccanica to about a third of all shares from the current 83%." (*Wall Street Journal,* June 5, 2000, p. A4)

GREENSPEAK. The coded and guarded language employed by U.S. Federal Reserve Board Chairman Alan Greenspan. Greenspeak phrases like "soft patch," "short-lived," and "considerable period" became front-page business news during 2003–2004.

"Harking back to his infamous 'irrational exuberance' speech, Greenspan again said stock prices may be 'excessive.' But he added the best way to deal with a possible bubble is to pursue price stability. In typical Greenspeak, he said price stability can 'induce investors to take on more risk and drive asset prices to unsustainable levels.'" (Ed Carson, "Philly Fed says higher input prices aren't passed on," *Investor's Business Daily,* June 18, 1999)

GREEN WASHING. The attempt by businesses to clean up their practices in order to appear environmentally responsible.

GRIND TO A HALT/SCREECHING HALT. Stop suddenly.

GROSS. Total sales; a total before deductions; twelve dozen or 144 units.

GROSS IMPRESSIONS. The total number of exposures to a marketer's message. One person seeing an advertisement four times counts as four exposures.

GROSS RATING POINTS. Total gross impressions, expressed as a percentage of the population.

GROSS REACH. Total potential viewers of an advertisement.

GROUND RULES. The basic rules or procedures to be used or followed.

GROUNDWORK. Foundation; preliminary research, or contacts made in establishing business relationships.

"The prospect of a formal troop commitment by the North Atlantic Treaty Organization appears far out of reach. The question is whether Mr. Bush can use his five-day tour of Europe, including a NATO summit in Istanbul, Turkey, beginning on Monday, to begin laying the groundwork for more help." (*Wall Street Journal,* June 25, 2004, p. A6)

GROUND ZERO. The center of activity.

GROUP OF SEVEN (G-7). The seven largest industrial countries: Canada, France, Germany, Great Britain, Italy, Japan, and the United States. In the 1990s, representatives of Russia were first invited to attend G-7 meetings.

GS RATING. General Services Administration rating. Federal Civil Service job rating system.

GUARANTEED INVESTMENT CONTRACT (GIC). Retirement investment product offered by insurance companies.

"Overall, people in their 60s have only about 40% of their 401(k) portfolios invested in equities, and as they get closer to retirement, they tend to start going into much more conservative investments. In fact, guaranteed investment contracts and guaranteed-rate-of-return allocations are now up to nearly 20% of the asset allocations for that age group." (*Wall Street Journal,* June 24, 2002, p. R10)

GUERILLA MARKETING. The use of clever, attention-getting nontraditional advertising media and messages. Guerrilla marketing includes the use of street theater, people paid to spread the word about a product, and nontraditional messages.

"In the past few years, corporations have embraced attention-getting guerilla marketing tactics." (*Wall Street Journal,* July 8, 2004, p. B4)

GUESTIMATE. An informed guess regarding a fact or figure (a combination of the words guess and estimate).

GURU. A prominent and influential expert or leader.

H

HACKER. Someone who illegally enters computer systems; a poor golfer.

HACK IT. Succeed; put up with.

HAIL MARY. A desperate course of action. The term refers to a Roman Catholic prayer invoking the help of the Virgin Mary.

HAIRCUT (TO TAKE A). To lose money.

HALF TONES. Photographs used in advertisements and other publications.

HALO EFFECT. Situation where past positive perceptions influence current judgment.
"Auto dealers said heavily advertised no-interest-loan offers have brought consumers into nearly all brands' showrooms ready to buy. 'There's a halo effect,' said Oscar Suris, spokesman for AutoNation Inc., the largest new-car dealer in the U.S. At Honda Motor Co., which offers few sales incentives on its lineup, sales

so far in October are outpacing last year's record result." (*Wall Street Journal,* Oct. 11, 2002, p. A2)

HAMMER OUT (TO). Come to an agreement through difficult negotiation.

"Because of the complexity of these talks between companies, federal regulators had urged the parties to hammer out the details of a cohesive plan on their own." (*Wall Street Journal,* May 20, 2004, p. A6)

HAMMER THE MARKET (TO). Sell large quantities of a stock at one time.

HAND OVER FIST (TO MAKE MONEY). So profitable that one is overwhelmed taking in the money.

HANDS-ON (MANAGEMENT STYLE). Direct involvement with employees' activities.

"Mr. Dewald's drying school is widely credited as the first one to flood a house to teach drying theory and hands-on techniques, and so far about 2,500 students have attended." (*Wall Street Journal,* August 24, 2004, p. B1)

HANG IT UP. Quit; retire.

HANG OUT ONE'S SHINGLE. Start a business, announce the opening of a business.

"What you see: A place in the sun. This real-estate attorney hangs his shingle on a white-stucco, Mediterranean Revival-style building that he's restoring to its former radiance." (*Wall Street Journal,* Oct. 8, 2003, p. B8)

HANG TOUGH. Persevere.

HAPPY HOUR. After-work promotional specials at bars and restaurants. In the United States, happy hour is usually from 4:00 P.M. to 7:00 P.M.

"What starts out as a co-worker relationship develops into a friendship, then a deep friendship, and then into a relationship. In my wife's case, work led to business lunches. Business lunches led to 'nonbusiness' lunches and then to 'happy hours.' And the whole thing led to divorce." (*Wall Street Journal,* Nov. 13, 2003, p. D1)

HARDBALL. Aggressive competition (baseball).

"Playing hardball with Pfizer is tougher. Suppose for instance that a benefit manager gives Merck & Co.'s pain reliever Vioxx a better position than Pfizer's Celebrex. This could mean that the benefit manager will have to pay more for Pfizer's Lipitor and Zoloft. Other companies try similar tactics, but don't have such a broad menu of drugs to use as a negotiating tool." (*Wall Street Journal,* August 23, 2004, p. A1)

HARD CURRENCY. Money easily accepted worldwide.

HARD HAT. Manual laborer. See also BLUE-COLLAR WORKER.

HARD-HITTING. Forceful; strong-willed (football).
"'What it boils down to,' says Mr. Nadler, 'is that Republicans don't have the guts to run the kind of hard-hitting program attacking Democrats on Democratic turf.' When that changes, you'll know the GOP is getting serious about outreach." (*Wall Street Journal,* July 28, 2004, p. A12)

HARD LINE. A rigid negotiating position offering little compromise.

HARD-NOSED. Critical, inflexible.
"She argues that there is no foundation for believing that ST is the chief cause of the race gap, so we shouldn't let it lead us into putting our hopes into 'psychological' explanations over a hard-nosed focus on skills." (*Wall Street Journal,* May 4, 2004, p. A21)

HARD NUMBERS. Facts and data rather than estimates.
"Data Gap—Behind Outsourcing Debate: Surprisingly Few Hard Numbers; Counting Jobs Moving Abroad Is a Complicated Task; Benefits Are Less Tangible; One Report: A Little Wobbly" (*Wall Street Journal,* April 12, 2004, p. A1)

HATCHET MAN. Junior executive who is given the task of firing employees.
"Mr. Mulva started in 1973 in Phillips's treasury department, becoming treasurer in 1986 and chief financial officer in 1990. In the mid-1980s, after Phillips took on a heavy debt load to avoid a takeover bid, he was said to be the company's 'hatchet man,' who oversaw steep and painful cost-cutting." (*Wall Street Journal,* Nov. 21, 2001, p. B6)

HAUL. Large sum of money, sometimes obtained illegally.

HAWTHORNE EFFECT. Study that found that any changes in working conditions improved productivity.

"Hawthorne effect refers to the findings of a 1924 study that measured the correlation between specific working conditions and output. It showed that productivity increased (regardless of particular changes) whenever the workers sensed that they were regarded as valued members of the organization." (*Supervisory Management,* May 1990, p. 6)

HEAD HONCHO. Top boss. The term honcho comes from Japanese, *hancho,* the leader of a small group.

"Lots of studios were interested, but the final bidding came down to Fox Searchlight, Fine Line and Miramax. Midway through the auction, Harvey Weinstein, Miramax's head honcho, called James Dolan, chief executive of Cablevision, which owned the rights to the film, and asked if he could buy it." (*Wall Street Journal,* August 30, 2002, p. W7)

HEADHUNTER. Recruiter who find executives for companies; implies stealing people from other organizations.

HEADLIGHTING. To bring issues up for discussion and consideration before they become crises.

"Texas Instruments is doing some headlighting by listing, as much as a year in advance, which jobs are in jeopardy and asking those employees, What do we need to do to broaden you out to look for a job inside or outside TI?" (*Wall Street Journal,* Oct. 3, 1995, p. B1)

HEADS UP. An alert or advance notification.

HEALTH MAINTENANCE ORGANIZATION (HMO). Health insurance group that charges a fixed fee per member and provides a wide range of services to the members. From World War II until the 1990s, most U.S. health insurance programs allowed the insured person to choose any healthcare provider. The premiums for this insurance were usually paid by the employer. HMOs have expanded rapidly in the 1990s as a means to constrain healthcare costs for employers.

HEARTLAND. The noncoastal areas of the United States. The heartland in the United States is perceived to have more "traditional," conservative values.

HEAT (TO TAKE). To receive criticism.

HEAT-SEEKING WORKFORCE. Workers who move from business to business seeking employment in "hot" industries and companies.

HEAVY HITTER/HEAVYWEIGHT. Very important person or business.
"The Property Report—Building Value: Small Investors Look to Become Heavy Hitters," (*Wall Street Journal,* Dec. 10, 2003, p. B10)

HEDGE (TO). Insure or protect against losses.

HEDGEHOG CONCEPT. An idea or concept that, if it becomes the total focus and is done extremely well, can help a person or a company achieve its full potential.
"'Walgreens' hedgehog concept is to run the best, most convenient drug stores with high profit per customer visit,' Jorndt continued. 'We know who we are and what we are all about—running drug stores. We work like crazy to execute it in our stores.'" (Rob Eder, "Out-foxing the hedgehog's rivals," *Drug Store News,* March 25, 2002)

HELICOPTER (TO). Maintain a presence in a corporation; to observe the overall economic trends.
"The Ten Deadly Euphemisms, Part 2:1. Helicoptering. To advance, you must hover over the corporate scene to observe the broad economic tides that push companies into new businesses that create opportunities, or out of old businesses that eliminate them." (*Wall Street Journal,* Oct. 3, 1995, p. B1)

HEM AND HAW (TO). To stall or be evasive, not answering the question asked.

HEMLINE THEORY. U.S. stock market phenomenon correlating fashions for short skirts with BULLISH markets and longer skirts with BEARISH markets.

HERD INSTINCT/MENTALITY. Everyone follows the leaders.
"'I don't think many places have carefully evaluated their odds of success,' says Joseph Cortright, co-author of the Brookings report and an economist in Portland, Ore. The hot pursuit of biotech, he adds, is driven more by what he calls the 'tremendous herd instinct' of state and local development officials. 'It's unlikely many of these biotech companies will grow into full-fledged manufacturing firms that produce lots of jobs.'" (*Wall Street Journal,* June 11, 2002, p. B1)

HEYDAY. Good times, enthusiasm.

"The obvious implication of so much of the 9/11 Commission's report is that the real failing of the Clinton and pre-9/11 Bush Administrations wasn't so much one of intelligence but of mindset. Neither was committed enough to acting pre-emptively against our enemies, and to doing so without legal restrictions (such as the Ford-era executive order banning assassinations) that were imposed starting in the anti-CIA heyday of the 1970s." (*Wall Street Journal,* August 4, 2004, p. A12)

HICCUP. A temporary, unexpected deviation from the expected path or plan.

HIDDEN AGENDA. Important issues that are not officially part of a meeting; personal antagonism between managers.

HIDDEN COST. Unexpected or difficult-to-measure costs.

HIERARCHICAL COMMAND. Traditional, from-the-top-down management.

HIGH COTTON (IN). Conceited (Southern).

HIGH END. More expensive; powerful; up-to-date.

HIGHER GEAR. A faster pace.

HIGHER-UPS. Senior administrators. See TOP BRASS, MUCKY-MUCKS.

"Mr. Turner's firm was responsible for one of the chief embarrassments to hit the Edwards campaign, when a law clerk stated publicly that firm higher-ups had assured staffers that they'd be reimbursed if they donated to the senator's White House run; the Justice Department's Public Integrity Section opened a criminal probe." (*Wall Street Journal,* July 12, 2004, p. A16)

HIGH FLYER. A stock or investment whose price has risen rapidly; implies that it may be a risky investment at the time.

HIGH-LEVEL ANALYSIS. An executive summary or outline of the conclusions.

HIGH ROAD. The ethical way of doing business or handling a situation.

HIGH-WIRE ACT. Risky decision.

"South Korea's High-Wire Act—Seoul Tries to Cool Consumption as Exports Slow; Asia Watches" (*Wall Street Journal,* Oct. 8, 2002, p. A20)

HIKE PRICES (TO). Increase prices.

HILL (THE). Capitol Hill in Washington, D.C., site of the legislative branch of the U.S. government.

HILL OF BEANS. Insignificant, of no value.

HIRED GUNS. Lawyers, accountants, and other business strategy consultants.

"If you want to understand the president's underlying motives, read the new book on his guru, Karl Rove, 'Bush's Brain.' Penned by two crack Texas reporters, it discloses that in 1994 Mr. Rove, a hired gun for Philip Morris, persuaded the gubernatorial candidate George W. Bush to make tort reform a priority." (*Wall Street Journal,* March 6, 2003, p. A13)

HIT. A success or a huge loss. Rapid sales of a new product suggest the product is a hit; a sudden, significant decline in a firm's sales or profits is also called a hit.

HITCH. A problem; to become attached or associated with.

"But there's a hitch. There's no definition of operating earnings in accounting rules." (*Wall Street Journal,* August 24, 1999, p. B1)

HIT LIST. Projects or programs that may be cut from a budget.

"War, not business, has driven Libya's recent rapprochement; he says the main driving force behind President Gadhafi's surprise move last year to give up Libya's arms program was his concern that Tripoli was next on Washington's hit list after the U.S. toppled Iraqi leader Saddam Hussein." (*Wall Street Journal,* August 5, 2004, p. A8)

HIT PAY DIRT. To succeed beyond expectations.

HIT THE COVER OFF THE BALL. A very strong performance (baseball).

HIT THE FAN (TO). Refers to the onset of chaos or panic. Often part of the larger phrase, "the shit hit the fan."

HIT THE GROUND RUNNING. To begin immediately and fully prepared.

HIT THE NAIL ON THE HEAD. Be exactly right.

HIT THE PANIC BUTTON. Become very alarmed.

HIT THE WINDSHIELD. To fail miserably.

HOCKEY STICK. Not very smart.

HOG-CORN RATIO. The ratio of the price received for a hog to the price of its primary input, corn. Developed by Dr. Earl O. Heady, the hog-corn ratio is used to determine whether it is more profitable to sell the corn or feed it to the hog.

HOI POLLOI. The many, the masses; people who have a high opinion of themselves (Greek).
   "To that end Stronach has installed a giant television screen in Santa Anita's infield, opened a glassed-in restaurant half the length of the homestretch where patrons can eat a $40 lunch while watching the races on table TVs, and terraced, retiled and generally fancied up the railside area where many of the hoi polloi hang out." (*Wall Street Journal,* Dec. 28, 1999, p. A16)

HOLD FEET TO THE FIRE. To put pressure on.

HOLDING THE BAG (TO BE LEFT). To be left responsible for something after it has been abandoned by others.

HOLD THE LINE. Not change, as in maintaining on offering price or controlling costs.

HOLD THE PHONE. Delay, wait a minute (command).

HOLY GRAIL. Sacred creed or value; a worthy but difficult or unobtainable goal.
   "For people who rely on a smart phone or wireless PDA to do e-mail and access the Web, the Holy Grail has been to get a device that can work on both a cellphone network and on faster Wi-Fi wireless networks." (*Wall Street Journal,* July 29, 2004, p. B4)

HOMEGROWN. Local.

HOME INDUSTRY ARGUMENT. Protection of local companies.

HOME IN ON (TO). Concentrate, focus.

"The original creation called for sour apple schnapps and became an instant local hit. It didn't take long for the DeKuyper brand team to home in on the recipe and promote it nationwide in industry trade publications." (*Wall Street Journal,* March 1, 2002, p. B1)

HOME RUN. A success (baseball).

"Coke and Pepsi officials insist it's still too soon to conclude the new health-conscious colas are going flat. 'Everybody in this category gets hyped up for a short-term home run in week one or two,' said Dave Burwick, chief marketing officer for Pepsi-Cola North America in Purchase, N.Y." (*Wall Street Journal,* July 15, 2004, p. D4)

HOME TURF. Domestic or local market.

"Delta has gone from being one of the strongest airlines to a financial mess, piling up losses of more than $3.6 billion in the past three years. It faces pressure to slash overhead so it can compete against lower-cost carriers ... that have invaded Delta's home turf on the East Coast." (*Wall Street Journal,* July 2, 2004, p. C1)

HONEYMOON. Extra cooperation at the beginning of a relationship.

"Charles Flocard, chairman of the Federation of European Air Transport Users, said he expects the two airlines to try to raise fares on routes that they dominated after a brief honeymoon period of low fares this summer." (*Wall Street Journal,* Feb. 12, 2004, p. D3)

HONORARIUM. Stipend; small fee paid to a speaker.

HONORARY LIFE MEMBER (HLM). Private groups and organizations often bestow honorary life membership to people who have made significant contributions to their cause.

HOOK (TO). Gain control of; promotional device designed to bring in new customers.

HOOPLA. Excitement.

"With all the hoopla over higher interest rates, here's one lending sector where rates actually dropped after the Federal Reserve's decision to boost interest rates last week: federal student loans." (*Wall Street Journal,* July 6, 2004, p. D2)

HORIZONTAL CAREER LADDER. Sarcastic description of a job environment that has no opportunities for advancement.

HORSE OF A DIFFERENT COLOR. Something different.

HORSE'S MOUTH. Official source, from the person in authority.

HORSE TRADING. Deal making, particularly in politics.

HOSTILE TAKEOVER. Unfriendly buyout, purchase of control of a business by a CORPORATE RAIDER.

HOT AIR. Meaningless talk, boastfulness.

HOTBED. Popular or controversial; under pressure to produce.
"Meanwhile, U.S. forces appeared to be gearing up to move into the hotbeds of Najaf, where Shiite militants loyal to a radical cleric were holed up, and Fallujah, which is controlled by Sunni insurgents." (*Wall Street Journal,* April 26, 2004, p. A4)

HOT BUTTONS. Topics to which one is sensitive; management philosophy that employees should make decisions themselves without going to upper management—employees should push the hot buttons.

HOT CARDING. When an ATM retains old credit cards and cards with liens against them.

HOT-DESKING. Practice of not assigning permanent desks to employees; instead, workers share a pool of desks.

HOT ISSUE. A new stock that is popular among investors.

HOT POTATO. An issue that is controversial.
"By not making their provisioning 'clear and public,' the other banks can gain some advantage of their own. Not disclosing how much they set aside for a possible Fiat loss keeps the banks from commenting on Fiat's financial prospects—a political hot potato in Italy." (*Wall Street Journal,* May 26, 2004, p. C3)

HOT SPOT. A dangerous or risky situation.

HOT TIP. Information received in advance of others.

HOT UNDER THE COLLAR. Angry.

HOUSE-CLEANING. Reorganization of a business, usually including the dismissal of many employees.

"With some $4 billion in revenue and $268 million in net income for its most recent fiscal year, Starbucks says its international business is on track to turn a profit next year for the first time since 1996. Results in the U.K. are improving following a new real-estate strategy and a house-cleaning in which U.S. managers were replaced with Brits." (*Wall Street Journal,* Dec. 15, 2003, p. B1)

HOUSE-MONEY EFFECT. The observation that people are more willing to take risks with money they obtained easily or unexpectedly.

"The Flemings lot are now talking about 'regret aversion,' investors' inclination to sell their winners and stick by their losers, and the 'house money effect,' where people are more likely to bet recklessly in casinos with money they have recently won." ("The Psycho Path," *Investment Week,* March 17, 2003)

HOW WILL IT PLAY IN PEORIA? What will average Americans think? Peoria represents the middle or HEARTLAND of the United States.

HUD. See DEPARTMENT OF HOUSING AND URBAN DEVELOPMENT.

HUDDLE (TO). Come together to discuss strategy (football).

"What you see: Economy. When Mr. Ted Waitt took back the lead of the struggling personal-computer maker with cow-spotted boxes, one of his first cost-cutting moves was to consolidate offices. So he corralled workers from seven facilities and found a new headquarters, where they huddle together in one big room." (*Wall Street Journal,* July 23, 2003, p. B6)

HUMAN RESOURCES (HR) DEPARTMENT. Department responsible for hiring, training, and the management of worker benefits.

HUMDRUM. Mediocre, ordinary.

HUMP DAY. Wednesday, the middle of the work week.

HUNT AND PECK. Typing, using only one's index fingers.

HUSH-MONEY. Bribe; payment to keep someone quiet.

"It is difficult to see how a 16-year-old black girl in Edgefield, S.C., could refuse advances from the randy son of one of that town's most prominent white lawyers—but rather by the yearly hush-money he gave her ('very substantial,' but less than a million, her lawyer is quoted as saying), and the clout he used to help Ms. Williams and her son." (*Wall Street Journal,* Dec. 23, 2003, p. A14)

HYPE. Superfluous promotion.

"Mr. Heinz says he has heard predictions of Xiaolingtong's demise for at least three years, particularly as the hype over 'third-generation' mobile gizmos—those offering high-speed Internet access for viewing TV clips and playing online games—has reached new heights." (*Wall Street Journal,* July 8, 2004, p. B1)

HYPERLINK. Buttons or other points on a Web page that, when clicked on, move (or link) the viewer to another Web page.

HYPERMARKET. A large retail store that sells a broad array of goods.

HYPERTEXT MARKUP LANGUAGE (HTML). A standard protocol used to define the text and layout of Web pages.

HYPERTEXT TRANSFER PROTOCOL (HTTP). A standard protocol used to define how information is transmitted across the Internet between Web browsers and Web servers.

I

ICANN. Internet Corporation for Assigned Names and Numbers. ICANN is a nonprofit business responsible for Internet protocol address space allocation.

ICEBERG PRINCIPLE. The idea that in any situation only a small part of the problem will be initially visible.

"Adds Andrew Brimmer, an economist and financial consultant who sits on the boards of several major corporations: 'It's like the iceberg principle. The 8% of the iceberg above the water is what we see—large corporations that have institutionalized affirmative action. The vast bulk of firms are below the surface—the smaller corporations have done virtually nothing.'" (*Wall Street Journal*, March 20, 1995, p. B1)

IDENTITY THEFT. Stealing someone's identification including theft and use of credit cards and the creation of fraudulent identification. Identity theft is a major problem and difficult to overcome.

IDIOSYNCRATIC RISK. The stock investment risk associated with unexpected changes specific to that company. Idiosyncratic risk contrasts with market risk, which is associated with changes in overall market conditions.

IF I TELL YOU, I WILL HAVE TO KILL YOU. A phrase used jokingly, meaning that the information is proprietary and cannot be divulged.

ILLEGAL ALIENS. People from another country without proper documentation.

ILLEGAL PARKING. Stock market practice of having another firm purchase securities in its name but guaranteed by the real investor.

"Michael Milken and Ivan Boesky made the practice of illegal parking famous in the 1980s. Illegal parking allowed Boesky to circumvent SEC net capital requirements." (Jim Reilly, Robinson-Humphrey Co., 1996)

ILLIQUID. Lacking cash.

IMPRESSION. One exposure to a brand message.

IN ABSENTIA. In the absence of (Latin).

IN BED WITH. In close agreement or financially connected.

IN CAMERA. In private (Latin).

INCENT (TO). Provide incentives for employees.

"One of their weapons is an underground game called buzzword bingo, which works like a surreptitious form of regular bingo. Buzzwords—'incent,' 'proactive,' 'impactfulness,' for example—are preselected and placed on a bingo-like card in random boxes. Players sit in meetings and conferences and silently check off buzzwords as their bosses spout them; the first to fill in a complete line wins. But, in deference to the setting, the winner typically coughs instead of shouting out 'bingo.'" (*Wall Street Journal,* June 8, 1998, p. A1)

IN CONCERT WITH. Working closely and cooperatively.

IN DEEP WATER. In trouble.

INDEXING. Creating a portfolio of securities representative of an overall group of stocks. Index mutual funds have enjoyed popularity as a passive investment strategy.

INDIVIDUAL RETIREMENT ACCOUNT (IRA). Tax-deferred retirement savings program created in the 1980s to try to get Americans to save. With restrictions, workers can put up to $2,000 per year in an IRA account and not pay income taxes on the money or interest until they withdraw the funds.

INFANT INDUSTRY. New manufacturing companies. Infant industries have the potential for economies of scale if they survive long enough to grow. Governments frequently protect these firms from international competition through tariff barriers.

INFOMERCIAL. An extended (ten- to thirty-minute) television advertisement; a television commercial presented as if it was entertainment or an informative report.

"The recall affects the Bowflex Power Pro XL, XTL and XTLU systems with the 'Lat Tower' attachment. The machines were sold through infomercials or retail stores January 1995 through December 2003 for $1,200 to $1,600." (*Wall Street Journal,* Jan. 29, 2004, p. 1)

INFORMATION SUPERHIGHWAY. The combination of Internet, cellular, and satellite communication technologies.

INFRASTRUCTURE. Vital services and capital assets of a country.

IN-HOUSE. Done within the company, as opposed to OUTSOURCING.

INITIAL PUBLIC OFFERING (IPO). The first time a company's stock is offered to investors. In the 1990s, IPOs offered significant profits to investors who FLIPPED the stock.

INK (TO). To sign a deal.

IN KIND. Barter, countertrade.

IN LOCO PARENTIS. In the place of a parent (Latin).

IN ONE FELL SWOOP. All at once.

"Defenders of the planned acquisition say their case is clear-cut. Buying Noranda would allow CVRD to diversify its portfolio of metals in one fell swoop." (*Wall Street Journal,* July 9, 2004, p. C14)

IN PLAY. Still available or not determined (baseball).

INS AND OUTS. The details associated with getting something done.

INSHORING. Gaining domestic jobs when foreign companies add or expand upon local operations.

"At a recent conference in the palatial Venetian resort, the people who help U.S. companies shift white-collar work overseas offered potential clients a Vegas buffet of outsourcing options: 'nearshoring,' for those willing to stray no farther than Canada or Mexico; 'inshoring,' for those who prefer to bring foreign workers to America, and 'rightshoring,' for those desiring a custom package of in-house and offsite, foreign and domestic." (Warren Vieth, "Outsourcing Variations Have Some Appeal," *Los Angeles Times,* April 27, 2004)

INSIDE CANDIDATE. Employee being considered for a new position within the company.

"The news that the company has chosen an inside candidate will surprise investors and analysts, who are concerned that the company will repeat past missteps. Mr. Robert DiNicola originally retired from the company in August 2000 and was succeeded at the helm by his hand-picked protégé Beryl Raff, who had been named CEO the previous year." (*Wall Street Journal,* June 24, 2002, p. B2)

INSIDER TRADING. The trading of shares of stock by a company's board of directors, officers, senior employees, and shareholders with a significant percentage of the company stock. Under Securities and Exchange Commission rules, insiders can only buy and sell shares at certain times and must disclose their actions. Insider trading is also the illegal practice of buying or selling shares based on information not available to the investing public.

INSIDE TRACK. An advantage. In a race, the competitor on the innermost lane travels a shorter distance around a curve than other competitors, thereby having an advantage.

"Meanwhile, PeopleSoft offered to cut $13 million from its list price for Albertsons Inc., the grocery chain, when it appeared Oracle had the inside track. 'We were late to the party,' said a PeopleSoft executive vice president, Phil Wilmington." (*Wall Street Journal,* June 21, 2004, p. B1)

INSTITUTE OF SUPPLY MANAGEMENT (ISM). Trade organization of supply management professionals, formerly the National Association of Purchasing Management (NAPM).

INSTITUTIONAL INVESTORS. Large investment companies, pension funds, insurance companies, banks, mutual funds, and endowments that are major investors in securities markets. Institutional investors often heavily influence market direction.

INSURABLE INTEREST. A life insurance requirement that the beneficiary of a policy have an economic interest or loss if the policyholder died.

INTERFACE. To interact with.

INTERLOCKING DIRECTORATE. A situation in which members of the board of directors sit on two or more companies that compete with each other. Interlocking directorates were made illegal in the United States by the Clayton Antitrust Act of 1914, but are still common in other countries.

INTERNAL RATE OF RETURN (IRR). Discount rate at which the present value of future cash flows from an investment equals the cost of the investment.

INTERNAL REVENUE SERVICE (IRS). U.S. government agency charged with collecting most federal taxes, including personal and corporate income, social security, estate, gift, and excise taxes.

INTERNATIONAL BANK FOR RECONSTRUCTION AND DEVELOPMENT (IRBD, WORLD BANK). Created at BRETTON WOODS in 1944, the World Bank financed the reconstruction of Europe and Asia after World War II. World Bank loans, a major source of financing for global economic development, have recently been criticized for overemphasis on large-scale projects and lack of sensitivity to cultural and environmental impacts.

INTERNATIONAL MONETARY FUND (IMF), THE FUND. The IMF functions as the regulator of foreign exchange rates and as a source of international liquidity. IMF assistance comes with conditions, including monetary and fiscal spending restrictions, that are often painful and controversial.

INTERNATIONAL ORGANIZATION FOR STANDARDIZATION (ISO). Swiss-based organization that coordinates and sets quality control standards. ISO 9000 certification has become a requirement for many companies wanting to do business in Europe.

INTERNET SERVICE PROVIDER (ISP). A company that provides access to the Internet.

INTERSTITIAL. An Internet pop-up advertisement.

IN THE BAG. Certain.
"U.S. trade officials and many U.S. companies say they have been surprised by how the capital-control issue has blown up out of nowhere. The Bush administration figured that both the Singapore and Chile deals were in the bag weeks ago. For Mr. Robert Zoellick, completing these deals is key to much larger ambitions to liberalize world trade." (*Wall Street Journal,* Dec. 9, 2002, p. A4)

IN THE BALL PARK. Close to what was expected (baseball).
"One Mandalay shareholder said he found it hard to believe Mandalay executives would pass up a deal, given the big run-up in the company's stock price already in recent months and the fact that Mandalay Chairman and Chief Executive Michael Ensign, as well as Vice Chairman William Richardson, sold most of their stakes last fall at about $40 a share. 'They better not tell me they're not in the ballpark price-wise when they were sellers at $39,' the investor said of the executives." (*Wall Street Journal,* June 8, 2004, p. A3)

IN THE BLACK. Operating profitably.
"The only time the government has been in the black was from 1994 to 1997, thanks to surpluses largely from the sale of assets." (*Wall Street Journal,* Sept. 8, 2004, p. B10)

IN THE CARDS. Likely to happen.
"'I can't say I thought they'd drop it today, but it was in the cards over the next couple of months,' said William Gross, chief investment officer at Pacific Investment Management Co., of Pimco. Mr. Gross says he still expects the Fed to hold off on raising rates until the second half of the year—probably until the fourth quarter—but adds the Fed's statement yesterday was a small step toward making an interest-rate increase 'easier to swallow' for the bond market." (*Wall Street Journal,* Jan. 29, 2004, p. C1)

IN THE CLEAR. Out of danger.

IN THE DRIVER'S SEAT. In charge, in control.
"'People are too pessimistic,' he says. 'Companies are very focused on keeping profitability and productivity high, and they're not about to give back gains achieved in recent years. And labor

isn't exactly in the driver's seat.'" (*Wall Street Journal,* June 22, 2004, p. C1)

IN THE KNOW. Well informed.

"Top this: Bush advisers try to stanch talk he'll beat an already jaw-dropping $20 million fund-raising goal for June. But besides the president's own events, others starring his wife and Cheney lift expectations further. 'These guys are rocking and rolling,' a Republican in the know says." (*Wall Street Journal,* June 20, 2004, p. A4)

IN THE LONG RUN. Over a considerable period of time. Economist John Maynard Keynes, whose economic models focused on the importance of short-run economic policy adjustments, is famous for the statement, "In the long run we are all dead."

IN THE LOOP. In the circle of power.

IN THE MONEY. An option contract where the current market price is greater than the STRIKE PRICE for a call option and below the strike price for a put option.

IN THE PIPELINE. Being prepared; not ready for distribution at this time.

IN THE RED/RED INK. Operating at a loss.

"The Standard & Poor's 500 Index shed 8.53, or 0.76%, to 1113.88, now less than two points away from joining the Dow industrials and the Nasdaq in the red for the year." (*Wall Street Journal,* April 30, 2004, p. C4)

IN THE RUNNING/RACE. Under consideration.

"Although five or six institutions have shown interest in Aplus, only Japan's Shinsei Bank Ltd. and HSBC Holdings PLC of the U.K. remain in the running." (*Wall Street Journal,* August 17, 2004, p. 1)

IN THE TANK. Declining.

INTRANET. An internal computer communications network.

IN TRANSITION. Unemployed, usually executives; changing.

"Mr. Bush's economic and Capitol Hill teams are also in transition, and efforts to advance the latest tax package have suffered as a result." (*Wall Street Journal,* Feb. 10, 2003, p. A4)

INTRAPRENEURSHIP. Entrepreneurship within a business organization.

INVENTORY RUNS. Computer analysis of inventory levels.

INVENTORY TURNS. How many times inventory is sold and replaced per year.
"Food sales fueled Wal-Mart's growth, climbing 34% in the quarter. Food carries lower margins, but it brings in customers more frequently, increases inventory turns and bolsters the sale of general merchandise—'a powerful combination for profits,' said Mr. Church." (*Wall Street Journal,* Feb. 20, 2002, p. B3)

INVENTORY YIELD. Financial analysis term derived by taking a firm's profit for the past year as a percentage of its spending on new inventory for the same period.

INVERTED MARKET. Financial market characterized by short-term interest rates being higher than long-term rates.

INVESTMENT GRADE. Bonds that do not have a high default risk. Corporate and municipal bonds that receive at least a BAA rating from MOODY'S or a BBB rating from STANDARD AND POOR'S agencies.

INVISIBLE HAND. Power of the marketplace.
"Every individual endeavors to employ his capital so that its produce may be of greatest value. He generally neither intends to promote the public interest, nor knows how much he is promoting it. He intends only his own security, only his own gain. And he is led by an invisible hand to promote an end which was no part of his intention. By pursuing his own interest he frequently promotes that of society more effectively than when he really intends to promote it." (Adam Smith, *Wealth of Nations,* 1776)

INVOLUNTARY REDUCTION IN FORCE (IRIF). Corporate layoffs made after attempting to encourage workers to terminate voluntarily. Large U.S. companies will offer workers a PACKAGE of incentives to avoid involuntary reductions in force.

IN YOUR FACE. Aggressive action.

IRONCLAD. Solid, guaranteed, as in an ironclad promise.
"Pyongyang's chief envoy at the six-nation talks that end today in China said his nation intends to formally declare it has atomic

arms and to test one as proof, an event sure to set off a chain of dangerous reactions across Asia. He also promised a demonstration of an improved missile delivery system. Pyongyang has hinted that the only thing that might stave off all of this is an ironclad nonaggression deal with Washington." (*Wall Street Journal,* August 29, 2003, p. A1)

IT'S NOT OVER UNTIL THE FAT LADY SINGS. Do not assume everything will get done or work out until all the details are finalized. The term comes from opera, where the ending is sometimes signaled by an aria sung by a diva.

J

JACK OF ALL TRADES. A person with many different skills but who is not an expert in one particular area.

JACKPOT JUSTICE. The awarding of huge monetary settlements to plaintiffs in court cases.

"The U.S. Chamber of Commerce has warned companies about doing business in Mississippi, calling the state the 'lawsuit mecca of America.' Corporate lawyers believe jackpot justice is so bad there that they rate its civil litigation system the worst in the nation, according to a Harris poll this year." (Tom Wilemon, Beth Musgrave, Lawyers' influence over judges probed," *Charlotte Observer,* Nov. 3, 2002)

JANITORS' INSURANCE. Life insurance taken out by a company on its employees often without the knowledge of the employee.

"Court Finds 'Janitors Insurance' a Tax Sham at Camelot Music" (*Wall Street Journal,* August 23, 2002, p. C13)

JANUARY EFFECT. The typical increase in the stock market, particularly smaller stocks, in January due to an increase in tax-deferred investment funds at the beginning of the year.

"There is a 'January effect' afoot in the stock market, but it isn't the one people expected." (*Wall Street Journal,* Jan. 13, 2003, p. C1)

JARGON FILTER. An email program filter configured to automatically delete incoming messages that contain certain jargon terms or buzzwords.

"The daily deluge is so bad many media have created bozo and jargon filters on their e-mail to automatically delete messages that contain words such as 'solutions, first, leading, cutting-edge, best, first mover, state-of-the-art, and end-to-end,'" (Jerry Walker, "Website Spots Bad Releases," Jack O'Dwyer's Newsletter, Dec. 20, 2000)

JAWBONE (TO). Talk someone into doing what you want; persuade with pressure.

"Worried that overheating could strain resources and lead to wasteful investment, painful inflation or burst bubbles, Beijing has been attempting to jawbone banks and local authorities into curbing investment, particularly in sectors such as steel, property and automobiles." (*Wall Street Journal,* May 14, 2004, p. A10)

J CURVE. Graphic representation of the impact of currency devaluation on a country's balance of trade. Currency devaluation results in immediate relative price changes, but the quantity of exports and imports responds more slowly. Initially after devaluation, the quantity of exports and imports does not change, but imports become more expensive and exports become cheaper; thus, a country's balance of payments will worsen. Over time the change in relative prices will cause exports to increase and imports to decline, improving the country's balance of payments.

JERK AROUND (TO). To manipulate someone with false promises or lies.

JERRY-RIGGED. Temporarily fixed, not a permanent solution. From the pejorative for German used in World War I.

"A large cause of this jerry-rigged democracy is the bipartisan gerrymandering that carves out 'safe' districts." (*Wall Street Journal,* Nov. 13, 2002, p. A24)

JET LAG. Tired feeling after an airplane trip that includes changes in time zones.

JILLION. A very large number. See also ZILLION.

JINGLE. Telephone call; lyrics or melody in a commercial.

"In the twilight of his career, Mr. Keith Reinhard, 69 years old, has formed Business for Diplomatic Action, a nonprofit organization that is trying to combat anti-Americanism abroad. The enormous task will take more than his famous 'two all-beef patties' jingle to achieve, now that photos of abused Iraqi prisoners have circulated and anti-U.S. sentiment has grown." (*Wall Street Journal,* June 9, 2004, p. 1)

JOB HOP (TO). Change employment frequently.

JOB LOCK. Situation of employees who want to leave their current positions but feel they cannot because they would lose their health benefits. In the United States, health benefits are provided primarily by employers, but most benefit programs do not cover pre-existing conditions. This "locks" many employees with health problems to their current job. A new law passed in 1996 was intended to create portability of health benefits, thereby reducing employees' sense of job lock.

JOB TRAINING PARTNERSHIP ACT (JTPA). Federal government worker training regulations providing incentives for employer education programs.

JOCKEY FOR POSITION (TO). Promote and sell oneself or one's products in order to compete (horse racing).
    "The new PRI is split into ideological and personal factions whose differences will become more pronounced as the party's multitude of presidential contenders—many of them governors who command the allegiances of congressional deputies—jockey for position in the coming presidential race." (*Wall Street Journal,* July 9, 2003, p. A12)

JOG (TO). Recall after concentration or suggestion, as in to jog one's memory.

JOHN HANCOCK. Signature. John Hancock, as president of the Continental Congress, was the first to sign the Declaration of Independence; he did so with such flourish that his name became synonymous with signature.

JOHNNY–COME-LATELY. A newcomer. A company late in entering a market.

JOURNAL (THE). Nickname for the *Wall Street Journal.*

JPEG, JPG. Joint Photographic Experts Group. A common type of digital photographic image format employing compression.

JUICE. Connections, power; to exhaust or squeeze out every last bit.

JUMP AT. Eagerly take advantage of an opportunity.

JUMP BALL. Undecided situation (basketball).
"It helped that Warren Buffett, whose Berkshire Hathaway Inc. owns both Geico and the Buffalo News, was a Buffalo booster. 'I was cheering for Buffalo,' he said in an interview. 'If it's a jump ball [between Buffalo and some other city], I want it to go to the home team.'" (*Wall Street Journal,* May 24, 2004, p. A4)

JUMP ON THE BANDWAGON. Join what is popular.
"He adds that his organization's numbers suggest that the growth in the percentage of companies offering entry into a 401(k) plan within the first three months of employment plateaued this year at about 50%, after growing for several years since the rule changes in the late 1990s. Schwab's Mr. Ben Brigeman, however, expects still more companies to jump on the bandwagon. 'Human-resources staff have been tied up with other things, like laying people off,' he says. 'But this year, we've seen a pickup in plans reducing their eligibility requirements.'" (*Wall Street Journal,* Nov. 25, 2003, p. D1)

JUMP SHIP. To abandon a project or company.
"'To be honest, we are more concerned about having them [PC makers] jump ship than be late,' Mr. Silverberg said." (*Wall Street Journal,* June 6, 1995, p. B16)

JUMP-START (TO). Initiate, get something going.
"Delta's pilots union signaled that it was preparing new concessions to jump-start wage-cut talks." (*Wall Street Journal,* June 18, 2004, p. A1)

JUMP THE GUN (TO). Start too soon (track and field).
"Election 2000: Some European Leaders Jump the Gun, Offering Early Congratulations to Bush" (*Wall Street Journal,* Nov. 9, 2000, p. A17)

JUMP THROUGH THE HOOPS (TO). Do all that is required, overcome barriers.

"'They all dream of getting their documents,' says Mr. Rosales. And helping an immigrant jump through the hoops to achieve legal residence—for which Mr. Rosales charges, on average, $550—can lead to a lasting relationship." (*Wall Street Journal,* April 4, 2002, p. A1)

JUNGLE. A highly competitive environment.

JUNIOR DEBT. Debt claims that are payable only after payment of senior debt claims.

JUNIOR LEAGUERS/JUNIOR LEAGUE. Affluent nonworking women under forty years old.

"She accepted her appointment to the authority, she says, because it was 'better than the Junior League.'" (*Wall Street Journal,* Nov. 29, 1995, p. F1)

JUNK BOND. A high-risk, less-than-INVESTMENT-GRADE corporate bond. Junk bonds became very popular among investors in the late 1980s.

"Riskier high-yield, or junk bonds, which pay more income in exchange for the increased uncertainty surrounding the companies that issue them, have also been on a tear and look a bit pricey, but Mr. Auwaerter thinks the right issues still can spice up portfolios." (*Wall Street Journal,* July 4, 2004, p. 3)

JUNKET. A trip, offered to politicians usually with all expenses paid, designed to enlighten or influence them.

JUST-IN-TIME (JIT). Management practice minimizing inventories. Materials arrive just in time to meet production schedules.

K

KAHUNA. An expert. From the Hawaiian term for witch doctor.

KAIZEN. Japanese term for continuous improvement through incremental change. In the 1980s, so many American managers studied Japanese production methods that the term has become part of American business jargon.

"Kaizen: This Japanese term for continuous improvement involves constant small steps to improve efficiency." (*Wall Street Journal,* April 9, 2004, p. A1)

KEEP A CLOSE EYE/TAB ON. Watch carefully.

"Aetna still keeps a close eye on costs, but it is trying to make allies out of former enemies. Aetna's chief medical officer, William Popik, cites a case last year when his department tracked down three hemophilia experts, seeking advice about treating a hemophiliac boy whose care was costing $500,000 a month." (*Wall Street Journal,* Aug. 13, 2004, p. A1)

KEEP A LOW PROFILE. To act discreetly without drawing attention to oneself.

KEEP IT SIMPLE, STUPID (KISS). A business slogan suggesting that plans should be kept clear and logical.

"Most insurance agents in the work site marketing arena were weaned on the KISS (keep it simple, stupid) method of payroll deduction installations." (*Broker World,* Aug. 1995, p. 10)

KEEP ONE POSTED. Keep one informed.

KEEP UP WITH THE JONESES (TO). Strive, especially beyond one's income, to socialize and spend like others in the same neighborhood.

"This allows for the idea that households care about their relative standard of living, or the saying goes, they want 'to keep up with the Jones.'" (*Journal of Money, Credit and Banking,* Feb. 1994, p. 1)

KEOGH PLAN. A tax-deferred retirement savings plan for small business owners and self-employed people.

KEY. Essential.

KEY LOGGER. A form of spyware that records each keystroke or other activity of a computer user. Key logger software can capture credit card numbers, passwords, and other sensitive information and transmit it to third parties without the computer user's knowledge.

KEYSTONE (TO). Mark up the price of a good 100 percent of its cost.

"The art dealer will double the price I give him, and the retailer will keystone it too." (Chet Allenchey, CAMMEO Art and Photography, 1996)

KICKBACK. A bribe.

"The suits accuse the brokers of failing 'to adequately disclose … under-the-table payments or kickbacks received from insurers.' As a result, they allege, 'defendants are able to reap tens of millions of dollars in additional fees while purporting to provide independent and unbiased brokerage advice.'" (*Wall Street Journal,* August 11, 2004 p. C3)

KICK BUTT. Outwit or overwhelm the competition.

"Alfred Chuang, chief executive and co-founder of BEA, says a recent slowdown in BEA's sales growth 'is totally macroeconomic. I'm not seeing the competition.' Moreover, computer-services businesses such as Accenture, of Hamilton, Bermuda, that compete with IBM often recommend BEA because of the company's technology. 'Our stuff kicks butt,' he says." (*Wall Street Journal,* Nov. 1, 2001, p. B6)

KICKER. Something added to a contract proposal to make it more attractive. See SWEETENER.

"The real kicker is that each DVD-R disc—which can be recorded upon only once—costs about $6.50. And the re-recordable DVD-RW discs cost $10 apiece. Some retailers sell these discs for less, but they're still costly." (*Wall Street Journal,* July 21, 2004, p. D4)

KICK OFF. Beginning; to initiate (football).

"The fall TV season kicks off later this month with more new characters than ever." (*Wall Street Journal,* Aug. 20, 2004, p. W1)

KICK/PUSH UPSTAIRS. Promote out of the way.

"Mr. Roberts, 36 years old, didn't want the usual kick upstairs to chairman, with its out-to-pasture connotations. So he dreamed up a title with more flair. FireDrop's main product is an e-mail program named Zaplet." (*Wall Street Journal,* Sept. 5, 2000, p. A1)

KIDDIE TAX. Special Internal Revenue Service tax treatment of investment earnings of children less than 14 years old.

KILLING. A large, quick profit.

"Yet almost no one expects to make a killing by selling or licensing browser software. The real money is in the overall Internet products and services business, of which the browser business is but a small part." (*Informationweek,* Oct. 23, 1995, p. 81)

KILLJOY. Unenthusiastic person.

"But debunking such bunk and mocking believers is part of this sport's attraction. 'Ruining people's day is fun,' says Mr. Lasner, a self-confessed killjoy who works from a home office cluttered with computer carcasses and empty peanut cans." (*Wall Street Journal,* Sept. 22, 1993, p. A1)

KIND OF NEAT. Somewhat interesting.

"Mrs. Tucknott, a nurse who still works part time in a local hospital, says what sold her on the neighborhood, and Beaufort in general, is that they feel like real places, not a retirement village. 'This could actually become a small town,' she says. 'That's kind of a neat feeling, that I could be part of founding a city.'" (*Wall Street Journal,* Aug. 9, 2004, p. R7)

KINGPIN / KINGFISH. Boss, important person.

"Loyal, Web-savvy customers are giving PC kingpin Dell a lift in its nascent printer line. The company sold 1.5 million printers in the last 9 months of 2003, according to Gartner Inc." (*Business Week,* April 19, 2004, p. 87)

KISS A LOT OF FROGS. Keep looking until one finds what one wants. The saying comes from the story *The Frog Prince,* wherein a prince is doomed to be a frog until he is kissed by a princess.

KISS OF DEATH. Final blow; signal that something will fail.

KISS UP TO. Flatter; BROWN-NOSE.

KIT AND CABOODLE. Including everything.

KITCHEN CABINET. Close advisors to a president of the United States. The term originated with President Andrew Jackson, when he suspended Cabinet meetings and met with close friends.

KITE A CHECK (TO). Write a check without sufficient funds to cover it.

KITING. Writing checks before the funds are available. Taking advantage of the FLOAT, the time between when a check is written and when it clears the bank account.

KNEE-JERK REACTION. To act without thinking, thoughtless response.

"'The common knee-jerk reaction that a minimum-wage hike hurts small entrepreneurs is not a calculated economic response,' says Kathryn Wylde, president of Partnership for New York City, a powerful nonprofit group of CEOs founded by David Rockefeller." (*Wall Street Journal,* July 27, 2004, p. B3)

KNOCKOFF. An unlicensed copy of a product.

"Piracy is such a way of life in China that people are surprised when a movie, software package or handbag bought there is not ripped off. Months before General Motors began selling its $7,500 Chevrolet Spark in China in December, a $6,000 knockoff version, the Chevy QQ, with the same grinning front end but missing some subtle details (like an airbag), was cruising Chinese streets." (*Forbes,* Feb. 16, 2004, p. 58)

KNOCK OUT COLD, KO. Overwhelm the competition (boxing).

KNOCK THEIR SOCKS OFF. Defeat the competition; astonish.

"Shares of the seller of nutritional and personal-care products look cheap: The more expensive of its two classes of shares trades for a mere seven times trailing earnings. And Herbalife's dividend yield 'is enough to knock your socks off,' says analyst Patricia Negron of Adams, Harkness & Hill in Boston." (*Wall Street Journal,* July 23, 1999, p. C2)

KNOW-IT-ALL. Someone who shows off his or her knowledge; conceited person.

"The wide-ranging freelance intellectual of a few generations ago has given way to the Ph.D. know-it-all, an arrogant specialist who, gratifying his ego and padding his wallet, gladly pronounces on matters about which he is an idiot." (*Wall Street Journal,* Jan. 15, 2002, p. A14)

KNUCKLE DOWN (TO). Focus; work hard.

"According to David Drinkwalter, a former executive at Ontario Hydro who is now a consultant with Resource Associates Canada Inc. of London, Ont.: 'Governments need to knuckle down and display real intestinal fortitude in their commitment to deregulation.'" (*Maclean's,* Feb. 5, 2001, p. 35)

KNUCKLE UNDER (TO). Give in, concede.

KOHLBERG, KRAVIS, ROBERTS (KKR). KKR is a merger and acquisition firm most famous for arranging the $29 billion buyout of R.J. Reynolds Company in 1989.

"Although a formal auction for Amadeus isn't under way, companies that have made the most progress in putting together bids to buy out Amadeus's core shareholders include U.S. private-equity firms Bain Capital Inc., Carlyle Group LP and Kohlberg Kravis Roberts & Co., say people familiar with the situation." (*Wall Street Journal,* August 18, 2004, p. A1)

KONDRATIEFF CURVE. Economic theory, named after a Soviet statistician, suggesting that the world economies move in fifty-year cycles.

KOOSHING. Rejecting someone for a job.

KOWTOW (TO). Cater to; defer to (Chinese).

"'The Fed is almost taunting them [the GSEs] a little bit, and letting them know the Fed is going to call the shots, and is not going to bow down or kowtow to the GSEs,' said Bert Ely, a banking analyst who is critical of the mortgage giants." (*Wall Street Journal,* Feb. 6, 2004, p. A2)

K&R INSURANCE. Kidnap and ransom insurance.

"Commercial policyholders with operations in Iraq are increasingly seeking kidnap and ransom insurance coverage for their staff in the region following a spate of kidnappings. In the past month, about 50 foreign workers in Iraq have been kidnapped, prompting some governments to advise civilians working there to leave the country." (*Business Insurance,* May 3, 2004, p. 25)

KUDOS. Congratulations, approval (Greek).

"Mr. Crocker joined Wachovia's mutual-fund team in February 1997, when Wachovia, then called First Union Corp., was expanding its stable of funds. By 2000, Mr. Crocker was the portfolio manager of $1 billion in high-yield bonds and winning kudos for his savvy investment strategies." (*Wall Street Journal,* Aug. 6, 2004, p. C3)

L

LABOR FORCE. Workers. U.S. Department of Commerce labor force statistics include employed and unemployed persons sixteen years old or older who either have jobs or are actively looking for and available for employment.

LABOR-INTENSIVE. Production method requiring many workers relative to other inputs.

LADDERING. Investment strategy of owning a series of bonds of staggered durations, in order to reduce the risk associated with changing interest rates.

LAFFER CURVE. 1980s economic idea, espoused by Arthur Laffer, suggesting that lowering marginal tax rates stimulates increases in output, thereby increasing government tax revenue. See also SUPPLY-SIDE ECONOMICS, DYNAMIC SCORING.

LAGNIAPPE. Anything given beyond what is obligated or expected. A surplus benefit. (Creole, pronounced lan-yapp).

LAISSEZ-FAIRE. Hands off, to let be free (French). Laissez-faire economic doctrine was advocated by Adam Smith in *The Wealth of*

Nations (1776). Conservatives in the United States have adopted the term as a symbol for reducing government influence in the economy.

LAME DUCK. Politician who is still in office but who has announced retirement or has been defeated in a recent election. The term originated in Britain in the eighteenth century, when it meant a bankrupt businessman.

LARGE CAP. A company with a market capitalization of more than $500 million.

LARGE SCALE. Big picture; broader view.

LAST IN, FIRST OUT (LIFO). A method of assigning cost to the ending inventory which assumes that the cost of the remaining units consists of the costs of the earliest units purchased.

LAST MILE. The last link between a communications provider and a customer. Communications companies, particularly those attempting to bypass the existing monopoly telephone companies, have struggled to develop efficient last-mile technology.

LAST-MOVER ADVANTAGE. The advantage a company gains by learning from the mistakes made by the first businesses in a market and benefiting from improved technology, quality, or lower costs, especially during an economic downturn.
  "Dynegy's announcements even included a dig at Enron's 'first-mover' braggadocio. Dynegy would take advantage of ever-accelerating advances in technology to capture what it called the 'last-mover' advantage." (Michael Rieke, "Enron Envy Costing Dynegy Big Bucks," *Dow Jones Energy Service,* May 6, 2002)

LAST STRAW. Mistake or problem that causes a manager to take action.
  "Even Green Street's Mr. John Lutzius sees only a 10% upside in the share price near term. And some analysts estimate that Crescent's 2004 adjusted earnings will fall between $25 million to $50 million short of covering the dividend at current levels of $175 million annually. The company is covering it through land sales. Another dividend cut would be the last straw for investors, 'a kiss of death,' says Dave Copp, a real-estate analyst with RBC Capital Markets." (*Wall Street Journal,* Dec. 26, 2003, p. C3)

LATTE FACTOR. Relatively insignificant daily purchases that add up to a significant amount of money over time.

"The advisor also suggested that they carefully watch their spending on little things—such as buying a cup of coffee every day. 'You get a mocha at Starbucks and it costs $3. You buy a biscuit for $1.50. At work, you get a diet Coke and Snickers. Before you know it, you've spent $10 a day,' Holt said. 'It's the latte factor.'" (Deborah Adamson, "Money makeover," *Honolulu Advertiser,* Oct. 19, 2003)

LAUNDER. Put illegal funds through a legitimate business, thereby cleaning the money of its "dirty" origin.

"The mini-crisis has refocused attention on the institutional weakness of Russia's banking system, which increasingly has become a bottleneck as Russia's economy rebounds. Many of the country's 1,300 banks are small and undercapitalized, and some do little more than launder money and channel cash offshore." (*Wall Street Journal,* July 12, 2004, p. A15)

LAYAWAY. A purchasing installment plan in which the product is kept at the store until the buyer has made full payment.

LAY CARDS ON THE TABLE. To show all the facts, to be totally honest.

LAY DOWN ON THE JOB. To be unproductive; to loaf.

LAY-OFF. Terminate workers because there is no work.

LAYOFF LUST. The strong desire to be laid off from one's job.

"A new term has entered the language: layoff lust, the sudden desire to be sent away with a severance package, providing time at last to search for meaning and cultivate the soul." (Cullen Murphy, "Fast-Free Living," *Atlantic Monthly,* April 2002)

LAYUP. Something that is easily accomplished (basketball).

LEAD BALLOON. A dismal failure.

"Much of the dissent heard here focused more on the U.S. government than on U.S. corporations. The president's State of the Union address, which played well in U.S. living rooms, fell on this crowd 'like a lead balloon,' observed one GOP member of Congress in attendance." (*Wall Street Journal,* Feb. 4, 2002, p. A1)

LEAD TIME. Time between the initiation of a new project and its delivery date.

"'Since we had no idea when the auction would be, it would have been impossible, with our lead time, to time that.' Playboy told

Google in advance when the article would run, Mr. Randall says." (*Wall Street Journal,* August 18, 2004, p. A1)

LEAPFROG (TO). Bound forward. Employees climbing the CORPORATE LADDER sometimes leapfrog past others on the way to the top.

"Boeing Co., Lockheed Martin Corp. and Northrop Grumman Corp. are among those that have bet heavily on Defense Secretary Donald Rumsfeld's vision of 'transformation,' which aims to leapfrog today's weaponry to a higher plane of technology, speed, lethality and communication among all the armed services." (*Wall Street Journal,* July 26, 2004, p. B6)

LEAPS AND BOUNDS. Large jumps, amounts, or quantities.

"A technological shift is underway that advances search quality by leaps and bounds. By leveraging the wealth of information around employees' interactions with content, the searcher is empowered to find precisely the information he needs." (*Information Today,* July/August 2004, p. 22)

LEAP TO NEW HEIGHTS. Attain levels never before reached.

"In February 1995, South Korea's Citizen National Bank changed its name to Kookmin Bank and adopted a new logo, a multicolored stick-man in a shape reminiscent of the ginseng root, which many Koreans believe has energizing, even aphrodisiac, qualities. Management may have chosen the logo to inspire the inefficient government-owned bank to leap to new heights of financial activity." (*Euromoney,* April, 1995, p. 20)

LEARNING ORGANIZATION. A company that values intelligence and initiative by personnel to continually improve their skills.

LEAVE IN THE DUST. Leave behind; defeat one's competitor.

LEFT-BRAIN PERSON. A person with strong organizational and mathematical skills; someone obsessed with order.

LEFT FIELD (FROM). "Out of left field" or "from left field" means out of nowhere, a total surprise (baseball). If a person is said to be "out in left field," it means he or she is confused or does not understand the situation.

LEFT-HANDED COMPLIMENT. Praise that is in fact subtle dispraise.

LEGAL EAGLE. Clever lawyer.

LEGAL MACHINE. The legal system; a machine meeting legal standards.

LEG UP (TO HAVE A). To have an advantage, sometimes derived through unethical or illegal activities.

"Money managers who make campaign contributions to officials who head public pension funds have received an unfair leg up on other firms competing to manage the retirement money of municipal and state employees." (*Wall Street Journal,* Dec. 17, 1999, p. C1)

LEMON. A defective product, especially a car. Lemon laws in the United States typically allow a manufacturer four attempts to fix a recurring problem.

"A Lemon of a Loan. Leading Italian banks face possible losses stemming from a 3-billion-euro loan to Fiat SpA." (*Wall Street Journal,* May 26, 2004, p. C3)

LEMON LAW. Laws, mostly associated with automobiles, that require companies to replace products if they cannot fix them.

LENDER OF LAST RESORT. Any government agency that provides loans to borrowers who have exhausted other options. The Small Business Administration and the Federal Reserve act as lenders of last resort to their markets.

LESS THAN TRUCKLOAD (LTL). Transportation prices are usually quoted for full loads and LTL shipments.

LET SLIDE. Ignore; not criticize.

"The modus operandi in the 16 trades that the SEC let slide followed the same pattern of the 11 trades for which the commission extracted the settlement, Mr. Kevin Marino says." (*Wall Street Journal,* Oct. 20, 2001, p. C1)

LEVEL (PLAYING) FIELD. Everyone being treated the same (sports).

"The bourse originally planned to make the rules compulsory for its Neuer Market segment. But now compliance will be on a voluntary or 'best practice' basis to ensure a level field for all IPOs in all segments." (*Wall Street Journal,* June 11, 2002, p. C18)

LEVERAGE. Use borrowed funds to make an investment; the ratio of borrowed funds to invested capital in a business; influence.

"Many aim to emulate Samsung Electronics Co. of South Korea, using sharp design to leverage their contract manufacturing business into a global brand." (*Wall Street Journal,* Sept. 1, 2004, p. A10)

LEVERAGED BUYOUT (LBO). The purchase of a company with borrowed funds.

"Leveraged-buyout firm Thomas H. Lee Partners acquired a majority stake in futures brokerage firm Refco Group in a deal valuing the firm at $2.25 billion. Both sides described the transaction as the latest offshoot of the broader boom in futures trading." (*Wall Street Journal,* June 9, 2004, p. C5)

LEVITTOWN. Suburbia; specifically, a town on Long Island, New York, built by Arthur Levitt as the first mass-produced suburban housing constructed to meet consumer needs after World War II.

"Michael O'Young pitched management at Far East Consortium International with the idea of introducing single-family housing to Shanghai, a sort of Levittown of the Far East." (*Forbes,* Oct. 16, 2000, p. 172)

LICK AND A PROMISE (GIVE IT A). Quick and not thorough.

LIE DOWN ON THE JOB. Not be productive.

LIFELONG STUDENT. Someone who is always learning.

LIGHTNING ROD. Person who initiates change, particularly dramatic and potentially dangerous changes in an organization; something that attracts or diverts attention to or from a related matter.

"Mr. Jeffrey C. Barbakow's compensation has been a lightning rod for criticism of Tenet since its troubles emerged in November 2002." (*Wall Street Journal,* April 6, 2004, p. B1)

LIKE A MILLION BUCKS. Very good.

LIMIT ORDER. An order to buy or sell a stock at a specific price.

LINE. Profession; products one sells.

LINE OF CREDIT. A guarantee that a lender will provide up to a specified amount of credit to a company during a specified period of time.

LINE UP THE BULLETS. Make a list of the issues or problems.

LINGO. Slang.

"Fund companies' lust for assets also underlies the sales abuses involving mutual-fund B shares. In the late 1980s, most funds either were sold through brokers and charged a large upfront commission or they were offered directly to investors without a 'load,' as sales commissions are known in mutual-fund lingo." (*Wall Street Journal,* August 1, 2004, p. 3)

LINUX. A collaborative computer operating system first developed by Linus Torvalds in 1991 using Unix technology.

LION'S SHARE. Largest part.

"Still, with the lion's share of the company's sales in products like traditional Oreos and Maxwell House coffee, Mr. Deromedi also defended Kraft's existing lineup." (*Wall Street Journal,* May 21, 2004, p. A1)

LIP SERVICE. Official agreement with, while having private reservations about the issue.

"Central bankers and finance ministers may pay lip service to 'stability,' but when they go home they conduct monetary policy with an eye to what they see as the 'national interest' and the dictates of domestic politics." (*Wall Street Journal,* Feb. 10, 2004, p. A17)

LIPSTICK BOARD. Plastic surface on which advertising messages are written.

LIPSTICK EFFECT. During a recession, the tendency for consumers to purchase low-priced, comforting items such as lipstick rather than expensive luxury items.

"If you've been following domestic news in recent weeks, you've probably heard about the 'lipstick effect.' As described in such outlets as NBC, The New York Times, and The Wall Street Journal, the idea is that, during a recession, women substitute small, feel-good items like lipstick for more expensive items like clothing and jewelry. And indeed, between August and October, lipstick sales were up 11 percent over the same period last year." (Norm Scheiber, "Replacement Killers," *The New Republic,* Jan. 7, 2002)

LIQUID. Easily converted to cash.

"MTS said the trades involved 200 instruments on EuroMTS, where the most 'liquid,' or easy-to-trade, euro-zone government bonds are traded, and other MTS markets in Europe." (*Wall Street Journal,* Aug. 19, 2004, p. C3)

LITMUS TEST. Basis for determining (chemistry).

"Analysts view the budget for the fiscal year ending March 31, to be announced tomorrow, as a litmus test of how Mr. Singh intends to balance market-opening policies that have driven India's rapid economic growth with a commitment to help the rural and working-class voters who backed the Congress-led coalition." (*Wall Street Journal,* July 7, 2004, p. A8)

LITTLE GUY. Small investor; low-level employee.

"How shocking to find liberal activists involved in the misrepresentation of financial figures, crony capitalism and sticking it to the little guys by allowing them to work without pay and without air conditioning." (*Wall Street Journal,* July 8, 2004, p. A15)

LIVELIHOOD. Job, how one earns one's living.

LIVING DEAD. A company or investment that is not successful but not in bankruptcy proceedings, but may soon be so.

LIVING ON BORROWED TIME. Being in a situation about to fail.

"Jakarta, Indonesia—It was once Southeast Asia's tallest hotel and Indonesia's finest. Now, it's a shabby, unfashionable hostelry living on borrowed time." (*Wall Street Journal,* August 28, 2004, p. 1)

LIVING PROOF. Actual evidence.

"Andrew Tomkins, Bob Carlson and the Web Fountain EBO are living proof of the big, new payoff IBM is getting from throwing open the doors of its vaunted research labs and turning its scientists loose in the marketplace." (*Fortune,* June 9, 2003, p. 133)

LOAD. Sales charge associated with the purchase of a mutual fund.

LOADED. Very rich; fully equipped.

LOADED GUN. Something that could dramatically change an existing situation for the worse, or something that can be used to threaten or influence a decision.

LOADING THE BOSS'S PISTOL. A list of issues or problems often organized by the vice president for finance.

LOAN-TO-VALUE RATIO (LTV). The ratio of the amount of money borrowed to the fair market value of the asset against which the loan is secured.

LOCAL AREA NETWORK (LAN). Group of computers that are linked together.

LOCKED AND LOADED. Ready to use. From the military term for a rifle ready to be fired.

LOCKED INTO. Forced to stay with, having no other option.

LOCK HORNS. Disagree.
"This week, creditors of the country's biggest credit-card issuer, LG Card, continued to lock horns with the state-run Korea Development Bank (KDB) over the terms of a proposed bail-out." (*The Economist,* Jan. 10, 2004, p. 65)

LOCK, STOCK, AND BARREL. Everything.
"Coram's Chapter 11 bankruptcy plan, if accepted by the bankruptcy court, would give the company, lock, stock and barrel, to the debt holders. And they want it." (*Forbes,* Oct. 30, 2000, p. 86)

LOCK UP. Complete, finalize, gain control of.

LOCK-UP PERIOD. Typically, a 180-day period following an initial public offering when officers of a company are barred from selling shares of stock.
"LECG, a provider of expert services, fell 1.58, or 9%, to 16, after a lock-up period expired, enabling insiders to sell shares for the first time since the Emeryville, Calif., company's initial public offering six months ago." (*Wall Street Journal,* May 13, 2004, p. C4)

LOG. Official records; to record.

LOMBARD. Acronym for "lots of money but a real dodo." A wealthy, simple person.

LOMBARD FACILITY. The discount window lending practice by the Federal Reserve to member banks for short-term loans to meet reserve requirements.
"Yesterday, the Bundesbank slashed its discount rate to 3.5% from 4% and its Lombard rate to 5.5% from 6%, the lowest level since January 1989. The two rates, which set the lower and upper limits for Germany's money market, were last cut in March. Germany's discount rate offers banks a limited amount of inexpensive refinancing under fixed borrowing quotas. Borrowing from the Lombard facility is unlimited and serves as a ceiling for short-term money-market rates." (*Wall Street Journal,* Aug. 25, 1995, p. A2)

LONDON INTERBANK OFFERED RATE (LIBOR). The interest rate charged to highest-quality customers for loans in the Eurodollar market. Less creditworthy customers pay the LIBOR rate plus varying percentage points. Like the PRIME RATE in the United States, the LIBOR is the standard by which interest rates are established.

LONELY AT THE TOP. The price of leadership may be a lack of friends.

LONG BOND. Thirty-year U.S. Treasury bond.

LONG ON (TO BE). Supportive of; own a financial interest in; lengthen.
"Going Long on Your Loan: Some of the various lenders that offer vehicle loans stretching six years or more." (*Wall Street Journal,* Sept. 30, 2003, p. D1)

LONG RUN. Time frame in which all inputs are variable.

LONG SHOT. Something that has a low percentage chance of being successful.

LONG-TAIL BUSINESS. Insurance industry jargon for hard-to-predict, long-term liabilities.
"This makes almost all the insurance companies with so-called long-tail business—insurance for something like medical malpractice that requires uncertain payout years down the line—unappealing." (*Wall Street Journal,* Feb. 5, 2003, p. C1)

LOOKS GOOD ON PAPER. Appears to have potential but is untested.

LOOPHOLE. Legal way to get around the law.
"'They were actually proud of how cunning and sly they were in getting around the rules,' says Mr. Lawson of the Malaysian and Singaporean timber dealers he met. The traders described how they easily exploited loopholes in Malaysian export rules." (*Wall Street Journal,* Aug. 4, 2004, p. 1)

LOOSE CANNON. An uncontrollable person (nautical).
"On the other hand, Mr. Toledo is a relative newcomer, whose emotional declarations in the tense days following the first vote made him look to many analysts like more of a loose cannon than a statesman." (*Wall Street Journal,* May 11, 2000, p. A18)

LOOSE CREDIT. Federal Reserve policy of lowering interest rates to make credit more available.

LOOSE ENDS. Unsettled business issues or details. To resolve the issue, one "ties up" the loose ends.

LOOT. Money.
"Mr. Rogers has been famous in financial circles for so long that some might be tempted to believe he was born famous. In fact, as a youngster he helped launch George Soros's Quantum Fund, then retired in 1980 with a bundle of loot." (*Wall Street Journal,* May 30, 2003, p. W10)

LOSE ONE'S SHIRT. Lose a significant amount of money.
"Mitsubishi had to lose its shirt to be persuaded to 'retool' its sales pitch to a more 'mature' buyer." (*Wall Street Journal,* Dec. 19, 2003, p. W15)

LOSS LEADERS. Products offered at very low prices to attract customers.
"For companies such as Nike and Adidas, however, breakout sales of an Olympic-related line are only part of the longterm goal. 'You justify it as a loss leader,' says the Warsaw Center's Mr. Swangard of the Olympics efforts. 'I'm not sure the next billionaire category will come off the pole vault runway. But you still want to be authentic to your brand, and that means you would help any athlete, even if it's a small-market niche.'" (*Wall Street Journal,* Aug. 27, 2004, p. B1)

LOTTERY EFFECT. Stock market strategy of buying stocks that have fallen significantly in price, hoping the stock will surge again.
"Part of the lottery-effect thing is people are looking at the stock price now and thinking it was once [at] that humongous price, maybe it will reach there again." (*Wall Street Journal,* August 28, 2002, p. C2)

LOW-BALL (TO). Reduce, as in a bid; a very low estimate. See COME IN LOW.
"Mr. Mehta, whose portfolio includes about $5 million in stocks, once planned to bid for several thousand Google shares. Now he is wavering, considering a low-ball bid of $60 to $65 a share—a level he thinks won't win him any Google shares in the auction." (*Wall Street Journal,* Aug. 9, 2004, p. C1)

LOW-END. Lowest priced. See also TOP-OF-THE LINE.

"The auction—and the intense spotlight on Google's every move—have spawned multiple strategies by investors. Barry Randall, portfolio manager of the First American Technology fund in Minneapolis, said he bid for shares at a price 'materially lower' than Google's $108 low-end estimate." (*Wall Street Journal,* Aug. 16, 2004, p. C1)

LOW-HANGING FRUIT. Easy sales or profits.

LOW MAN/WOMAN ON THE TOTEM POLE. Lowest position in an organization (offensive to Native Americans).

LUDDITES. Workers who feel their jobs are threatened by changing technology, or those who oppose technology in general. The original Luddites, early 1800s British craftsmen, were followers of the mythic figure, Ned Ludd. They rioted, destroying textile machines that had replaced them.

"A quarter of all Americans now work in jobs that weren't listed in the Census Bureau's occupation codes in 1967. Technophobes, neo-Luddites, and antiglobalists be warned: You're on the wrong side of history. You see only the loss of old jobs. You're overlooking all the new ones." (*Wall Street Journal,* Dec. 26, 2003, p. A10)

LUMP SUM. One-time payment.

"Taking Stock—Strategy: If you hold company stock in your 401(k) and retire or change jobs, gains will be taxed at the lower capital-gains rate if you take the shares as a lump-sum distribution." (*Wall Street Journal,* Aug. 18, 2004, p. D1)

M

MA BELL. American Telephone & Telegraph.

"There is no love lost between Vonage and AT&T. When AT&T launched its CallVantage service in March, Vonage sued Ma Bell, claiming it was trying to piggyback on its name. The suit is pending." (*Wall Street Journal,* May 17, 2004, p. A16)

MACHIAVELLIAN. Ruthless (reference to Niccolò Machiavelli, author of *The Prince,* 1532).

"To some, the suggestion that we should work for money, period, will not seem especially heretical. But for others—lots of others—it will verge on sacrilege. Yet it is hard to argue with such Machiavellian ideas. 'In every profession that is followed not for the sake of money but for love,' wrote the novelist Robert Musil, 'there comes a moment when the advancing years seem to be leading into the void.'" (*Wall Street Journal,* May 18, 2004, p. D10)

MADE UP OF. Consists of.

MADISON AVENUE. Advertising agencies; New York City street with many ad agencies.

"The new school of thought is more than welcome on Madison Avenue. Executives have been grumbling that many students finish college or graduate programs unprepared to deal with the rapidly changing advertising landscape." (*Wall Street Journal,* June 15, 2004, p. B1)

MAD MONEY. Money saved and spent on impulsive purchases.

MAGALOG. A combined magazine and catalog.

MAGIC. Art, charm.

MAGIC BULLET. An ideal solution to a problem.

MAKE A BUCK. Make money.

MAKE A FEDERAL CASE OUT OF IT. Overreact, over-emphasize.

MAKE A MARKET. Be willing to buy or sell. In the stock market, a dealer who buys and sells over-the-counter shares of a stock is called a MARKET MAKER.

MAKE ENDS MEET. Get by, be able to pay the bills.
"Local governments, like businesses, have to look at ways to save money when times are tight. They can cut services, lay off employees, raise taxes or privatize to make ends meet." (*Waste Age,* August 2004, p. 18)

MAKE GOOD. Make an adjustment or special allowance when a problem arises; a free repeat of an advertisement when there has been a mistake.
"Ms. Hanrahan, who teaches six signs of a child's 'readiness,' offers parents a guarantee that if they follow her advice and their child isn't trained by age 3, she'll go to their house and train the child herself. She says she's never had to make good on her offer." (*Wall Street Journal,* Aug. 27, 2004, p. A1)

MAKE INROADS. To make progress, particularly to expand into new markets or territories.

MAKE IT WORK. Be successful.

MAKE OUT LIKE A BANDIT. Emerge from a business transaction very successfully.

MAKE WHOLE. Repay all that is owed.

"For months, Western bankers hoped Beijing would make foreign creditors whole." (*Wall Street Journal,* Jan. 12, 1999, p. A14)

MAKING IT. Becoming successful.

"Making it is relative, though, and even the most optimistic estimates are now a far cry from the original BULLISH projections." (*Wall Street Journal,* July 19, 1996, p. R6)

MALARKEY. Nonsense.

MALTHUSIAN. Person who advocates population control; follower of the ideas of Thomas Malthus, nineteenth-century philosopher who predicted that population would grow faster than the ability to produce food. Malthusians ignored the contribution of technology improvements to increasing productivity.

MANAGED CARE. Healthcare system in which a third party, usually the government or an insurance company, reviews and controls payments to healthcare providers.

MANAGED FLOAT. Exchange rate policy under which the government intervenes to maintain exchange rates at a predetermined level. Also called a dirty float.

MANAGEMENT-BY-EXCEPTION. Theory that managers should focus their attention on areas that differ from normal.

"Broadly speaking, tight budgetary controls seem more stringent than simply monitoring bottom-line budget deviations in a hands-off management-by-exception basis." (*Management Accounting Research,* March 2001, p. 119)

MANAGEMENT BY OBJECTIVES (MBO). Management technique of setting goals and then reviewing performance against them.

"On the one hand, MBO is seen as a traditional management tool which forms part of the foundation of effective public management, while at the same time it is viewed by others as being out of date, ineffectual, and inconsistent with contemporary management and thought practices." (*Public Administration Review,* Jan.–Feb. 1995, p. 48)

MANAGEMENT BY WALKING AROUND (MBWA). Informal management style where decisions and changes are made based on supervisors' observations.

"Managers literally walk around making informal visits to work areas. This enables them to collect data, form impressions, and generally keep their finger on the company's pulse." (*Across the Board,* Nov./Dec. 1993, p. 42)

MANAGEMENT GURU. Well known management author or consultant.

"Every profession needs its cheerleaders and for HR and the business world, they are management gurus, industry experts who diagnose what's wrong with businesses and then later tell people how to fix it. An essential 10-step guide on how to win at the guru game and make it big is presented." (*Personnel Today,* June 29, 2004, p. 21)

MANO A MANO. Face-to-face. To compete directly (Spanish).

MANUFACTURER'S SUGGESTED RETAIL PRICE (MSRP). Manufacturers are not allowed to dictate prices to retailers in the United States but many have "suggested" prices. Fair trade laws enacted in the 1930s allowed manufacturers to stipulate prices retailers could charge. The Consumer Pricing Act (1975) ended resale price maintenance agreements.

MAQUILADORA. Foreign-owned or -controlled factories in Mexico that assemble parts and materials primarily for export to the United States.

MARATHON SESSION. Lengthy business meeting.

MARCH ALONG THE PATH. To follow company policies, even if one disagrees with them.

MARCHING ORDERS. Plans or directives.

MARGIN. Profit margin, the difference between the selling price and the initial cost of a good.

MARGIN CALL. Brokerage house requirement that a stock trader either put up more funds against stock purchased with borrowed money or the stock will be sold.

MARK. Person who is the object of a deceptive business practice; target.

"Tribune's decade-old system may sound like an easy mark for big, sophisticated companies eager to muscle into the European market." (*Wall Street Journal,* June 19, 1995, p. B4)

MARKDOWN. Downward revision of the value of a security due to changes in market prices.

MARKET CAP, MARKET CAPITALIZATION. A measure of the size of a company derived from the current price of a stock multiplied by the number of shares issued. Investment analysts divide companies into small, medium, and large cap categories.

MARKETING CONCEPT. The idea that businesses should focus their efforts on anticipating and fulfilling the needs of customers.

"Implementation of the marketing concept in service firms is accomplished through individual service employees and their interactions with customers." (*Journal of Marketing,* Jan. 2004, p. 128)

MARKET LETTER. Investment news and advice distributed to clients.

MARKET MAKER. Market specialist who commits to buying and selling particular stocks.

MARKET PENETRATION. Marketing strategy designed to increase sales of existing products in present markets.

"Fearing that it may be losing a new generation of diners and worried by the rapid market penetration of several upstart competitors, ... S&A Restaurant Corp. is experimenting with an ambitious reimaging project to make the Steak and Ale chain more competitive and appealing." (*Nations Restaurant News,* Aug. 28, 1995, p. 1)

MARKET SWEEP. An additional offer of stock to an investor after an initial tender offer. A market sweep expands the investor's position in the company to be acquired, giving the investor a controlling interest.

MARKET TIMING. Investment strategy of attempting to buy and sell stocks based on analysis of economic cycles.

MARK TO MARKET. Banking term for valuing assets at their market price.

MARQUEE. A symbol or trademark identifying a company (French).

MARRY UP. Auctioneering technique of putting low-valued goods with more-valued merchandise.

MARSHALL PLAN. U.S. investment and loans to redevelop Europe after World War II. Also known as the European Recovery Program, this foreign-aid program was named after then–U.S. Secretary of State George C. Marshall.

MASSAGE. Manipulate; carefully or gently adjust; manipulate data.

MASS CUSTOMIZATION. Mass production with special features to meet individual customer needs. Allows consumers to customize options. Also called flexible manufacturing or targeted mass production.

MASSTIGE. Marketing jargon combining mass markets and prestige markets. Masstige goods are a retail category that includes relatively low-priced goods that come with a relatively prestigious brand name.

"Although masstige products in new categories have great potential, they can be attacked by products that offer similar benefits at a lower price or by premium products that deliver a greater number of genuine benefits for a small price increment. Every masstige product, therefore, is a candidate for death in the middle." ("Luxury for the Masses," *Harvard Business Review,* April 2003)

MASTHEAD. The banner on the front page of a newspaper.

MATRIX ORGANIZATION. Business structure where employees report to more than one supervisor, crossing functional lines in the organization.

"A matrix organization helps solve various corporate problems, but managers must report to more than one boss." (*Wall Street Journal,* Aug. 12, 2003, p. B1)

MAVEN. An outspoken expert, often self-taught.

"The president's call last week for a new era of ownership needs work from the marketing mavens." (*Wall Street Journal,* Aug. 17, 2004, p. A4)

MAX OUT (TO). Reach the limit.

"Some strategies presented for playing the odds include: 1. Defer income. 2. Accelerate deductions. 3. Max out retirement accounts. 4. Follow the tax debate." (*Forbes,* Dec. 23, 2002, p. 362)

MCCARTHYISM. Character assassination. Joseph McCarthy was a senator from Wisconsin in the 1950s who gained national attention by his claims that the State Department and other agencies of the U.S. government were full of communist sympathizers.

"Pictures of Ken Starr were greeted with boos as the narrator talked of 'police-state type of tactics,' 'McCarthyism' and 'lynch mobs.' Notable by their absence in the film were words such as 'perjury,' 'presidential pardons' and 'White House FBI files.'" (*Wall Street Journal,* June 18, 2004, p. W17)

MCJOB. Low-paying positions in service companies. The term is a derogatory reference to McDonalds Company.

M-COMMERCE. Mobile commerce.

MEA CULPA. My fault (Latin), an apology.

"Such audits are more commonly requested of big businesses, not budget-constrained schools. Soon after, Microsoft, in a rare mea culpa, apologized and said it should have been more sensitive." (*Wall Street Journal,* Sept. 17, 2002, p. B1)

MEALYMOUTHED. Garrulous; not plain or straightforward.

MEANS TEST. Criteria used by government agencies to determine eligibility for social welfare programs.

MEAT AND POTATOES. Basics; main ideas.

"The conference sessions are largely focused on Apache, Linux, Perl, PHP, and Python. These are the meat and potatoes of open source development." (*InfoWorld,* August 9, 2004)

MECHANIC'S LIEN. A legal claim against property registered by contractors or suppliers who have not been paid for their product or service.

MEDIA BLITZ/HYPE. Short-term, intense advertising campaign.

"Greece's Tourism Ministry presented a new promotional T-shirt this summer with the slogan, in English, 'The Year of Greece.' But the shirt isn't linked to an Olympics media blitz: It was created only after the Greek national soccer team unexpectedly triumphed in the European soccer championships in Portugal earlier this month." (*Wall Street Journal,* July 21, 2004, p. B1)

MEGA. Very large, significant.

MELTDOWN. Product failure, a complete collapse (nuclear reactors). See also ECONOMIC MELTDOWN.

MENSCH. An honest, respectable person (Yiddish).

MERC. Nickname for Chicago Mercantile Exchange.

MERGE AND PURGE. Marketer's term for combining mailing lists and eliminating duplications.

"A prospect database represents a new direction that breaks the mold of traditional merge/purge-based mailing strategies. Instead of renting names for a single use, the mailer, or its service bureau, makes an offer to list owners to permit it to rent their names for a full year, paying the list owners for each use." (*Wall Street Journal,* June, 2004, p. 41)

MESSAGE CENTER. Answering service.

METROPOLITAN STATISTICAL AREA (MSA). Census Bureau classification of a city with at least 50,000 residents.

MEZZANINE FACILITY. Junior debt, a loan that is placed privately with equity investors.

MICKEY MOUSE. Unsophisticated.

"Tax humor: Tax Notes, a weekly publication, ran a provocative 'viewpoints' column this week on tax shelters by 'Mickey Mice,' identified only as 'a tax lawyer in New York.'" (*Wall Street Journal,* July 8, 2004, p. D2)

MICROCREDIT. Loan programs that offer small, short-term loans to help establish business enterprises.

"Microcredit got its start in Bangladesh in 1976, when Muhammad Yunus, an economics professor, gave a $27 loan to a small group of women in a local village without demanding collateral. The women defied expectations by repaying the loan, developing a sustainable business, starting savings accounts, and helping this simple economic model expand to millions of borrowers worldwide." ("Women Entrepreneurs," *Boston Globe,* July 2, 2002)

MICROMANAGE. To manage every detail of a company or operation.

MICROMARKETING. Marketing strategy targeting very small groups or individual customers.

"Digital is the word and individual is the target. No longer is it necessary to mass market to millions. Micromarketing has the potential to produce even greater returns." (*Wall Street Journal,* March 20, 2000, p. 16)

MID CAP. A company with capitalization between $1 billion and $5 billion.

MILE-HIGH CITY. Denver, Colorado.

MILITARY-INDUSTRIAL COMPLEX. The combined influence of military manufacturers and government bureaucracies. President Dwight D. Eisenhower warned, "In the councils of government, we must guard against the acquisition of unwarranted influence, whether sought or unsought, by the military-industrial complex." (Farewell Address, Jan. 17, 1961)

"Albright's broadside hits as Democratic leaders privately grouse that party experts have been too timid to criticize Bush, given their post-government ties to the military-industrial complex." (*Wall Street Journal,* August 15, 2003, p. A4)

MILK (TO). Exploit, to get the maximum out of. See also CASH COW.

"But the apparent game plan is to milk Kmart's retailing operation, sell undervalued real estate and then use the company's growing cash hoard for acquisitions or a large share-repurchase program." (*Barron's,* July 19, 2004, p. 21)

MILK A MOUSE. To pursue a trivial issue and consume an inordinate amount of time in the process.

MIND THE STORE (TO). Take care of routine business.

MIND YOUR OWN BUSINESS (MYOB). Don't get involved (impolite).

MINT. New; place where money is produced; to make.

MISERY INDEX. The combined inflation and unemployment rates. Republicans created the term during the 1980 U.S. presidential elections as a "sound bite" criticism of the Carter administration.

MISSIONARY SALESPEOPLE. Sales support people who concentrate on promotional activities and new product introductions.

MISSION-ORIENTED. Focused on a particular goal.

MISS THE MARK. Fail.
"The reasons that many companies miss the mark on safety may be subtler than expected. It might just be a kind of cultural inertia—that the old ways of doing things continue in spite of attempts by outside forces such as safety professionals, OSHA, and insurance carriers to change them." (*Occupational Health and Safety*, April 2004, p. 76)

MISTER SOFTEE. Microsoft.

MODIFIED AMERICAN PLAN. Hotel price that includes the room, breakfast, and dinner.

MODUS OPERANDI. Method of operating (Latin).

MOGUL. Powerful, rich person.
"Cable mogul Ted Turner's Turner Broadcasting System Inc. owns the Atlanta Braves baseball team and controls the Atlanta Hawks basketball team and Tribune Co., which has various media holdings, also owns the baseball Chicago Cubs." (*Wall Street Journal*, March 18, 1996, p. B7)

MOM-AND-POP. Small store or family-owned business.
"India's retail sector, which is still dominated by mom-and-pop stores and has few modern shopping malls, has stifled the industry from keeping pace with its counterpart in booming China, according to Russell Farmery, ACNielsen's managing director for India." (*Wall Street Journal*, August 31, 2004, p. B2)

MOMENTUM INVESTING. Stock market technical analysis charting price and volume of trade changes.

MOMMY TRACK. Damaging, dead-end career status, often of people with family responsibilities.
"But in practice, many women (and men too, though in smaller number) who need to use them [flexible schedules] resist for fear of being relegated to the Mommy Track." (*Wall Street Journal*, Dec. 13, 1995, p. B1)

MONDAY MORNING QUARTERBACK. A critic after something has gone wrong; a KNOW-IT-ALL (football). See also 20-20 HINDSIGHT.

MONEY ILLUSION. The false perception of increased income when inflation is greater than the increase in income.
   "In the spirit of Keynes' General Theory, behavioral macroeconomists are rebuilding the microfoundations that were sacked by the New Classical economics. It is argued in this lecture that reciprocity, fairness, identity, money illusion, loss aversion, herding, and procrastination help explain the significant departures of real-world economies from the competitive, general-equilibrium model." (*American Economist,* Spring 2003, p. 25)

MONEY LEFT ON THE TABLE. Profit that is not realized when something is sold at a price lower than what it could have been sold for. In initial public offerings, it is the difference between the offering price and the price in the open market when the stock begins to trade.

MONKEY BUSINESS. Pranks, silliness; less-than-ethical behavior.
   "Known for its over-the-top marketing punctuated by Super Bowl ads featuring a chimp riding on a horse and cavorting with the company's CEO, E*Trade is cutting the monkey business to focus on its more staid, more profitable revenue streams." (*Brandweek,* Feb. 10, 2003, p. 3)

MOOCH LIST. A list of potential buyers, particularly people who are easily scammed.
   "Well, in French they call it a 'mooch' list. That's a slang term that's used in the industry to describe people who have the [right] personality traits—they have *got* to have a deal." (*Wall Street Journal,* August 9, 2004, p. R3)

MOONLIGHT (TO). Work a second job.
   "Kelly K. Spors's article last week on how to moonlight as a 'mystery shopper' certainly brought out the letter writers among you." (*Wall Street Journal,* August 29, 2004, p. 4)

MOORE'S LAW. The tendency for computer technology to improve rapidly. Named after Gordon Moore, who observed that computer chip capacity doubled approximately every 18 months.
   "Moore's Law, which says that the number of transistors per square inch on an integrated circuit board will double every couple

years, has long been a driving principle behind Intel's success." (*Wall Street Journal,* Oct. 12, 2004, p. C1)

MORAL HAZARD. The risk that insuring against a potential calamity will make the insured person take fewer precautions. For example, does flood insurance cause people to build homes in places known for flood risk?

MORAL SUASION. Pressure, influence, as opposed to citing laws and regulations. The FED has been known to use moral suasion to influence bank practices.

MORDIDA. A bribe, Spanish for a little bite.

MORPH. To change rapidly. Morph comes from metamorphosis.

MOST FAVORED NATION (MFN). GATT* trade understanding that no other nation will receive special privileges. If a trade barrier is reduced between any two members of GATT, the benefit is extended to all other GATT members under the MFN principle.

MOTHER-OF-ALL/MOTHER LODE. Largest, huge (Persian Gulf War/mining).
  "Broadcast television is poised to leap into the digital age. The transformation will mean 2 things for public network carriers: a revitalized competitor for video customers and a mother lode of spectrum greater than the PCS bonanza." (*America's Network,* July 15, 1995, p. 18)

MOTOWN/MOTOR CITY. Detroit, Michigan, home of Motown music and the BIG THREE automobile manufacturers.

MOUSE NUTS. An insignificant contribution.

MOUSE POTATO. Internet equivalent of a COUCH POTATO. Someone who spends significant amounts of time on the Internet.

MOUSETRAPPING. A computer programming technique that keeps replacing pop-up ads with other pop-up ads as the user attempts to close the ads.
  "Using a programming technique called 'mousetrapping' Zuccarini designed his pop-ups ads to spawn new ads when users tried to close them, the FTC said." (*DM News,* June 2, 2002, p. 11)

MOUTHPIECE. Spokesperson; sometimes refers to a lawyer.

MOVERS AND SHAKERS. Important people.
"Talk to the folks on Bay Street, and a few of the major movers and shakers will even tell you that labour has more right to be angry than creditors in some restructuring cases." (*Canadian Business,* May 24–June 6, 2004, p. 88)

MOVE THE GOAL POSTS. To change the standards or rules, usually in one's favor; to cheat.

MOVE UP IN LIFE. Make more money.

MUCKY-MUCK/MUCK-A-MUCK. Person in charge, decision-maker.
"The expression is still often heard as 'high muck-a-muck' because of its probable derivation from Chinook [Native American] jargon, hiu (plenty) muckamuck (food); hence, one who has plenty to eat, or a man of power, a BIG WHEEL." (*Safire's New Political Dictionary,* 1993, p. 469)

MULTILEVEL MARKETING. Direct marketing system where sellers recruit other people into the organization as sales representatives, earning a commission on their sales. Critics refer to such practices as PYRAMIDING; multilevel marketing sounds more professional.

MULTIPLE LISTING SERVICE (MLS). Cooperative real estate system advertising many companies' properties.

MURPHY'S LAW. If something can go wrong, it will.
"It is quite natural for an entrepreneur to pay little or no attention to the legalities of doing business. With the energy and commitment level needed to get started, business owners need some degree of optimism. In reality, running an enterprise is complicated, and Murphy's Law rears its head quite regularly." (*Black Enterprise,* July 2001, p. 45)

MUSHROOM (TO). Expand.
"Treasury departments' use of the Internet for increasingly varied and complex activities is expected to mushroom in the next year or two." (*Business Finance,* Aug. 2004, p. 45)

MUSHROOM JOB. Derogatory reference to any distasteful work; deceive. From the joke, "Treat them like mushrooms: keep them in the dark, and feed them manure."

N

NADER'S RAIDERS. People working with noted consumer advocate and environmental lawyer Ralph Nader.

NAG FACTOR. The influence nagging children have on their parents' purchasing decisions.

"Trade conventions are held across the country to develop strategies to entice children to certain products and then get them to cajole their parents into buying the products. Those in the industry call it the 'nag factor' or 'pester power.'" (Jenny Deam, "Targeting kid consumers," *Denver Post*, July 23, 2002)

NAKED CALL. An option to buy a stock that is not actually owned by the seller of the option.

"Writing, or selling, covered calls is a fairly conservative strategy. A much riskier strategy is to sell naked calls—options on shares that the seller does not already own." (*Barron's*. July 3, 2000, p. 13)

NAME OF THE GAME. The basic purpose or idea.

NANNY STATE. A NEWT description of excessive government involvement in social issues and problems.

"The challenge for Dominican leaders is to free themselves from the harmful ideology that holds that income redistribution and the nanny state can make people better off." (*Wall Street Journal,* Feb. 27, 2004, p. A9)

NARROWCASTING. Broadcasting to a small, specific audience. Technological advances increasingly allow marketers to appeal to small target markets.

NARROWING THE SPREAD. Reducing the difference between the bid and asked prices for a stock.

NASCAR EFFECT. The promotional effect produced by an article of clothing, Web site, or other object that displays a large number of logos or advertising images. NASCAR (National Association of Stock Car Automobile Racing) is a U.S.-based association devoted to professional car racing. Almost all the cars are covered with sponsors' logos.

"Until recently, many doctors' offices had signs showing logos of the dozens of health plans they accepted, usually with an invitation to patients to speak up just in case their plan wasn't listed. 'We call it the NASCAR effect,' Breen says." ("Managed care: Evolution brings myriad choices," *Memphis Business Journal,* Feb. 25, 2000)

NATIONAL ASSOCIATION OF SECURITIES DEALERS AND AUTOMATED QUOTATIONS (NASDAQ). Computerized market for securities of smaller companies in the United States.

NATIONAL BANK. A commercial bank operating under a charter from the U.S. Comptroller of the Currency. National banks were created during the Civil War and are an alternative to state-chartered banks.

NATIONAL CREDIT UNION ADMINISTRATION (NCUA). Federal agency supervising credit unions in the United States.

NATIONAL INSTITUTES OF HEALTH (NIH). Federally funded center for health-related research.

NATIONAL LABOR RELATIONS BOARD (NLRB). The NLRB administers the National Labor Relations Act (1935), which prohibited employers and employees from engaging in unfair labor practices.

NEAR MONEY. Liquid assets, assets that can be quickly turned into cash.

NECK-AND-NECK. In close competition.
"WPP's acquisition of Grey Global would push WPP neck-and-neck with Omnicom as the biggest ad-holding company." (*Wall Street Journal,* Sept. 14, 2004, p. B.14)

NEED IT YESTERDAY. Needed immediately or as soon as possible.

NEGATIVE CASH FLOW. A business situation requiring more cash than it produces from existing sales.

NEGATIVE INCOME TAX. A federal program providing tax refunds greater than taxes withheld for lower-income families, also called earned-income credit.

NEGAWATT. The conservation of electrical power. The term was coined by Amory Lovins, leader of the Snowmass Institute and critic of government energy policies that encourage production rather than conservation.

NERVE. Self-importance; willingness to take risks; courage, confidence.
"A Fed retreat now might do more damage to financial markets by showing a failure of anti-inflation nerve and lead to even higher oil and commodity prices." (*Wall Street Journal,* August 10, 2004, p. A10)

NEST EGG. Funds set aside for a specific purpose, often for retirement.
"This 56-page publication is designed for people who are about five years from retirement and helps you estimate (among other tasks) your expenses later in life, and whether your nest egg will cover those expenses." (*Wall Street Journal,* August 8, 2004, p. 2)

NET. Amount left after expenses and taxes; abbreviation of Internet.

NET ASSET VALUE (NAV). The value per share of a mutual fund; the total assets of a company less liabilities and intangible assets, divided by the number of shares outstanding.

NETIQUETTE. Internet etiquette.

"Many Internet recruiting seminars teach 'netiquette.' Consultants try to encourage polite online behavior to prevent recruiters from, say, spamming every user of a popular chat room about a job vacancy, according to Barbara Ling, president of RISE Internet Recruiting Seminars Inc. in Pelham, N.Y." (*Wall Street Journal,* Oct. 3, 2000, p. B1)

NET LEASE. A rental agreement under which the renter is responsible for property taxes, maintenance costs, insurance, and other costs associated with the property.

NET-NET. The end result.

NET THIRTY. The balance is due in thirty days.
"Throughout that period our standard terms were 1/3 with purchase order, 1/3 on delivery and the final 1/3 net 30." (*Canadian Plastics,* Feb. 2003, p. 15)

NETWORK. Build friends and contacts; link computer systems.

NEUROMARKETING. The study of a person's mental state and reactions while being exposed to marketing messages.
"When we reached the M.R.I. control room, Clint Kilts, the scientific director of the BrightHouse Institute, was fiddling away at a computer keyboard. A professor in the department of psychiatry and behavioral sciences at Emory, Kilts began working with Meaux in 2001. Meaux had learned that Kilts and a group of marketers were founding the BrightHouse Institute, and she joined their team, becoming perhaps the world's first full-time neuromarketer. Kilts is confident that there will soon be room for other full-time careers in neuromarketing." ("There's a Sucker Born in Every Medial Prefrontal Cortex," *New York Times,* Oct. 26, 2003)

NEWBIE. Someone new to an online computer network.

NEW BLOOD. People who bring new ideas or energy to a situation.

NEW CHIP. Describes stock from a relatively young technology company, as opposed to a BLUE CHIP, established company.
"Blue chips vs. new chips; Bedrock investors used to sneer at tech stocks, decrying the neophytes who eagerly snatched them up. Now, they've been transformed, loading up on these hot new shares."

(Aaron Lucchetti, "Blue chips vs. new chips," *Wall Street Journal*, March 12, 2000)

NEW DEAL. The economic programs of the Franklin Roosevelt administration (1932–1945). Elected during the height of the Great Depression, Roosevelt enacted numerous social and economic programs, including Social Security, the Works Project Administration (WPA), and the Civilian Conservation Corps (CCC).

NEW ECONOMY. 1990s term for fast-paced, technology-driven globalization.

NEW KID ON THE BLOCK. New competitor.

NEWLY INDUSTRIALIZED COUNTRIES (NICs). Developing countries that pursue an outward-oriented market strategy. The original NICs included Hong Kong, South Korea, Taiwan, and Singapore. Based on their success, many other countries are pursuing similar strategies.

NEWT. Referring to or related to Newt Gingrich, former Republican Speaker of the House, 1994–1998.
"Newt Portfolio, stocks that would do well with the policies Congressman Gingrich advocates." (*Wall Street Journal,* Feb. 14, 1995, p. C1)

NEW YORK MINUTE (IN A). Without hesitation.

NIBBLING. Sales negotiation strategy in which the buyer requests a small add-on or extra to the deal that has been negotiated.

NICE GUYS FINISH LAST. Look out for yourself (Leo Durocher, famous baseball manager); the notion that an agreeable, friendly personality often does not correlate with success.

NICHE MARKETING. Marketing strategy of serving a unique (often small) market segment. Niche marketing is considered a step toward RELATIONSHIP MARKETING, because it reinforces the concept that companies must anticipate and satisfy customer needs.

NICKEL-AND-DIME. Small amounts; quibble over minor issues.
"Each manager was given the 29-page playbook laying out 'Five Steps to Victory,' against WaMu. One: Blunt the appeal of WaMu's

'no nickel and dime fees' advertising campaign." (*Wall Street Journal,* Nov. 6, 2003, p. A1)

NICKEL TOUR. A quick overview.

NIELSEN. Rating of the number of households watching a television program (named after marketing researcher Arthur C. Nielsen).
    "Nielsen feels it's being unfairly pilloried but isn't getting much sympathy. Major clients—including Walt Disney Co.'s ABC, Viacom Inc.'s CBS and General Electric Co.'s NBC—say Nielsen made the switch unnecessarily difficult by allowing its current system to become so outdated." (*Wall Street Journal,* Sept. 16, 2004, p. A1)

NIFTY. Creative, well done.

9-11. Referring to the September 11, 2001 terrorist attacks in the United States.

911. Pronounced nine-one-one; emergency telephone number in the United States.

NINE-TO-FIVE. A regular day job (9:00 A.M. to 5:00 P.M.), usually salaried.

NINTH INNING. At the last moment (baseball).
    "Even though Schwab, based in San Francisco, is getting into the 401(k) game in the ninth inning, its arrival is sure to ruffle some competitors, especially given Schwab's reputation for low-cost service." (*Wall Street Journal,* April 3, 1996, p. C1)

NITTY-GRITTY. Most basic parts.
    "Once specific medical conditions are mentioned, television drug ads are required to discuss all sorts of medical nitty-gritty. Why do pharmaceutical concerns tap this technique?" (*Wall Street Journal,* April 8, 2004, p. 1)

NO-BRAINER. An easy decision.
    "Still, 'those two weeks would cost me $10,000, an enormous splurge,' she says. 'Compared to that, the insurance was a no-brainer.'" (*Wall Street Journal,* August 15, 2004, p. 2)

NO-FRILLS. Without any extra features. See also VANILLA MODEL.
    "Founded in 1982, Nicole Miller Ltd. for years followed a no-frills, low-key strategy, in sharp contrast to today's young designers who

often jump into the fray with pricey, avant-garde collections and fashion shows." (*Wall Street Journal,* Sept. 8, 2004, p. B1)

NOISE. Anything that distracts from a marketer's message.

NOISY WITHDRAWAL. A requirement that lawyers who believe a client is committing a securities-law violation, announce they are quitting for "professional considerations."

"A majority of the five commissioners is currently leaning toward instituting some form of 'noisy withdrawal' requirement, according to people familiar with the matter." (*Wall Street Journal,* Jan. 9, 2003, p. A1)

NO LOAD. Without any added fees.

NOLO CONTENDERE. Choosing not to contest (Latin), as in a legal dispute. Many Americans first learned the term when Vice President Spiro Agnew resigned from office in 1973, pleading nolo contendere to charges of tax evasion.

NON-ACCELERATING INFLATION RATE OF UNEMPLOY-MENT (NAIRU). An inflation rate that creates jobs but not pressure to raise wages.

"Inflation phobes at the Federal Reserve and on Wall Street 10 years ago were obsessed with something called the Non Accelerating Inflation Rate of Unemployment. Widely known as Nairu, this was supposed to be the economy's natural rate of joblessness. Now, with Nairu mostly discredited, the buzz in financial circles is about a different kind of natural rate: the natural rate of interest." (*Business Week,* April 22, 2002, p. 32)

NON-COMPETE AGREEMENT. A clause in a buyout or employment agreement preventing an owner or former employee from working in or starting a business in direct competition with the firm they were associated with.

NONCOMPETITIVE BID. A bid accepting the average price at an auction.

NON-D. Abbreviation for nondisclosure agreement. Employees, especially research and development staff, are often required to sign a nondisclosure agreement as a condition of employment. The agreement commits the person to not sharing information with others.

NONLINEAR (TO GO). To take a problem or issue to upper management without going through the organizational hierarchy.

NO-NOS. Convertible bonds that pay no interest.
"In the arcane world of convertible bonds, they are called 'no-nos,' but a number of companies are saying 'yes-yes' as they peddle these no-interest bonds to investors." (*Wall Street Journal,* June 3, 2003, p. C1)

NONPERFORMING ASSET. An asset that is not generating income. Under accounting rules, banks and other businesses are required to list nonperforming assets when payments are overdue for more than a set period of time, often 90 days.

NO SCRAPS HIT THE FLOOR. Competitors will immediately replace firms that make mistakes.
"There is so much competition out there that no scraps will hit the floor." (Jami Martin, USC Corp., 1995)

NOSEDIVE. A steep, rapid decline.

NOTE. A promise to pay.

NOT IN MY BACKYARD (NIMBY). Local opposition to environmental threats. Critics have suggested that environmentalists are not really concerned with pollution but instead are interested in making sure it is not in their backyards.
"The affordable housing crisis squeezing working-class families in the US' largest metropolitan areas may finally be diffusing some of the NIMBY sentiment that led many communities to oppose building housing for low- and moderate-income households for at least a generation." (*Builder,* August 2004, p. 35)

NO WONDER. Not surprising; "I'm not surprised."
"No wonder Mylan, the second-largest generic-drug firm in America, has opted for a spot of complementary medicine." (*The Economist,* July 31, 2004, p. 58)

NUKE (TO). Eliminate, terminate.
"'I know what you're thinking,' it tells Burgess. 'You're going to nuke me.'" (*Canadian Business,* April 17, 2000, p. 46)

NUMBER-CRUNCHER. Accountant; technical financial analyst.
"Investors also have a sense that the quality of earnings isn't high—and they are correct. Traditionally, the difference between

generally accepted accounting principles net income and operating earnings is 12% to 18%, according to S&P's number-cruncher Howard Silverblatt." (*Wall Street Journal,* Oct. 27, 2003, p. C1)

NUMERO UNO. Oneself; person in the highest position; Spanish/ Italian for "number one."

"Before he left for Westchester and Montana, Brokaw told people both inside and outside NBC that he was taking the summer off to reflect on his future as NBC's Numero Uno news anchor." (*Electronic Media,* August 27, 2001, p. 27)

NURSE AN ACCOUNT (TO). Give special attention or consideration to a problem account.

NUTMEGGED. Fooled, from soccer, when the ball goes through an opposing player's legs. Originally, from colonial times when merchants would sell wood-shaped imitation nutmeg.

NUTS AND BOLTS. The basic parts or activities.

O

OCCUPATIONAL SAFETY AND HEALTH ADMINISTRATION (OSHA). OSHA was created in 1970 to protect workers. The many confusing and contradicting OSHA regulations have turned the acronym into an epithet in management circles.

ODDBALL. Loner, person or thing left out of the group; strange, unusual.

"In the process of building his fortune, Jimmy A. Pattison turned Ripley's Believe It or Not!, a struggling little outfit with a giant brand name and a cache of oddball collectibles, into a thriving business." (*Forbes,* March 17, 2003, p. 159)

ODD LOT. Stock trades of less than one hundred shares. One hundred shares is considered a ROUND LOT.

ODD MAN OUT. All alone.

"For years, it has been software hackers, whose tools are a keyboard and mouse, who embodied the computer subculture. Now, hardware is getting cooler, says Mr. Grand, who felt like the 'odd man out' in his days as a member of the Boston hacker collaborative known as the L0pht in the 1990s." (*Wall Street Journal,* Sept. 7, 2004, p. A1)

OFF BASE. Not informed, not understandable.

"Coke's new chairman and CEO warned that third-quarter profit would fall well short of Wall Street expectations, making clear that his initial upbeat assessment of the beverage titan's prospects and strategy was off base." (*Wall Street Journal,* Sept. 16, 2004, p. A1)

OFFERING PRICE. The asking price; the price paid by investors at the initial public offering.

OFFICE OF MANAGEMENT AND BUDGET (OMB). The NUMBER CRUNCHING arm of the executive (White House) branch of government.

OFFICE OF THE INSPECTOR GENERAL (OIG). The internal investigation division within the federal government.

OFFPEAK PRICING. Energy pricing with lower rates during periods of low demand.

OFFSHOOT. Derived from or variation of.

"Virgin Blue Holdings' strong run in the Australian aviation market has skidded to a halt, with earnings threatened by oil prices and the launch of Qantas Airways' domestic budget offshoot, Jetstar." (*Wall Street Journal,* August 5, 2004, p. 1)

OFFSHORE FUNDS. Investments registered outside one's home country for tax advantages.

"Investors are often confronted with the issue of investing in an offshore investment vehicle and hedge fund managers are often confronted with the issue of whether to set up a domestic fund, an offshore fund or both." (*Journal of Taxation of Investments,* Winter 2004, p. 187)

OFFSHORE PRODUCERS. Overseas companies.

OFFSHORING. Relocation of business processes to an overseas location, taking advantage of lower wages or other tax and legal advantages.

OFF THE BOOKS. Cash or barter; business done without records to avoid taxation.

"These obscure partnerships could be kept off the books—with no footnote disclosures—if an independent investor owned 3% of an entity's equity." (*Wall Street Journal,* Sept. 22, 2004, p. A1)

OFF THE CHARTS. Beyond expectations or projections.

"According to Ameritech CEO Richard Notebaert, reaction to the new service was off the charts in tests this summer with 200 customers." (*Wall Street Journal*, Sept. 23, 1998, p. B10)

OFF-THE-CUFF. Informal, initial opinion.

"The move points Starwood toward more traditional corporate leadership and away from Mr. Sternlicht's off-the-cuff style." (*Wall Street Journal*, Sept. 21, 2004, p. B1)

OFF THE RECORD. Unofficially, not for quotation. Many times politicians and government bureaucrats will only speak off the record.

OFF-THE-SHELF/RACK. Readily available, not custom made.

"If you want something that is customized and made for you, you are going to get one that is tailor-made and not off the rack." (*Wall Street Journal*, April 28, 2004, p. D4)

OFF THE TOP. Before any deductions are made; from the most profitable part.

"Next Sunday, Kitty Kelley's anti-Bush book, 'The Family,' will knock John O'Neill's Kerry-bashing book, 'Unfit for Command,' off the top spot on the New York Times best-seller list." (*Wall Street Journal*, Sept. 28, 2004, p. A4)

OFF THE WALL. Crazy.

"While Mr. John Malone wasn't available to comment, and people close to him play down the idea of a sale, the notion isn't off the wall." (*Wall Street Journal*, Dec. 24, 2003, p. C3)

OIL PATCH. The U.S. oil industry; specific regions of the United States noted for oil production and refining, including Texas, Oklahoma, Louisiana, California, and Alaska.

"It's a reality that experienced oil-patch investors learned to live with long ago." (*Wall Street Journal*, March 11, 2004, p. C1)

OK/OKAY. All right. The term may have come from President (1837–1841) Martin Van Buren's nickname, "Old Kinderhook."

OLD AGE, SURVIVORS, AND DISABILITY INSURANCE (OASDI). The official name for Social Security.

OLD BOYS CLUB/NETWORK. Closed network of established business relationships.

"Perhaps the biggest surprise of 'girls club' is that it lacks the one thing that definitely does exist: the old boys club." (*Wall Street Journal,* Oct. 20, 2003, p. B1)

OMBUDSMAN. Third party who acts as an arbitrator within an organization. The term comes from the Swedish word *ombud,* meaning authority to act for another.

ON ACCOUNT. Buying on credit rather than with cash.

ON ALL FOURS. Ready to go.

ON A MISSION. Highly motivated.

ON A ROLL. Experiencing a series of successes.
"The two were on a roll. They'd worked to re-elect Gov. Zell Miller of Georgia, and, speaking of Hail Marys, Carville had rallied Harris Wofford from 40 points down in the polls to an upset victory in Pennsylvania's Senate race." (*Wall Street Journal,* Sept. 16, 2004, p. A16)

ON A SIGNATURE BASIS. Based on one's reputation or signature, without review.
"While credit cards operate almost exclusively on a signature basis, debit transactions in the majority of countries are undertaken by using the cardholder's PIN, or by a combination of signature and PIN." (*Credit Card Management,* April 1994, p. 100)

ON BOARD. Hired; in agreement. The phrase is most often associated with jobs in government.
"After that meeting, the agency began the bold work of trying to hook up Oprah and Pontiac in a promotional deal. Ironically enough, getting GM on board was at first an uphill battle." (*Wall Street Journal,* Sept. 14, 2004, p. B1)

180. An about-face, a complete reversal.
"The Senate retreat on the debt-ceiling strategy was announced by Senate Appropriations Committee Chairman Ted Stevens. It represented a 180-degree turn by the Alaska Republican, who had earlier encouraged the House to take the approach it did." (*Wall Street Journal,* June 25, 2004, p. A2)

ONE-MAN SHOW. To work alone and therefore perform many tasks, sole proprietor.

"With the earnestness of a schoolboy and the dramatic flourishes of a one-man show, the 28-year-old channeled the voices of his boss and his No. 1 client." (*Newsweek,* March 15, 2004, p. 28).

ONE-TWO PUNCH. Two actions taken quickly one after the other (boxing).

"The entertainment retail industry was dealt a one-two punch this month when Tower Records filed for Chapter 11 Bankruptcy protection and Viacom announced plans to spin off Blockbuster Entertainment." (*DSN Retailing Today,* Feb. 23, 2003, p. 3)

ONE-UPMANSHIP. Keeping a subtle psychological advantage over an opponent.

ON HIS/HER WATCH. While he or she was in charge (military).

ON PAPER. In theory, for official or tax reporting purposes, but not in reality.

"Stein propelled KPMG to the forefront of a tax-shelter frenzy, which saw rival auditing firms pushing a new generation of shelters, often designed to create large losses on paper that company could use to erase taxable income. Now, KPMG is one of more than 100 tax-shelter promoters facing IRS scrutiny." (*Wall Street Journal*, Feb. 25, 2005, p. A1)

ON THE BALL. Alert, effective.

"'It's fairly urgent,' says Philip Lim, an economist at the Korea Development Institute, or KDI. 'The Korean government and Kogas have to get on the ball pretty soon.'" (*Wall Street Journal,* August 4, 2004, p. 1)

ON THE BLOCK. For sale, on the auction block.

ON THE CHEAP. Inexpensively.

"Health Management buys existing hospitals in small cities, mainly in the southeastern U.S., usually financially ailing hospitals that can be had on the cheap." (*Forbes,* Aug. 28, 1995, p. 90)

ON THE CLOCK. Working.

Customer: "He's on the clock. He can't sit down."

Manager: "Yes I can, I'm SCHMOOZING with customers!"

(A conversation overhead by the author while working on the first edition of this book, June 6, 1996)

ON THE FENCE. Undecided.

"While the big banks seem to want to beef-up the services in branches, others are either sitting on the fence or, as in the case of Alliance & Leicester with its decision to close some branches in favor of internet or telephone channels, going in the opposite direction." (*Financial World,* August 2004, p. 24)

ON THE FIRING LINE. In the path of the action, under pressure.
"But are the woes of governors, who are saddled by balanced-budget requirements and are often on the firing line during hard times, indicative of a broader rebellion against elected officials and special-interest politics? So far, no—but that could change." (*Business Week,* Oct. 20, 2003, p. 39)

ON THE LAM. Hiding.

ON THE LINE. At risk.
"Computer security breaches are a recurring problem for companies, particularly those that conduct business online. A company's corporate reputation is on the line if it does not adequately secure customer information." (*Network World,* Sept. 13, 2004, p. 49)

ON THE MONEY. Accurate.
"Besides the small fact that the BULLS have been absolutely on the money and the BEARS dead wrong all year, what has fed investor complacency has been the supposed lack of feverish speculation, that universally perceived telltale sign that trouble is brewing." (*Barron's,* August 28, 1995, p. 3)

ON THE ROCKS. Failing; a nautical reference to a ship hitting rocks and sinking.

ON THE SAME PAGE. In agreement.

ON THE SAME WAVELENGTH. Thinking similarly.

ON THE SIDELINES. Not involved, not participating in decision or action. The term comes from sports; if you are on the sidelines you are not in the game.

ON THE SPOT. Immediately; under pressure.
"The aide, Andy Blocker, was momentarily flummoxed. 'You really put me on the spot there,' Mr. Blocker said to Mr. Shuler later, both men recalled. 'I'd appreciate it if you didn't do that again.'" (*Wall Street Journal,* August 27, 2004, p. C1)

ON THE TABLE. UP FRONT, up for discussion.
"Just this week in an interview with Fox's Bill O'Reilly, Mr. Bush said about Iran's bomb program, 'We've made it clear, our position

is that they won't have a nuclear weapon.' Diplomacy, he said, was the first option, but 'all options are on the table.'" (*Wall Street Journal,* Oct. 1, 2004, p A14)

ON THE TAKE. Accepting bribes or illegal payments.

"Carriers say shippers and receivers are on the take, while shippers say carriers are more unabashed than ever about trying to buy their business with entertainment and bribes." (*Distribution,* March 1994, p. 34)

ON THE WINGS OF. With the support or assistance of.

"The NASDAQ* is up some 35% since 1995 started, mostly on the wings of the technology stocks." (*Barron's,* August 28, 1995, p. 3)

ON THIN ICE. A dangerous or risky situation.

OP. CIT. (OPERE CITATO). In the work cited (Latin).

OP/ED. Opinion/editorial section of a newspaper.

OPEN-COLLAR WORKER. A person who works at home and therefore does not need to dress for work.

"Home-based entrepreneurship is attracting growing numbers of recruits to its ranks. These 'open-collar workers' come from a variety of backgrounds: lifelong entrepreneurs, homemakers, downsized workers, graduate students, stay-at-home parents, homebound disabled people and retirees. But their goals are similar: to be their own bosses, work flexible hours and devote their efforts to projects they love. ("It's Home Suite Home for Brave Entrepreneurs," *Los Angeles Times,* May 20, 2001)

OPEN-DOOR POLICY. Management policy advocating access for employees from all levels within the organization.

"It seemed simple enough a task to carry out, and terrifically symbolic, as well, for the new president of WPP Group's J Walter Thompson, New York, but it turned out to be far more time-consuming to achieve than she'd expected. Hopefully, the difficulties she encountered in establishing—literally—an open-door policy are not a harbinger of things to come for the former president of Kirshenbaum Bond & Partners, New York." (*Advertising Age,* August 30, 2004, p. 16)

OPENING PRICE. The price paid for a stock when it is first traded on the open market. Often the opening price is considerably higher than the offering price, allowing investors who first purchased the stock to make a quick profit.

OPEN INTEREST. The number of outstanding futures contracts.

"More than 4,500 of Procter & Gamble's October 55 puts crossed the tape, compared with open interest of 6,152. The stock fell $1.88 to $54.38 in New York Stock Exchange composite trading at 4 P.M." (*Wall Street Journal,* Sept. 21, 2004, p. C5)

OPEN ORDER. An order that is good until canceled.

OPEN SKIES. Available to everyone.

"In Asia, the era of the low-cost carrier has arrived and perhaps sooner than most would have expected in a region still making the transition from tightly drawn bilateral agreements to freewheeling open skies arrangements." (*Air Transport World,* August 2004, p. 28)

OPEN SOURCE. Internet term for a cooperative agreement among programmers. LINUX is the most widely known open-source agreement.

OPEN THE KIMONO. To open a company's accounting records for inspection; to expose something previously hidden.

"The phrase 'opening the kimono' can mean 2 things in the context of public relations (PR). It can mean being straightforward in client and media relations, and it also applies to the issue of how far an agency should go in new business presentations." (*PR Casebook,* Feb/March 1984, p. 14)

OPERATING EXPENSES (OE). All the expenses of running a business except the cost of goods sold.

OPERATING RATE. The percentage of operating capacity being used.

OPPORTUNITY COST. The value of the next best use of a resource. The cost of something in terms of an opportunity lost or missed.

"By parceling trades—known as slicing and dicing—institutions could be paying a high opportunity cost as well." (*Pensions and Investments,* June 28, 2004, p. 3)

OPTIMIZE. Develop to full potential.

ORDERING AND SHIPPING IMPROVEMENT SYSTEM (OASIS). Computerized shipping and production control system.

ORDER OF THE DAY. Common; objective being pursued (military).

"New products, new brands combined with new advertising is the order of the day." (*Marketing,* Sept. 7, 1995, p. 9)

ORGANIZATION OF AMERICAN STATES (OAS). U.S.-dominated regional political alliance including South and Central American countries.

ORGANIZATION OF PETROLEUM EXPORTING COUNTRIES (OPEC). Thirteen-member international commodity organization that seeks to limit petroleum production in order to control the price of oil.

ORPHAN STOCK. A stock that is not followed by research analysts, usually because the company is quite small.

OTHER PEOPLE'S MONEY (OPM). Borrowed funds.

OUT OF THE BALLPARK. Beyond the predicted range; excessively high (baseball).
"This [increasing the minimum wage] is going to knock the budget numbers out of the ballpark." (*Wall Street Journal,* April 24, 1996, p. A1)

OUT OF THE LOOP. Not part of the decision-making group, not in the network. During the Iran-Contra investigations, then Vice President George Bush claimed that he was out of the loop.
"With $1.7 billion to $2 billion in annual supply-chain spending, HP has become more assertive. But HP's new strategy doesn't mean the company is cutting its third-party logistics providers out of the loop." (*Journal of Commerce,* Sept. 6, 2004, p. 1)

OUT OF THE MONEY. A stock option that has no value.

OUT OF THE WOODS. No longer in danger.
"Still, convinced that it is not out of the woods yet, Aqualon recently turned to the Manager's Network to help it tackle new challenges." (*CIO,* May 1995, p. 31)

OUT OF THE WOODWORK. Appear unexpectedly.

OUT OF TOUCH. Not informed, not understanding.
"'George Bush has proven that he's stubborn, out of touch, unwilling to change course,' Mr. Kerry told an Orlando rally on Saturday." (*Wall Street Journal,* Oct. 4, 2004, p. A4)

OUT OF WHACK. Not right; out of balance.

OUTPLACEMENT. Services provided to recently terminated employees.

"'Younger workers will seek employers who will further their development as professionals,' says David Craig, vice-president and managing consultant of Drake Beam Morin, an international outplacement and career transition firm based in New York." (*Benefits Canada,* Sept. 2004, p. 51)

OUTSOURCE (TO). Replace company production with subcontractors.

"P & O is refusing to comment on reports it intends to outsource its ferry operation to a third party ship management company, said to be Monaco-based V Ships, to prepare the way for a sale of the business that will free it to focus on its fast-growing and profitable global container terminal." (*Journal of Commerce,* Sept. 27, 2004, p. 1)

OUT THE WINDOW. Discarded; no longer in consideration.

OVERBOOK. When demand exceeds supply. Airlines often overbook seats, and initial public offerings frequently have considerably more buy orders than the number of shares being offered. Also, someone with a very full calendar might be characterized as overbooked.

OVERDRAFT. An account without sufficient funds to pay the check that has been written. Banks often offer overdraft protection, of course, for a fee.

OVERHANG. A large quantity of stock that is available in the market; looming problem.

"Another overhang continues to be whether options will be expensed in 2005, this would be a big negative for many technology stocks." (*InformationWeek,* Sept. 13, 2004, p. 70)

OVERHEAD. Management cost associated with a specific activity.

OVERRUN. Production in excess of requirements.

OVER THE COUNTER (OTC). Stock market transactions that take place through telephone and computer networks rather than through market specialists on the exchanges.

OZONE-FRIENDLY. Products without chlorofluorocarbons.

"Their common replacement, hydrofluorocarbons, although ozone-friendly, have been found to be extremely powerful greenhouse gases." (*Appropriate Technology,* April–June, 2001, p. 40)

OZZIE AND HARRIET. Traditional two-parent, two-children household.

"Looking backward makes the importance of families obvious. Looking forward makes families look like an outmoded television sketch called, variously, 'Leave It to Beaver' or 'Ozzie and Harriet.'" (*Wall Street Journal,* Jan. 7, 2003, p. A12)

P

PACESETTER. Person or product that sets the standard for others who follow (horse racing).

PACKAGE. Parts of an agreement; to bring together parts of a business strategy.

PACKAGE DEAL. An agreement including several parts.
   "To entice the pros, Mr. Neville described the accommodations at Doral, the special package deals for families, and the chance to ride by helicopter to nearby Homestead auto racetrack, where the pro golfers could drive Ford race cars 140 miles an hour with Nascar drivers in the passenger seat." (*Wall Street Journal,* April 19, 2004, p. R15)

PACK IT IN. Quit; close a business.

PAC-MAN STRATEGY. Corporate strategy of buying up the shares of the company attempting to take over one's company (computer games).

PAD (TO). Add to, as in a budget or an expense account.

PAINTING THE TAPE. Illegal stock market tactic where a large order is divided into many small orders to give the appearance of interest on the part of many investors.

"The action on the floor was dominated by pools, which would rig the market and paint the tape with phony trades. The public would see a stock moving and figure that something must be going on. The suckers would all rush in, ... and then the pool operators would sell at a profit." (*Wall Street Journal,* May 28, 1996, p. R18)

PANDORA'S BOX. An array of potential problems. In Greek mythology, Pandora, the first mortal woman, opened a box, releasing the ills of the world.

PAPER. A contract, agreement; abbreviation for COMMERCIAL PAPER.

PAR. Face value of a security.

PARADIGM SHIFT. A change in focus, or of fundamental assumptions.

"In a paradigm shift: a) your company's structure and work will change profoundly, forever altering your career; b) someone in management has been to a seminar—don't worry, it will pass; or c) many people will be fired to convince investors that real change is taking place." (*Wall Street Journal,* Oct. 3, 1995, p. B1)

PARALLEL ECONOMY. Informal, unregulated economy. See also BLACK MARKET.

"Spread across the Middle East and beyond are more than 200 Islamic financial institutions: banks, mutual funds, mortgage companies, insurance companies—in short, an entire parallel economy in which Allah, not Alan Greenspan, has the final say. Industry growth has averaged 10% to 15% a year." (*Fortune,* June 10, 2002, p. 154)

PAR FOR THE COURSE. What would be expected, average.

"The economy probably lost more than a million jobs last month, but that would be par for the course." (*Wall Street Journal,* August 6, 2004, p. C1)

PARKING. Financial strategy of placing assets in a safe investment while looking for other opportunities. See also ILLEGAL PARKING.

PARKINSON'S LAW. The observation that work expands to fill the time available to do it.

PARLIAMENTARY PROCEDURE. Rules of order for running meetings based on those used in the British Parliament.

PARTNERING. Forming a business alliance.

"A substantial stake in the pipeline also would give Alaska more control over the project, officials say. Still, Ethan Berkowitz, House minority leader in the Alaska Legislature, worries Alaska could turn out the loser by partnering with the powerful oil companies." (*Wall Street Journal,* June 10, 2002, p. 154)

PART OF THE EQUATION. Something that must be included when considering a situation or problem.

PARTY LINE. The official response or position.

PASS THE BOOK. Daily transfer responsibility for an investment bank's current trading positions from one office to another around the world.

PAT ON THE BACK. Support; to encourage.

"The federal government's major law enforcers crowded the lectern yesterday to pat themselves on the back for indicting Ken Lay. But all the self-congratulation over the Enron founder and former CEO's perp walk couldn't conceal the sense of anticlimax." (*Wall Street Journal,* July 9, 2004, p. A10)

PAVE THE WAY. Make easier for; provide access to.

"The bigger question is whether the vote can take place in something resembling a calm and orderly environment. If it does, that's a big boost for President Bush and his argument that the wars in Afghanistan and Iraq will pave the way to democracy and, hence, stability in the Middle East." (*Wall Street Journal,* Oct. 6, 2004, p. A4)

PAVLOV'S DOGS. Reference to conditioned responses; people who respond to management's stimuli. Refers to the research of Russian psychologist Ivan Pavlov, who conducted stimulus-response experiments with dogs.

PAYMENT IN KIND. Payment without the use of cash, instead paying with goods or services. In agriculture, a government support program in which farmers are paid with crops for diverting land from production.

PAYOLA. Bribe; secret payments.

PAY ON THE LINE. Pay promptly.

PAY THE PIPER/FIDDLER. Pay what one owes; take the consequences. The phrase comes from the proverb "He who dances must pay the piper."
"But he who pays the piper calls the tune, and the biggest piper-payer is the American Treasury." (*The Economist,* July 17, 2004, p. 79)

PAY THROUGH THE NOSE. Pay an excessive amount.

PAY TO PLAY. The use of campaign contributions to gain access, often to win municipal-bond contracts.
"That rule, known as G-37, is designed to prevent big Wall Street firms from using campaign contributions as a way of winning lucrative municipal-bond deals, a process known as pay to play." (*Wall Street Journal,* Dec. 17, 1998, p. C1)

PEARL-DIVING CONTEST. A sales-force incentive program.

PECKING ORDER. Rank, seniority (social behavior of fowl).
"For every chief planner who retires, a chain reaction begins and officers further down the pecking order are bumped up a grade." (*Planning,* Feb. 20, 2004, p. 14)

PEEK. A very brief look or reading.
"Many of the objects will have to travel through the museum's public spaces, offering visitors a rare and fleeting peek at seldom-seen pieces of the collection." (*Wall Street Journal,* August 30, 2004, p. A1)

PEERING. Internet term for the practice of not charging other Internet providers for access to each other's systems.

PENALTY BOX. In trouble or in a position of low esteem. From ice hockey, in which someone who breaks the rules is sent to the penalty box.

PEN DRIVE. Data storage device that looks like a pen, which can be connected to computer USB ports.
"These 'pen drive' devices are making stealthy but steady inroads onto the computing scene." (*Wall Street Journal,* August 7, 2002, p. D5)

PENDULUM SWING. A change to the opposite direction.

"While recent data have been upbeat, 'the bond market has been resilient,' and it is 'waiting for when the pendulum swings.'" (*Wall Street Journal,* Dec. 1, 2003, p. C10)

PENETRATION PRICING. Marketing strategy of initially setting a low price to gain market share with the goal of raising prices once one's product is the established leader in the market.

"Penetration pricing is perhaps the most abused pricing strategy. It can be effective for fixed periods of time and in the right competitive situation, but many firms overuse this approach and end up creating a market situation where everyone is forced to lower prices continually, driving some competitors from the market and guaranteeing that no one realizes a good return on investment." (*Management Marketing,* Summer 1998, p. 30)

PENGUINHEAD. People who use the LINUX open-source operating system. The Linux mascot is a penguin.

PENNY-ANTE. Of little consequence or importance.

"All those $5, $10, or $20 bills may prove irresistible to dishonest employees—or lunch money bandits, as one practice administrator calls these penny-ante embezzlers." (*Medical Economics,* August 23, 2002, p. 45)

PENNY-PINCHER. A derogatory term for someone who is cheap or excessively focused on cutting costs.

PENNY STOCK. Stocks that sell for less than $1 per share. Penny stocks are traded over-the-counter at regional stock exchanges. The penny stock market has frequently been the subject of investigations for price manipulation.

PEOPLE PILL. Anti-takeover tactic in which managers all threaten to leave if the company is purchased by outsiders.

PEP TALK. Motivational speech.

"The government's Exhibit A will presumably be a videotape of Mr. Lay's now-famous pep talk to employees in August 2001, telling them Enron was still 'doing extremely well' and encouraging them to hold on to their stock." (*Wall Street Journal,* July 19, 2004, p. A10)

PERCUSSIVE MAINTENANCE. Sarcastic way of describing attempts to fix a machine by hitting it, hoping that will make it work.

PER DIEM. Expense allowance per day (Latin).

PERFORMANCE BOND. A surety bond that provides insurance against loss if one party does not fulfill its commitment.

PERK. Special benefit, privilege. (Short for perquisite.)
"The Schwab card is missing a few luxury perks that competitors offer. Smith Barney customers can trade their points for American Airlines miles, for instance, though they have to pay an annual fee for this version of the card." (*Wall Street Journal,* Oct. 7, 2004, p. D4)

PERMISSION MARKETING. A marketing strategy in which the marketer asks the consumer for permission to send him or her targeted ads based on personal data supplied by the consumer.
"A recent Vanderbilt University analysis of consumer responses . . . reported that more than 72 percent of Web users would relinquish their data if they were assured of 'a cooperative relationship built on trust'—specifically, if the sites would provide statements about how the data were going to be used. In Mr. Godin's lexicon, that cooperation is the essence of permission marketing, which has three basic components: it is anticipated, it is personal and it is relevant." ("Digital Commerce," *New York Times,* May 10, 1999)

PER SE. By or in itself; as such (Latin).

PERSONAL IDENTIFICATION NUMBER (PIN). Secret number used to secure telephone communications or financial transactions.

PERSONAL TIME OFF. The sum of vacation time, sick leave, and personal leave allowed by a company.

PERSONA NON GRATA. A person who is not welcome (Latin).

PER STIRPES. Legal formula for allocating the assets of an estate when the deceased did not leave a will.

PETER PRINCIPLE. Tendency of management to promote people one level above their competence. Dr. Lawrence Peter of the University of Southern California coined the term.
"The Peter Principle may be responsible for some employees' performance problems." (*Supervisory Management,* June 1994, p. 14)

PETRODOLLARS. Surplus revenues accumulated by oil-exporting countries. When OPEC* was established in the 1970s, members insisted on being paid in U.S. dollars.

PHANTOM INCOME. A tax and accounting issue in limited partnerships whereby tax credits taken earlier in the life of the investment result in a reportable income when otherwise there would be a loss. Tax shelters prior to 1986 often resulted in phantom income.

PHANTOM STOCK. A bonus given to corporate executives based on increases in the value of the company's stock without actually awarding the stock to the executives.

PHARMING. Technique used by Internet criminals to link consumers with their Web site, and then capture personal information.
"In pharming, thieves redirect a consumer to an imposter Web page even when the individual types the correct address into the browser. They can do this by changing—or 'poisoning—some of the address information that Internet service providers store to speed up Web browsing.'" (*Wall Street Journal,* May 17, 2005, p. B1)

PHILLIPS CURVE. Graph of the relationship between inflation and unemployment in an economy.

PHONE BOOTH GLUT. 1990s' overabundance of telephone booths due to the introduction of cellular phones.

PHONY AS A THREE-DOLLAR BILL. Deceitful; con-artist.

PICK AND SHOVEL COMPANY. A company that supplies equipment to an industry.
"The smart money is not just spreading bets on individual companies. Rival biotech firms are pursuing vastly different approaches to profiting from the basic research. There are, for example, the 'pick and shovel' companies, an allusion to the fact that the only people who made real money during the gold rush were those who sold supplies to the miners." ("The Gold Rush," *Newsweek,* April 10, 2000)

PICKET (TO). Demonstrate. Union workers form PICKET LINES.

PICKET LINE. Union protest technique, creating a line of union members that nonunion workers and customers must pass in order to enter or leave a business.
"The picket line, once largely honored by unionized and nonunion workers alike, appears to be losing its legs. 'There used to be families that grew up believing that crossing a picket line is

the equivalent of pushing an old lady off a curb.'" (*Wall Street Journal,* Jan. 17, 1996, p. A1)

PICK ONE'S BRAIN. Solicit ideas from someone.

"A good way to bring business into your firm would be to sit down with a RAINMAKER and pick his brain." (*Mechanical Engineering,* Dec. 1998, p. 34)

PICK UP. Start where one left off; a stimulant; a casual encounter.

PICKS UP. Increases.

PIECE OF CAKE. Easy.

PIECE OF THE ACTION/PIE. Part ownership; involvement in a project; some of the sales or profits.

"And it matters not just to the droves of foreign businessmen flocking there to carve out a piece of the action, or to the Chinese who are experiencing what some people compare with the 'British industrial revolution.'" (*Strategic Direction,* Sept. 2004, p. 21)

PIECE RATE. Amount a worker is paid per unit when doing PIECEWORK.

PIECEWORK. A job in which one is paid based on the quantity of goods produced.

PIGEON. A person who is easily deceived. See also MARK.

PIGEONHOLE (TO). Place in a category.

"Overall, there will be a wider range of loss scenarios, and the inability to pigeon-hole hospitality units in the way one might other commercial property types, driving more insureds to the excess and surplus lines market to obtain needed coverages." (*National Underwriter,* Oct. 6, 2003, p. 17)

PIGGYBACK. Intermodal transportation combining rail and truck transport.

PIGGYBACKING. Practice of one firm marketing another firm's products; making use of existing efforts. In stock markets, when a broker buys or sells based on the actions of a client, it is considered illegal piggybacking.

"The 'piggy-backing' of advertising programs isn't illegal because the P2P companies often bury notification in the terms-and-conditions form each user must agree to. Most computer users, however, don't wade through the legalese and never know they have these programs on their computers." (*Wall Street Journal,* Dec. 10, 2003, p. D1)

PIGS. Thirty-pound blocks of aluminum or other metal; greedy people.

PILOT FISH. Junior executives who follow close behind senior management. See also BROWN-NOSER, ASS-KISSER.

"Does anyone seriously think that Tuesday's results were going to be determined by elevating Bob Jones University, breast-cancer ads, Texas cronies or any of the other marginal, mindless 'issues' that seem to obsess campaign advisers and the media pilot fish who swim after them?" (*Wall Street Journal,* March 9, 2000, p. A6)

PILOT LAUNCH. Test marketing by limiting the initial distribution of a product.

"The pilot launch of the RSS-14 (Reduced Space Symbology 14-digit) bar code system is getting underway at Dayton, Ohio-based Dorothy Lane Market." (*Supermarket Business,* Dec. 15, 2000, p. 57)

PINCH HIT (TO). Substitute (baseball).

"ACD Systems' Canvas 9 Professional Edition is primarily for technical illustrators who need to design precision graphics. It can also pinch-hit as an image editor or an illustration program—plus, it can serve as a page-layout, drawing, presentation, and Web-site program." (*Macworld,* Feb. 2004, p. 38)

PINK SHEETS. Daily publication of stock quotations on the NASDAQ*.

"MCI shares, trading on the over-the-counter Pink Sheets, jumped 17% Monday, when MCI announced that Leucadia had made filings with regulators seeking permission to acquire more than half of MCI's stock." (*Wall Street Journal,* July 15, 2004, p. B4)

PINK SLIP. Dismissal notice.

"In the wake of the September 11 attacks and the downturn of the book business, Unger said that many PCP graduates received pink slips, victimized by the 'last hired, first fired' syndrome." (*Publisher's Weekly,* June 7, 2004, p. 13)

PIN MONEY. A small amount of money set aside for miscellaneous purchases.

PIPE DREAM. Unrealistic idea or expectation.

PISSED. Angry. The term is considered vulgar.
"It may be that Gavin is simply pissed off with the never-ending reviews of the business." (*Marketing,* July 21, 2004, p. 20)

PIT. The center of activity in futures and options markets.

PITCH. High-pressure sales presentation.
"The figures have significance because the company has been trying to pitch itself as an emerging high-tech player, particularly in southern China, where it operates a broadband network and hopes to expand its high-speed Internet services for home and business users." (*Wall Street Journal,* Oct. 19, 2004, p. C4)

PITCH MAN. Sales person.

PLAIN-VANILLA. Ordinary, without any extras. See also VANILLA MODEL.
"The company's new managers and a report prepared for prosecutors by an independent consultant contend that the Canadian deal and several other transactions were far from the plain-vanilla financings that global companies normally engage Wall Street to do." (*Wall Street Journal,* Sept. 28, 2004, p. A1)

PLANKTON. A company being taken over or swallowed by a much larger one.

PLASTIC. Credit card.
"With retail card executives questioning the relevance of their plastic, retailers are approaching a crossroads. They can either surrender to 3rd-party cards or retrench and find new ways to profit from growing their cards' share of sales." (*Credit Card Management,* July 1995, p. 6)

PLAY BALL. Cooperate; get started (baseball).
"Not all groups want to play ball with brands. Some denounce such collaborations." (*Marketing Week,* Sept. 9, 2004, p. 41)

PLAYBOOK. Corporate plans (football); standard procedure.

"Princess Diaries 2, is as reassuring and soothing as a nursery story—in fact it's straight out of the Disney playbook of the '50s." (*Wall Street Journal,* August 20, 2004, p. W1)

PLAYER. A noteworthy competitor in the market.
"The situation affected all industry players and was worse than expected." (*Wall Street Journal,* Oct. 19, 2004, p. B2)

PLAY HARDBALL. Be demanding, difficult to negotiate with (baseball).
"The book's hype prepared one for just this sort of drill sergeant's manual. 'It's time to play hardball.'" (*Wall Street Journal,* Oct. 15, 2004, p. W6)

PLAY IT BY EAR. Improvise, to use your best judgment in situations where you have limited or no experience or information.

PLAY THE FLOAT. Write a check today and deposit the funds to cover it tomorrow.

PLEAD THE FIFTH. Refuse to divulge information. The Fifth Amendment to the U.S. Constitution allows citizens not to answer questions in court when their response would incriminate themselves.

PLOW BACK. Put back into.
"They argue that sending some jobs overseas more than repays the U.S. with lower prices for imported goods, expanded markets for U.S. products and fatter profits that U.S. companies can plow back into more-innovative businesses." (*Wall Street Journal,* Nov. 13, 2003, p. A4)

PLUG A PRODUCT. Promote.

PLUM. A good investment or assignment.

POINT-OF-PURCHASE (POP) DISPLAY. Retailing strategy of placing impulse items near where customers make their purchases.

POINT PERSON. Person designated to take charge of a crisis situation.

POISON PILL. A financial maneuver to avoid being taken over by another company.

"The court said the fund's poison pill adhered to the 1940 act because, when triggered, 'it allows for all shareholders, except the Acquiring Person, to exercise their rights' and that the 'poison pill does not change the fact that all shares are granted equal voting rights.'" (*Wall Street Journal,* Oct. 25, 2004, p. C17)

POLISH A TURD. To edit or refine a piece of writing even though the material in the report is of little or no value. To make something that is worthless appear valuable or important. (Considered vulgar.)

POLITICAL ACTION COMMITTEE (PAC). Group created to lobby government.

"Then there is the Prosperity Project, an effort organized by the Business Industry Political Action Committee to get business leaders to communicate more with their employees about politics." (*Wall Street Journal,* Oct. 26, 2004, p. A4)

POLITICALLY CORRECT (PC). Accepted terminology; the notion of not using any language and practices that could be offensive to any social, cultural, or political group.

"The competition resulted, as you would have expected, in a festival of politically correct nihilism: cruise missiles vied with a wrecked red car covered in bird droppings on a gigantic scale." (*Wall Street Journal,* April 9, 2004, p. A8)

POLLUTION CREDIT/RIGHT. Market-based pollution control credit program, allowing firms that reduce their levels of pollution below what is required by law to sell the difference between the maximum amount allowed and their current amount produced to other firms. The economic logic is that firms that can easily reduce pollution will do so, while those firms for whom it would be expensive to reduce pollution will purchase credits instead.

PONZI SCHEME. A fraudulent financial proposition in which initial investors are promised very high rates of return; eventually the scheme collapses. The phrase is named after Charles Ponzi, who in 1919 created the Security and Exchange Company, promising investors a 40% return. Ponzi paid off the initial investors with funds of later investors. Auditors eventually revealed the scheme, and Ponzi went to jail. He later sold real estate in Florida. See also PYRAMID.

"More Charges Filed in Alleged Ponzi Case: Federal prosecutors file additional charges against Martin A. Armstrong, the jailed former financial adviser they have accused of orchestrating a $3 billion 'Ponzi' scheme." (*Wall Street Journal,* July 29, 2004, p. C3)

POOH-POOH (TO). Reject or be critical of.

POOL OF APPLICANTS. Potential employees.

POOL TOGETHER (TO). Combine.

"Regulators responded by proposing that insurers pool together more policyholders to produce smaller, across-the-board rate increases if necessary, and phase in any large increases over two to three years." (*Wall Street Journal,* June 23, 1999, p. F1)

POOR-MOUTH (TO). Deny one's wealth.

POP-UP, POP-UNDER. Internet ads that appear when closing a Web page or site.

"Talk about irony. Software firm Blazing Logic is using pop-up ads—those small ad windows that appear in separate browsers as people surf the Web—to sell software to help eliminate pop-up ads." (*DM News,* Sept. 9, 2002, p. 19)

PORK BARREL. Government spending designed to favor a politician's constituents.

"Boondoggle ('an extravagant and useless project') has long since entered the American vernacular, as has pork barrel (programs meant 'to ingratiate legislators with their constituents')." (*Wall Street Journal,* Oct. 22, 2004, p. W5)

PORTABILITY. The ability to take employee benefits, particularly retirement accounts, from one job to another.

PORTAL. A Web site that acts as a gateway to information services on the Internet.

PORTFOLIO. A collection of securities.

PORTFOLIO INVESTMENT. Purchasing stock in a number of companies.

POSITION. A company's financial condition; an investor's interest in a venture.

POSITION SQUARING. Option, currency, commodity, or stock market action of reversing the previously held position, buying back options sold or selling back options previously purchased.

"In the prevailing currency markets, fundamentals have taken a temporary back seat to technical trading signals and 'position squaring'" (*Review & Focus,* EverBank World Market report, April 1, 2004, p. 1)

POSITIVE CASH FLOW. More cash produced than spent.

POSTAL PRICING. Pricing telephone calls the same regardless of distance, like postal (mail) rates.

POTHOLES. Problems; obstacles.
"Concerns have risen that the economic expansion hit a pothole in June as payroll-job growth slowed, and retail sales softened." (*Wall Street Journal,* June 21, 2004, p. A2)

POUND OF FLESH. An exorbitant demand for payment. In Shakespeare's *Merchant of Venice,* SHYLOCK demands a pound of flesh as payment for his loan to Antonio.

POWER HITTERS. Strong, forceful individuals (baseball).

POWERHOUSE. Forceful person or group.
"During the mid-1990s, Uzbekistan maintained its Soviet-era status as a regional industrial powerhouse by hewing to Soviet-style state economic planning." (*Wall Street Journal,* Oct. 21, 2004, p. A17)

POWER LUNCH. Lunchtime business meeting between MOVERS AND SHAKERS.
"After flaming out in 1996 following a stormy 14 months as president at Walt Disney Co., Michael Ovitz is back doing deals, working the phones and taking lots of power lunches." (*Business Week,* July 24, 2000, p. 42)

POWER NAP. A short, five- to ten-minute rest. Some people have the ability to sleep for short periods of time and awaken refreshed and ready to go again.

POWER OF THE PRESS. Media's ability to change or affect public opinion.
"She says that these organizations understand the power of the press and make armchair activists believe they can make a difference by simply hitting the send key." (*The Masthead,* Autumn 2004, p. 8)

POWER PLAY. An attempt to overwhelm a competitor through a show of strength (hockey).

POWWOW. Meeting, discussion. The term comes from a Native American word for conjurer or medicine man.

"So it seems encouraging that they have now decided, as Yoriko Kawaguchi, Japan's foreign minister, announced this week, to start holding their own three-way powwow every year. Business and economic ventures are already blazing the trail for the diplomats." (*The Economist,* April 10, 2004, p. 56)

PRAIRIE DOGGING. When anything important happens, every-one in offices with cubicles pops their head up over the cubicle.

PREFAB. Abbreviation for prefabricated: already manufactured and ready for assembly.

PREMIUM. The excess of market price over the value of the good; in insurance, the payment due; an item given away or for a reduced price when customers purchase another product. Premiums are used to motivate consumers to try a new product or brand.

PRESS THE FLESH. Shake hands with everyone in a room. See also GLAD HAND.

PRESSURE-COOKER. Stressful environment.

"But she also acknowledges the office's workload and demands are a turnoff to qualified candidates. 'It's a pressure cooker,' she says." (*Wall Street Journal,* July 22, 2003, p. B8)

PRICES TUMBLING. Prices going down rapidly.

"A day after Iraq's restoration of its exports sent prices tumbling, rumors swirled through the market that President Bush's admin-istration, increasingly worried about the political and economic ramifications of record oil prices, is considering releasing oil from the 667 million-barrel emergency reserve known as the SPR." (*Wall Street Journal,* August 26, 2004, p. C4)

PRICE WAR. Competitive price-cutting, often below cost, in order to gain market share or drive competitors out of business.

PRIMA DONNA. Show-off ("first lady" in Italian).

PRIMA FACIE. On first appearance (Latin).

PRIME. Prime rate. The rate charged by banks to their highest-quality borrowers for short-term, uncollateralized loans.

PRIVATIZATION. The selling-off by government of nationalized industries; contracting privately for services previously done by government employees.

"The privatization of Telstra—Australia's largest full-service telephone company, which ranks itself as the 14th largest in the world by market capitalization—would be one of the biggest share sales anywhere when the offering is made, which bankers predicted would be late next year or 2006." (*Wall Street Journal,* Oct. 11, 2004, p. B3)

PROACTIVE. Taking a position in advance rather than reacting.

"Seagate Chief Financial Officer Charles Pope says the company didn't undercut rivals to win market share as it re-entered the laptop market, but he says it was surprised by 'proactive, reflexive' price-cutting by others." (*Wall Street Journal,* Oct. 14, 2004, p. A1)

PROBLEM CHILD. A low-market-share product in a fast-growing market.

PRO BONO. For the (public) good (Latin)—that is, without charge. Most state law associations require lawyers to do some work pro bono annually.

PRODUCER PRICE INDEX (PPI). The PPI measures inflation at the wholesale level. Changes in the PPI usually precede changes in inflation at the consumer level.

PRODUCT LIFE CYCLE (PLC). Stages a product goes through in the marketplace, including introduction, growth, maturity, and decline. PLC was once used exclusively among marketers, but it began to be used in the 1990s by accountants and finance managers concerned with whether a product would remain marketable long enough to be profitable.

PRO FORMA. As a matter of form (Latin). New companies often issue pro forma estimated income and expenditure statements.

PROGRAM TRADING. Pre-programmed computer orders to buy or sell shares of stock as prices of stocks or indices change. The New York Stock Exchange defines program trading as any trade valued at $1 million or more involving 15 or more stocks. Program trading sometimes accounts for as much as 40 percent of daily volume on the NYSE.

"Program trades in which firms buy or sell dozens of different stocks in one blast, often to keep pace with a major index, have long elicited muttering from smaller investors." (*Wall Street Journal,* July 24, 2002, p. C1)

PROGRESSIVE TAX. A tax whose percentage increases as income increases.

PROMO. Promotion.
"McDonald's global chief marketing officer Larry Light's ad/promo/product revitalization by summer's end had spurred 16 consecutive months of same-store sales growth." (*Brandweek,* Oct. 11, 2004, p. M12)

PROOF IS IN THE PUDDING. Whether something really works will be based on the actual performance or results.

PRO RATA. According to shares (Latin); a percentage based on past performance.

PROS AND CONS. Advantages and disadvantages.
"Six community bank presidents bashed out HR issues relating to communications, the pros and cons of a 'family' atmosphere, employee burnout, and training." (American Bankers Association, *ABA Banking Journal,* Sept. 2004, p. 20)

PROSPECT. Potential; a potential customer.
"While eager investors have driven up Google's stock 55% since its August initial public offering, many analysts believe that to cement its long-term prospects Google should get into the browser business." (*Business Week,* Oct. 11, 2004, p. 54)

PROTECTION MONEY. Bribe; money paid to avoid problems with authorities or criminals.
"Enron bathed the Beltway in money because the members demanded every penny. Like every corporate donor in America, Enron was paying protection money." (*Wall Street Journal,* Feb. 12, 2002, p. A2)

PROXY. One who represents another person's interests, or the agreement that allows another person to represent one's interests.

PRUDENT-MAN RULE. U.S. legal standard for the actions of someone charged with investing funds in trust for others. The administrator of the funds is expected to ask, "Would a prudent man or woman make this investment?"

PSYCHIC INCOME. Non-monetary value or satisfaction from a work activity.

P-TO-P. Peer to peer.

PUBLIC DOMAIN. Something that is no longer protected by patent or copyright and can be used by anyone. In the United States, government documents are in the public domain.

PUBLIC EYE (IN THE). Visible, widely publicized.
"Doing so serves to keep tort reform in the public eye." (*Business Insurance,* Sept. 13, 2004, p. 8)

PUBLICITY STUNT. An outrageous act designed to get media coverage.
"One marketer sees it as an 'incongruous' link amounting to a PR and publicity stunt." (*Marketing Week,* June 24, 2004, p. 28)

PUBLIC SERVICE ANNOUNCEMENT (PSA). Free advertising time for socially important messages. As part of their licensing requirements, radio and television stations in the United States are expected to provide time for public service announcements.
"During his set, Mr. Springsteen issued a short 'public service announcement' in favor of Mr. Kerry." (*Wall Street Journal,* Oct. 5, 2004, p. D8)

PUFF PIECE. HYPE; extravagant praise, often in flowery newspaper stories.
"Before the act, 'offering circulars' were often nothing more than puff pieces issued by unscrupulous promoters employing high-pressure sales tactics, said Joel Seligman, dean of Washington University's School of Law and author of a history of the SEC and a textbook on the securities laws." (*Wall Street Journal,* June 2, 2003, p. C5)

PULL IN. Bring in, as in people or money. See also DRAW.
"Chambers is confident that lineup changes will help pull in the young, upmarket viewers advertisers fall over themselves to reach." (*Campaign,* Sept. 10, 2004, p. 13)

PULL OFF. Succeed.
"Microsoft can pull this off because stations' playlists are matters of public record." (*Forbes,* Oct. 18, 2004, p. 62a)

PULL PUNCHES. Hold back, (boxing).

"Isaak Karaev, Multex.com's chairman, chief executive and president, still says his company can knock Thomson Financial off its perch. 'We don't ever pull punches,' says Mr. Karaev, who co-founded Multex.com." (*Wall Street Journal,* Dec. 13, 2000, p. C18)

PULL STRINGS. Use one's influence, manage, control; track a problem to resolution.

"To win a chunk of the Google business, Goldman, the nation's premier investment bank, unleashed its CEO, Hank Paulson, to pull some strings." (*Newsweek,* May 10, 2004, p. 42)

PULL THE PLUG. Put an end to, often by withdrawing funding or resources.

"The government-sponsored Industrial Revitalization Corp. of Japan yesterday told Daiei it will pull the plug on an evaluation of Daiei's assets—effectively barring the retailer from asking for aid from its turnaround fund, an official at one of Daiei's creditor banks said." (*Wall Street Journal,* Oct. 13, 2004, p. A14)

PULL THE RUG FROM UNDER. Undermine; suddenly cease support for.

"Companies keen to encourage trust in e-commerce, especially those, like Ebay, trying to promote radically new forms of trade, cannot expect consumers to trust them if they suddenly pull the rug from under their feet." (*Marketing Week,* March 27, 2003, p. 30)

PULL THE WOOL OVER SOMEONE'S EYES. Deceive.

PUNCH IN/PUNCH THE CLOCK. Report for work; punch a time card at a factory.

"Interest in pinkies among employees of the dinner-house group stems from Left Coast Restaurants' requirement that they use a fingerprint scanner device to punch in and out on a virtual time clock in the company's Menusoft Systems Digital Dining point-of-sale system." (*National Restaurant News,* Sept. 13, 2004, p. 76)

PUNT. Give up (football).

PURE PLAY. Investment in a company that is in only one market or industry; a company that only sells over the Internet.

PURGE AND MERGE. See MERGE AND PURGE.

PUSH COMES TO SHOVE (WHEN). A hostile or high-pressure situation.

"Reality #1: For all the enlightened talk of teamwork, when push comes to shove, people often look out for themselves and try to blame others for their failures." (*Business Week,* Feb. 2, 2004, p. 41)

PUSH MONEY. Payments paid directly to retail salespeople by manufacturers for selling the manufacturer's product.

PUSH THE ENVELOPE. Always trying to do better (aeronautical engineering).

"We then need to reach out to the team at CBS, the team at MTV, the team at Spike, and have a conversation with them about, how do we push the envelope?" (*Wall Street Journal,* Sept. 15, 2004, p. 1)

PUSH UPSTAIRS. Promote someone out of the way.

PUT A DAMPER ON. Discourage.

"Of course, the Justice Department's intervention in Oracle's bid for PeopleSoft put a damper on Oracle's plans—for now." (*Barron's,* July, 26, 2004, p. T3)

PUT EVERYTHING ON THE LINE. Risk everything on the business.

PUT IT ON THE BOARD (YOU CAN). It is accurate, without a doubt.

PUT IT ON THE MAP. To make known or important.

PUT ON THE SPOT. Challenge or pressure someone openly.

PUT OUT TO PASTURE. Pressure someone to retire.

PUT THE MEAT ON THE TABLE. Discuss the important parts of a business negotiation.

PUT THE SCOTCH TO IT. To cancel or stop something.

PUT THE SQUEEZE ON. Put under pressure.

"America's deregulation of wholesale power markets put a painful squeeze on the country's dozens of nuclear plants, many of which were run as one-shot investments by incompetent local utilities." (*Wall Street Journal,* March 30, 2004, p. A18)

PUT UP OR SHUT UP. Become part of the team or keep quiet; prove what you say is true.

"In addition, 1995 will be the year that vendors have to 'put up or shut up.' Instead of issuing yet another round of future oriented press releases, vendors must demonstrate successful implementations of large-scale management solutions in customer environments." (*Computer World,* Jan. 16, 1995, p. 56)

PUT YOURSELF IN SOMEONE ELSE'S SHOES. Try to understand the other person's perspective.

PYRAMID. An unethical or illegal financial scheme. See also PONZI SCHEME.

"Its longtime sales model, which relies on independent sales representatives selling door to door and deriving income from their recruits' sales, was declared illegal five years ago by a Chinese government directive that lumped direct sellers like Amway with illegal pyramid schemes." (*Wall Street Journal,* March 12, 2003, p. B1)

PYRRHIC VICTORY. A costly success or bittersweet victory. The term comes from the Greek king Pyrrhus's victory over the Romans at the cost of many lives.

Q

Q.E.D. (QUOD ERAT DEMONSTRANDUM). That which was to be proven (Latin).

Q1, -2, -3, -4. Abbreviation for first, second, third, and fourth quarter of a business year.

Q RATING. A measure of a celebrity's name recognition. Advertisers frequently use celebrity testimonials and want to know in advance which "stars" are currently most popular.

Q.T. (ON THE). Secretly, without others knowing.

QUALIFIED OPINION. The report of an independent auditor or certified public accountant stating any limitations or exceptions to a company's audit.

QUALITY AWARDS. Citations given by governments recognizing organizations that are leaders in TQM*. The three major awards are: the Malcolm BALDRIGE Award (U.S. private sector), the President's Award for Quality (U.S. public sector), and the Deming Prize (Japan). The Baldrige Award has become quite competitive, and winning corporations use the award in their marketing promotions.

QUALITY CIRCLES. Management and worker groups that focus on improving the substance and value of their products.

"Quality Circles showed that making it right the first time, and involving everyone, made better products cheaper." (*Wall Street Journal,* Jan. 7, 2002, p. A4)

QUALITY MANAGEMENT. Analysis of production processes and statistical error to improve efficiency and performance.

"Comptroller John D. Hawke Jr. directed the OCC's quality management division to examine how effectively regulators handled Riggs's compliance with federal regulations against money laundering." (*Wall Street Journal,* June 2, 2004, p. B2)

QUALITY OF LIFE. Living conditions.

QUALITY TIME. Short but satisfying periods of time spent with family members. Harried executives often talk about spending quality time with members of their family.

QUEEN BEE. Office matron; woman in charge of an office. The phrase is considered offensive, sexist.

"Queen bees tend to seek others' perspectives when planning or making decisions." (*Fortune Small Business,* May 2002, p. 67)

QUICK AND DIRTY. Cheap and easy, but often second-rate, solution to a problem.

"Allowing market forces to work sounds good to us, but first let's look at how China is failing to do so before jumping for the quick and dirty fix of currency manipulation." (*Wall Street Journal,* Sept. 3, 2003, p. A16)

QUICK ASSETS. A company's cash and other assets that could be easily turned into cash; current assets minus merchandise inventories.

QUICK BUCK. Money made fast.

"And two days earlier state attorney general Bill Lockyer filed charges against a second law firm engaged in what he called a 'quick-buck racket.'" (*Wall Street Journal,* July 22, 2003, p. A10)

QUID PRO QUO. Something for something (Latin). Many business agreements have implicit quid pro quo understandings.

"It's part of a quid pro quo relationship that aims to bolster the retailer and the supplier. In the case of Wal-Mart, the store gives a category leader exclusive access to market-share information of its rivals, food executives say." (*Wall Street Journal,* Oct. 28, 2004, p. A1)

QUIET PERIOD. The period of time during the registration and issuance of securities when the company is prohibited from promotional activity related to the securities. The quiet period is a Securities and Exchange Commission regulation.

"The SEC backed off. That was fortunate, because the violation was minor—though it was a demonstration of double standards. Quiet-period violations have led to delays of other offerings, most recently that of salesforce.com." (*Wall Street Journal,* August 18, 2004, p. C1)

R

RACE THE CLOCK. Work feverishly to complete something before a deadline.

"While he races the clock and fears eroding support, Bush is expected to ask as many as five House Democrats to join his administration. The lame-duck session of Congress will test whether his bipartisanship is real." (*Wall Street Journal,* Nov. 30, 2000, p. A1)

RACINO. A horse racing track that also includes gambling or other casino features.

"Here's how racinos work, and why fans, breeders, and track owners like the idea: Racetracks install slots, generally thousands at a time, on-site. Racing fans, presumably between races, spend a few dollars on the slots. The income made by the track, after sizable payouts to the state and the lottery system, is funneled back in the form of bigger purses for each race. The difference between a racino-funded purse and one without slot money can be as much as $175,000." (Heather Timmons, "Can slot machines rescue racing?" *Business Week,* Dec. 2, 2002)

RACKET. Noise; special business deal that is very profitable and may be illegal.

"He will be assisted at trial by James DeVita, a former federal prosecutor who helped win a tax-fraud conviction of hotelier Leona Helmsley, and Austin Campriello, a former chief of rackets in the Manhattan district attorney's office." (*Wall Street Journal,* Sept. 25, 2003, p. C10)

RACKETEER INFLUENCED AND CORRUPT ORGAN-IZATION (RICO) ACT. A federal law designed to address problems of organized crime in the United States. RICO has also been used to convict people of insider trading and other financial industry violations.

RACK-JOBBER. Distributor who monitors and stocks store shelves.

RACK UP. Accumulate.
"The reward redemption terms aren't as generous as one normally gets from credit cards. You'd need to rack up 4,000 points for a $10 gift certificate, or 20,000 for a $50 gift certificate." (*Wall Street Journal,* Oct. 17, 2004, p. 4)

RADAR SCREEN (APPEAR ON). New information that creates excitement or comment among members of that industry or market.

RAGS TO RICHES. Poor to wealthy.

RAG TRADE. Clothing industry.

RAIDER. Outside investor trying to take over a company.
"Reagan's 'decade of greed,' after all, was dominated by corporate raiders and junk-bond financed start-ups that upset the status quo in industry after industry." (*Wall Street Journal,* June 16, 2004, p. A15)

RAIN CHECK. A postponement. When an unscheduled conflict arises many Americans will apologize, saying, "I'll have to take a rain check." Businesses also offer rain checks to customers when they have run out of an advertised product. The rain check promises to allow the customer to purchase the product at the price advertised.

RAINMAKER. Person who uses his or her influence to benefit a client. The term originally referred to Native American shamans who would attempt to make it rain.

"His probation officer asks: 'What are you doing with your life?' Mr. Berstein used to be a prominent New York attorney, a self-described 'rain maker.'" (*Wall Street Journal,* Sept. 17, 2002, p. D1)

RAISE MONEY. Find investors.

RAKE IN. Bring in large amounts, usually money.
"Tired of playing defense, some industry officials say law firms such as Skadden, Arps rake in big fees for offering favorable legal opinions to justify shelters." (*Wall Street Journal,* July 16, 2004, p. A4)

RAMP UP. To expand output.
"When authorities recently reached out with another offer, however, HSBC pounced, signaling the bank's readiness to ramp up on the mainland in a major way." (*Wall Street Journal,* Aug. 20, 2004, p.C1)

RANDOM WALK THEORY. Stock market theory that past share movements are of no use in predicting future changes.

R & R. Rest and recreation (military) or rest and relaxation.

RASPBERRY. Disapproval, usually associated with a flatulent sound.
"By contrast 34% in laid-back Britain told the pollsters, in effect, to get lost, and only 49% gave Mr. Bush the raspberry." (*Wall Street Journal,* August 21, 2001, p. A19)

RATCHET. Incentive system where management increases its equity in a company if the firm does well.

RATEBUSTER. Worker who produces more than other workers doing the same task.

RATE CARD. Standard advertising prices for media. In the 1990s, increased competition forced most media in the United States to discount from published rates.

RATING. The television or radio audience, expressed as a percentage of the total population (see NIELSEN); evaluation of credit risk. The major rating services in the United States are Duff & Phelps, Fitch, Moody's, and Standard & Poors. Their rating scales vary slightly but range from AAA to D.

RAT RACE. High-pressure business environment.

"Some time in the 1960s Edmund apparently decided to escape the New York 'rat race' by fleeing to a farm in New England." (*Wall Street Journal,* Jan. 31, 2001, p. A20)

RATTLE THE CAGES. To make things happen.

REACH. The number of people who see or hear a commercial.

READ MY LIPS. A promise. President George Bush pledged, "Read my lips, no new taxes," but he then agreed to a compromise budget plan that raised taxes.

REAGANOMICS. The economic programs of the Reagan administration (1980–88). Reaganomics emphasized lower marginal tax rates, increased defense spending, and placed constraints on social programs. Originally the Reagan program also included promises to balance the budget, but Reaganomics resulted in higher U.S. budget deficits.

REAL ESTATE INVESTMENT TRUST (REIT). A company that manages a portfolio of real estate properties. REITs are usually publicly held trusts that, under special investment laws, must distribute 95% of their NET income annually to investors.

"Colonial Properties Trust agreed to acquire Cornerstone Realty Income Trust Inc. for stock valued at about $610 million, the latest deal among apartment real-estate investment trusts." (*Wall Street Journal,* Oct. 26, 2004, p. 1)

REAL INTEREST RATE. Nominal interest rate minus the inflation rate. Real interest rates measure the return investors receive after allowing for inflation.

REALITY CHECK. Comparison of perceptions with available evidence. Suggesting that someone needs a reality check is an unflattering comment that they have a distorted perspective of what is happening.

REALLY! That is amazing!

REAL TIME. Live, in the present. Computer-based communications occur in real time.

REAL WAGES. Wages adjusted for inflation.

RECORD PACE. Fastest rate.

RED CARPET/RED CARPET TREATMENT. Plush, fancy, fit for royalty; lavish welcome.

"Standard & Poor's soon may roll out the red carpet for real estate investment trusts, after years of excluding them from its indexes." (*Pensions & Investments,* Aug. 6, 2001, p. 3)

RED CHIPS. Shares of top-quality Asian companies.

"In early May China-based property developer Top Glory International Holdings became another buyout target, signaling that the takeover frenzy is spreading to the so-called red-chip sector, which includes Chinese companies with Hong Kong listings." (*Wall Street Journal,* June 10, 2003, p. C14)

RED-EYE (THE). Overnight flight.

RED FLAG. Warning sign.

"We haven't seen the red flags or the patterns that would give us a heightened level of concern in other areas, but that doesn't mean it isn't there." (*Wall Street Journal,* Oct. 28, 2004, p. C1)

RED HERRING. An act of deception; an advance copy of a prospectus for the issue of new securities; something that distracts or diverts attention from the real issue.

"That is a red herring, says Ken Broad, a portfolio manager at Transamerica Investment Management, a Los Angeles fund company that voted for the option-expensing proposal at Intel." (*Wall Street Journal,* May 25, 2004, p. C3)

RED INK. In accounting red ink is used to show losses.

RED-LINING. Illegal practice wherein lenders do not make loans in certain geographic areas red-lined on a map.

REDNECK. Low-class person (derogatory).

"The Democrats lost their affinity with the Scots-Irish during the Civil Rights era, when—because it was the dominant culture in the South—its 'redneck' idiosyncrasies provided an easy target during their shift toward minorities as the foundation of their national electoral strategy." (*Wall Street Journal,* Oct. 19, 2004, p. A18)

RED TAPE. Bureaucratic delays.

"While India is one of the world's fastest-growing economies, its share of global trade has hovered at about 0.8% for several years, due in part to local red tape and poor infrastructure at home." (*Wall Street Journal,* Oct. 18, 2004, p. A17)

REDUCTION IN FORCE (RIF). LAYOFFS.

RE-ENGINEERING. Reorganizing a company. See also DOWNSIZING.

"Aside from tax measures, Ms. Arroyo asked Congress to pass legislation that would arm her with the power to 'downsize' the government and provide a safety net for public-sector workers who may be displaced by the 're-engineering' process." (*Wall Street Journal,* July 27, 2004, p. A14)

REFLATION. Attempts by government to stimulate the economy.

"Essentially, reflation is the intentional effort by governments to ward off deflation by boosting demand and underpinning prices." (*Wall Street Journal,* Dec. 30, 2002, p. A2)

REHAB. Rehabilitation, often treatment for substance abuse.

REINVENT THE WHEEL. To do something that has already been done.

RELATIONSHIP MARKETING. Firm's attempt to develop long-term links with customers.

RENAISSANCE CONSULTING. Supposedly new ideas.

"Renaissance consulting is the new spin on what was called 'process consulting'—a continuing cycle of testing and monitoring." (*Wall Street Journal,* May 30, 1996, p. A1)

RENEGADE. Maverick, one who refuses to conform to norms.

REP. Representative.

REPURCHASE AGREEMENT (REPO). Financial market agreement in which the seller agrees to repurchase a security at a set price and stated time in the future. Repos are used in money markets for short-term investments and cash management.

REQUEST FOR PROPOSALS (RFP). Government agencies and grant foundations announce RFPs to solicit projects related to the issues and objectives of the group.

RESISTANCE LEVEL. Technical stock market analyst's term for a price level at which sellers add supply to the market, making it hard for the stock to continue to rise.

RESOLUTION TRUST CORPORATION (RTC). U.S. government agency created in 1989 to address the Savings & Loan crisis. The RTC took over bankrupt S&Ls, merging some with financially sound banks and liquidating the assets of others.

REST ON ONE'S LAURELS. Sit back, relax based on past performance.

RETIREMENT. Repayment of a debt.

REVECTOR. To change a business plan, especially as a means of reducing the size of a company's workforce.
"Responding to changing international market conditions, Teleglobe (NYSE,TSE: BCE), the e-World Communications Company, today announced plans to revector portions of its business during the next month which will result in the elimination of approximately 450 positions, or 20 percent of its workforce." ("Teleglobe Announces Rationalization Plan," *Business Wire,* August 30, 2001)

REVENUE-MANAGEMENT. 1990s use of computers to analyze past sales, predict patterns of consumer purchases, and adjust prices accordingly.
"Mr. Ford elevated the executive overseeing the revenue-management process, Lloyd Hansen, to a corporate vice presidency. Ford analysts track sales by model, color and optional features on a regional basis." (*Wall Street Journal,* May 7, 2004, p. A1)

REVENUE STREAM. Flow of money coming in over time.
"To make up the difference, some investors worry the firm is turning more to its trading operations—a revenue stream they deem risky." (*Wall Street Journal,* June 22, 2004, p. C1)

REVERSE ENGINEERING. To take apart a product in order to study and produce a similar one.

REVERSE MORTGAGE. Mortgage allowing an owner to borrow against the equity in their home. Reverse mortgages are increasingly popular among retirees but often include significant initiation fees.

REVOLVING-DOOR SYNDROME. When government officials and regulators quit or retire and then take employment with the companies they regulated.

"Ann Eppard for months has been Exhibit A for what critics call the revolving door between government service and lobbying. She became the transportation industry's most successful new lobbyist when her old boss, Rep. Bud Shuster, assumed the chairmanship of the committee that oversees such issues last year." (*Wall Street Journal,* Feb. 9, 1996, p. A4)

REVOLVING LINE OF CREDIT. An agreement providing a commitment to lend funds to a borrower as requested for a set period of time.

RICH. Expensive or overpriced.

RICHES TO RAGS. Wealthy to poor.

RICH MEDIA. Media that feature video or audio formats.

RIDE SHOTGUN. Oversee; to be ready to take on problems or conflicts (nineteenth-century American West).
    "The French are striking again. This time it is the security guards who ride shotgun in armored cars across the nation." (*Wall Street Journal,* May 19, 2004, p. A16)

RIDE THE MARKET. Making money with the general growth in the economy.

RIDING HIGH. Confident; successful.

RIDING ON. At risk; invested in.

RIG. Fix a machine; illegally predetermine an election; illegally manipulate a market; a truck or other piece of large machinery.

RIGHT-BRAIN PERSON. A person with creative skills.

RIGHT-HAND MAN/WOMAN. Trusted assistant; a person who works closely with the manager.

RIGHT OF FIRST REFUSAL. Part of a business contract giving a company the first chance to produce or distribute a new product. In the publishing industry, a publisher frequently asks for the right of first refusal of an author's next work.

RIGHT OFF THE BAT. From the beginning (baseball).

RIGHTSHORING. Restructuring a company's workforce to find the optimum mix of local jobs and jobs moved to foreign countries.

"Whatever the truth of the matter, there is no doubt that customers with complex queries requiring local understanding do not respond well to far-off operators repeating parrot-fashion a series of learned responses. Convergys, one of the world's biggest providers of "contact-centre services", advises companies to shift simple queries offshore while retaining the more complex ones on the same shore as the caller. It calls this process 'rightshoring', and estimates that about 80% of the companies that it is working with in Britain are planning to split their call-centre operations in this way." ("Relocating the back office," *The Economist,* Dec. 13, 2003)

RIGHT SIZE. To restructure a company or operation consistent with market demand or potential. Usually, right-sizing involves downsizing and/or outsourcing.

RIGHTS OFFERING. An offer to sell additional shares of stock to existing stockholders, often at a price less than the current market price.

RIGHT TO WORK. Rule allowing employees to work without being required to join a union. Most Southern states in the United States are "right to work" states.

RING A BELL. Stimulate memory; recall.

"Leak, of course, is what it did, and to no one other than CBS's '60 Minutes.' Funny how that rings a bell." (*Wall Street Journal,* Oct. 27, 2004, p. A16)

RINGER. An expert or professional who pretends to be an amateur. A ringer might be brought in to gain an advantage over the competition.

RING UP. Record a sale; to telephone.

"Major retailers, including Saks Inc.'s Saks Fifth Avenue and Bloomingdale's, report strengthening sales of fragrances and expect to ring up full-year increases." (*Wall Street Journal,* May 7, 2004, p. B1)

RIPOFF. A swindle, scam.

RIPPLE EFFECT. The series of consequences from an initial action or decision.

RISING STAR. Someone who is being promoted quickly within the organization.

"Maybe a rising star in Singapore's telecommunications sector, but the company's coming initial public offering of stock doesn't exactly sparkle." (*Wall Street Journal,* Sept. 24, 2004, p. C14)

RISING TIDE THAT LIFTS ALL BOATS. Something that benefits everyone. Originally used by President John F. Kennedy.

RISK-FREE RETURN. The interest rate on the lowest-risk investment, usually a U.S. government security, for that period of time. Investors compare the yield premium over the risk-free return versus the risk of the investment.

R.J. REYNOLDS (RJR). Originally a U.S. tobacco company, in 1989 RJR was the object of the largest takeover in U.S. corporate history.

ROACH BAIT. A marketing message delivered by an actor posing as a regular person with the intention of having that message conveyed to many other people.

"Then, there's the roach bait technique. Under this scenario, the paid huckster doesn't necessarily buy a drink for others. He's often found sitting in a prime spot at a bar or club, very visibly drinking Brand X. He talks up the brand big-time in the hope the good word will spread." ("Freebies take on brash new form," *USA Today,* May 15, 2001)

ROADBLOCK. An issue or disagreement that hinders accomplishment of a goal or change.

ROADKILL. People or companies that fail to keep up with changing market conditions.

ROAD MAPS. Guides.

"In May, Mr. Fields told managers and union leaders at Land Rover's Solihull, England, plant to draw up a detailed 'road map' for restoring the brand's quality after Land Rover finished below average in a widely watched quality survey by the research firm J.D. Power & Associates." (*Wall Street Journal,* Sept. 1, 2004, p. A2)

ROAD SHOW. Seminars held by investment underwriters to attract investors to a new issue.

ROAD WARRIOR. A businessperson who travels frequently.

ROBBER BARONS. Powerful companies who manipulate a market; American Industrial Revolution industrialists who monopolized markets.

ROBERT'S RULES OF ORDER. Book providing guidelines for managing official meetings.

ROB PETER TO PAY PAUL. Take funds from one account or project for use in another.

ROCKET SCIENTIST. Someone with a technical background or an intelligent person. Often used in the context of "You do not need to be a rocket scientist in order to figure out…"

ROCK THE BOAT. Cause trouble.
"'Investors don't want to see him rock the boat,' said Michael Holton, who manages a fund for T. Rowe Price Associates Inc. that holds Citigroup shares." (*Wall Street Journal,* Oct. 1, 2003, p. C1)

ROLL BACK (TO). Return prices to a previous lower level after regulatory action by government.

ROLLING STOCK. Wheeled vehicles collectively used on a railroad, including the engines, passenger coaches, and freight wagons.

ROLL-OUT. A full advertising campaign; the sale of corporate assets to investors; ceremony introducing a new aircraft.

ROLLOVER. The movement of money from one investment to another. Employees switching jobs will often rollover their retirement funds from one plan to another, avoiding the problem of creating taxable income.

ROLL-UP. Businesses that buy smaller companies, consolidating the industry.
"Industry consolidators, also known as roll-ups, usually roll along in a bull market, buying up small companies for stock instead of cash." (*Wall Street Journal,* Sept. 17, 2002, p. B7)

ROLODEX. Brand name for a popular business card index file; generic name for a list of contacts.

ROOF OVERHEAD. A building or shelter; basic necessities.

ROOT CAUSE. Primary reason.

RO-RO. Roll-on/roll-off maritime shipping.

ROSY. Very optimistic prediction.

"U.S. central bank should use next week's FOMC meeting to start a new era by foregoing manipulative hype and leveling with the American people about the true state of their economy—no rosy scenarios please." (*Wall Street Journal,* August 8, 2003, p. A8)

ROUND FILE. Waste basket.

ROUND LOT. A hundred shares of stock.

ROUND ROBIN. A discussion including all the people at a table, usually proceeding in a circular pattern with each person getting a turn to speak.

RUBBER CHECK. A check for which there are not sufficient funds, a bounced check.

RUBBER-STAMP (TO). Approve without review.

"No surprise, the so-called '10-day rule'—the Big Board allowed brokers to vote if they didn't hear from the owners 10 days before the annual meeting—has typically functioned as a rubber stamp for management." (*Wall Street Journal,* June 10, 2003, p. A10)

RUBE GOLDBERG. Less-than-professional, especially a repair job. Rube Goldberg was an early twentieth-century cartoonist whose works depicted complex machinery with improbable parts. The machines involved enormous effort that resulted in very little.

"Currently laying planks in a platform due out in a month or two, the group says it is looking to throw a wrench into traditional Polish politics, a Rube Goldberg-like machine that looks complicated but functions quite simply." (*Wall Street Journal,* Feb. 27, 2001, p.1)

RUB ELBOWS WITH. Interact with; work together.

"Prices range from less than $200 a day for Graham Baxter's bring-your-own-bike trips and VeloSport's self-guided tour, to more than $1,000 a day for one of U.S.-based Trek Travel's packages (promising VIP access to the Tour de France Village and the chance to rub elbows with the U.S. Postal Service team, including the current Tour de France champion, Lance Armstrong.)" (*Wall Street Journal,* June 3, 2003, p. D3)

RUG RANKING. Situation in which a secretary's or assistant's career path is tied to the fate of the boss.

RULE OF 72. Financial formula for determining how long it will take for an investment to double in value. Dividing 72 by the interest rate will yield the number of years needed for the sum or principal to double.

RULE OF THUMB. Basis for measuring, deciding.
"General rule of thumb: Don't give a guy potpourri." (*Wall Street Journal,* June 4, 2004, p. W1)

RUN. In banking, a sudden surge in withdrawals. During the Depression, many banks suffered runs and went bankrupt.

RUN A TIGHT SHIP. To be very organized.

RUN BY. Visit; repeat; discuss briefly with an associate or supervisor, usually as a courtesy rather than as a request for their input.

RUN INTERFERENCE FOR. Assist, protect (football).

RUN IT UP THE FLAG POLE AND SEE WHO SALUTES. Introduce a new product or idea and see what happens.

RUN-OF-THE-MILL. Ordinary.

RUN THE SHOW. Be in charge.

RUN UP. Incur.

RUN WITH IT. Implement an idea.

RUST BELT. Manufacturing areas in the Midwest that have lost jobs to competitors in other regions using newer technology.

S

SACK (TO). Fire, dismiss. See also SEND PACKING.

SACRED COW. Something that cannot be questioned or eliminated (Hinduism). Managers sometimes have favorite projects that
become sacred cows even if they are not profitable and have little
chance of becoming so.
 "Directors told her they felt free to challenge him because there
were no sacred cows." (*Wall Street Journal,* June 23, 2003, p. B1)

SAFE HARBOR LEASING. Financial measure to reduce tax
liability.

SAFEKEEPING. Out of danger; to be responsible for.

SAFETY CUSHION. A margin for error, additional resources that
can be utilized in an emergency.

SAFETY NET. Government social welfare programs designed to
assist the poor. The term is derived from the net protecting circus
high-wire performers should they fall.

"Long-term care insurance can provide a valuable safety net for healthy families who are modestly wealthy." (*Wall Street Journal,* August 9, 2004, p. R2)

SAIL THROUGH. Successfully complete or be approved with little or no difficulty. See SMOOTH SAILING.
"Since biotech drugs are often versions of the body's own proteins, the thinking was that they'd sail through safety tests." (*Wall Street Journal,* May 20, 2004, p. A1)

SALARY COMPRESSION. Situation in which new employees are paid more than current employees.

SALES FLOWS. Mutual fund account activity.
"Jargon: sales flow. Translation: account activity" (*Wall Street Journal,* Jan. 4, 1999, p. R8)

SALES PITCH. Sales presentation, sometimes an aggressive presentation.

SALLIE MAE. Nickname for government student loan marketing program, college loans. See also SLMA.

SALMON DAY. The experience of spending an entire day facing obstacles only to fail at the end.

SALT MINE. Work, drudgery.

SALVAGE VALUE. The value of an asset after it has been fully depreciated or no longer useful to the company.

SAMURAI BONDS. Bonds denominated in Japanese yen but issued by non-Japanese firms.

SANDBAG (TO). Mislead; attack from behind; sales representative's practice of not reporting sales in the current year once quota or bonus standards are reached.
"Mr. Ben-Veniste was the party's designated sandbag man on the Senate's Whitewater probe." (*Wall Street Journal,* Dec. 16, 2002, p. A12)

SATELLITE OFFICES. Branch offices.

SATISFICING. Aiming for a predetermined level of profit or sales, rather than profit maximizing.

SATURDAY NIGHT SPECIAL. Sudden attempt to buy a large share of stock in a company; a cheap gun.

SAVE OUR BACON. Save from disaster.

SCAB. A non-union worker; strikebreaker.
"I met him for the first time during a hospital strike, and the man running the consortium of hospitals, which included the Catholic hospitals, had decided to bring in strikebreakers. I heard O'Connor yelling in the corridor: 'Over my dead body will you bring in scabs!'" (*Wall Street Journal,* May 5, 2000, p. W17)

SCALABLE. Easily enlarged or reduced in size or scope.

SCALE. The wages paid for different types of jobs in a company.

SCALP (TO). Sell tickets at prices above their face value.

SCAM (TO). Cheat someone out of something; swindle.

SCAPEGOAT. Person who is blamed for a mistake.

SCARLET LETTER. Symbol of shame. The term comes from Nathaniel Hawthorne's *The Scarlet Letter.*
"Some lawyers think targeted employees may be able to accuse Ford of defamation. 'You are in effect painting them with a scarlet letter "A" for awful,' argues Peter Panken, a New York employment lawyer." (*Wall Street Journal,* July 22, 1998, p. B1)

SCHLEMAZEL. Bad luck; a person who has bad luck (Yiddish).

SCHLEMIEL. An awkward person; a nerd (Yiddish).

SCHLEP. Stupid, awkward person (Yiddish).

SCHLOCK. Inferior merchandise (Yiddish).

SCHMOOZE. Mingle with the crowd at a business function. See also GLAD-HANDING.
"High-profile auto shows have become less like industry excuses to schmooze and drink too much, and more like floating focus groups to test media reaction to the ideas coming to life on industry computer screens. Soon it might be necessary to stop using the word 'overcapacity' to describe the market's basic condition." (*Wall Street Journal,* March 3, 2004, p. A17)

SCHMOOZER. A person who interacts well with people, in the process finding news or opportunities.

SCHMUCK. Obnoxious person (Yiddish).

"Jacob, the SCHLEMIEL, has worked in the kitchen of a restaurant for years. One night the regular waiter is sick and Jacob is given the chance to replace him. Henry, the schmuck, is a rich powerful businessman who comes to the restaurant each night. David, the SCHLEMAZEL, is also at the restaurant on his first date with the girl of his dreams. Henry orders Jacob to bring him fresh soup, and when it is brought, angrily and loudly sends it back as too little. As Jacob, the Schlemiel, turns to return to the kitchen, Henry, the schmuck, sticks out his foot sending Jacob tumbling and the soup flying, landing all over David, the Schlemazel." (Jerry Rosenthal, Zip's Business Services, 1996)

SCOOP. A news story one is the first to report.

SCOPE CREEP. Urge by clients to require additional enhancements to product before acceptance.

SCORCHED-EARTH STRATEGY. Anti-takeover defense of selling off a company's most attractive assets (military).

SCORE CARD. A report comparing the performance of different individuals, departments, or other segments of an organization.

SCORE POINTS/BIG (TO). Impress.

"Ms. Lisa McGurn also is adding amenities to help students score points with recruiters. 'We teach students to dress to impress,' says Ms. McGurn, 'but trudging through the snow here isn't conducive to well-pressed suits.'" (*Wall Street Journal,* Sept. 9, 2002, p. R.10)

S CORP. See SUBCHAPTER S CORPORATION.

SCRAP (TO). Terminate a project.

SCUTTLEBUTT. Rumors, gossip.

"In other stock action, Kmart Holding (Nasdaq) jumped 4.33, or 7%, to 66.33 and Sears, Roebuck rose 2.11, or 5.5%, to 40.41 on industry scuttlebutt that Sears plans to buy some of Kmart's stores." (*Wall Street Journal,* June 9, 2002, p. C4)

SEAGULL MANAGER. A manager who drops in, makes a lot of noise, and then leaves.

SEA OF CHANGE. A period of uncertainty or turbulence in a business or market.

SEASONALLY ADJUSTED. Statistics that are adjusted for seasonal variations. Employment, sales, and other macroeconomic measures are often seasonally adjusted.

SEAT OF THE PANTS ESTIMATE. Based on experience or knowledge, without any research or analysis.

SECONDARY OFFERING. Public sale of shares in a company that was previously privately held.
"The panel found that a company sales book, relating to a planned secondary offering of a publicly traded company included nonpublic information concerning the company's fourth-quarter earnings." (*Wall Street Journal,* Sept. 3, 2003, p. B4A)

SECOND CLASS. Not as good, inferior.

SECONDS. Products with defects.

SECOND-STRING. Not the top-quality people (sports).
"It is one of his most treasured sayings, revealing the notorious Kaufman pessimism, an outlook that led him to keep his second-string drama post at the New York Times well into his illustrious and financially rewarding theater career." (*Wall Street Journal,* Sept. 17, 2004, p. W.1)

SECULAR TREND. Long-term, as opposed to cyclical or seasonal, trend.

SECURITIES AND EXCHANGE COMMISSION (SEC). Federal agency set up after the collapse of the stock market during the Depression. The SEC is responsible for oversight of the securities market.

SEED. Technicians who transfer manufacturing know-how from one department or division to another.
"Ms. Roughgarden is known inside Intel as a 'seed,' an unofficial title for technicians who transfer manufacturing know-how from one Intel chip factory to another." (*Wall Street Journal,* Oct. 28, 2002, p. B1)

SEED MONEY. Initial funds needed to start an enterprise.

SEIGNIORAGE. The profit made by government from the production and issue of coins.

SELF-ADDRESSED STAMPED ENVELOPE (SASE). Preaddressed, postage-included, envelope. When requesting information or submitting work to a publisher, an SASE is often expected.

SELL ONE, MAKE ONE (SOMO). Production management slogan or policy.
"SOMO companies enjoy increased efficiency: no inventory pile-ups, no excess paperwork." (*Across the Board,* Nov./Dec. 1993, p. 42)

SELL SHORT. To underestimate; to sell shares of stock that you do not own, hoping to buy back the shares at a lower price.

SELL SHORT AGAINST THE BOX. In the stock market, to sell borrowed shares while owning the same or similar shares that one delivers later to complete the transaction.
"The most popular is to 'sell short against the box.' To do this, you arrange through a broker to sell borrowed securities (a short sale) while owning essentially identical securities that you deliver later to complete the short sale." (*Wall Street Journal,* Oct. 27, 1995, p. A1)

SEND PACKING. Dismiss, fire from a job.
"Mr. Foley isn't the only Washington state incumbent the voters may send packing." (*Wall Street Journal,* Sept. 23, 1994, p. A14)

SEND TO SIBERIA. Transfer an employee to an insignificant or out-of-the-way division of the company.

SET ASIDES. Portions of government programs that are allocated to minority-owned businesses.

SET UP SHOP. Open for business.
"Far from hush-hush, ACT and TMF set up shop down the hall from the DNC Finance Committee." (*Wall Street Journal,* July 30, 2004, p. A10)

7 BY 24 SCHEDULE. Seven days per week and twenty-four hours per day. An overworked employee's perception of his or her workweek.

SEVEN S MODEL. Seven factors can be used to measure a company's performance: strategy, structure, systems, style, shared values, skills, and staff. The model was developed by Richard Pascale, Tom Peters, and Robert Waterman when they were consultants for McKinsey & Co.

SHADOW STOCK. An artificial stock created by privately held companies, used for performance evaluations and bonuses. Shadow stock prices mimic what the company's shares would have traded for in an open market.

SHAKE AND BAKE. To create and produce a product quickly with little concern for details or quality.

SHAKEDOWN. Pressuring someone for a bribe to ensure things work out correctly. See PROTECTION MONEY.

SHAKE-OUT. Period in which unprofitable businesses leave the market.
"The shift reflects a five-year shake-out in home businesses, which include independent contractors and other self-employed people." (*Wall Street Journal,* July 17, 2004, p. D1)

SHAM. A deceptive business practice or transaction. Sham transactions are used to inflate the value of property or to avoid taxation.

SHANK (TO). To make an ugly mistake (golf).

SHAPE UP OR SHIP OUT. Do the job or leave (command).

SHARE. The percentage of TV watchers (or radio listeners) who are watching (or hearing) a particular show.

SHAREHOLDER VALUE. The net worth of a company divided by the number of shares of stock outstanding.
"This type of POISON PILL destroys shareholder value because it's highly dilutive." (*Wall Street Journal,* Oct. 25, 2004, p. C17)

SHARK. Swindler.

SHARK REPELLENT. Any measure taken by a company to avoid a takeover attempt. See also POISON PILL.

SHELF OFFERING. The offer for sale of securities included in a prospectus but not offered through an underwriter.

SHELF REGISTRATION. A Securities and Exchange Commission rule that allows companies to register plans to issue stock up to two years in advance.

SHELL CORPORATION. An incorporated business with no major assets or business activities. Shell corporations are created to facilitate financing of new business ventures or as a means to hide business activities.

SHELL OUT (TO). To pay a large sum of money.

SHELTER FROM THE ELEMENTS (TO). Protect from the weather or adversity.

SHIFT DIFFERENTIAL. Added pay for working less desirable hours.

SHINDIG. Big party. See also BASH.

SHOESTRING (ON A). Small budget.

SHOOT FOR. Attempt, set as a goal.
"Jaguar and Ford luxury-group executives said in interviews this week that Jaguar will continue to shoot for its previously stated target of 200,000 annual vehicle sales, but will slow down the brand's growth rate in the short term." (*Wall Street Journal,* Sept. 26, 2002, p. D2)

SHOOT IN THE FOOT. To make a costly mistake.

SHOOT THE BREEZE. Talk casually.

SHOOT THE BULL. Exaggerate; engage in casual conversation.
"The innovative course is seen by some as a 'neat shoot-the-bull session' which cheats the kids, and by others as a remedy for teens who haven't been exposed to healthy relationships at home." (*Wall Street Journal,* Nov. 9, 1994, p. B1)

SHOP FLOOR EMPLOYEES. Lower level employees.

SHOP TALK. Discussion of the latest business news or rumors.
"At one Scott facility he clambered over machines, discussed their workings with the factory crew and easily slipped into shop talk." (*Wall Street Journal,* June 27, 1994, p. B3)

SHORT (TO). Sell stock not owned by the seller, based on the assumption that the stock's price will decline.

"Short selling is a trading technique that produces profits when a company's stock price falls. Shorting a stock, like the opposite practice of promoting it, can be perfectly legal—depending on how it is done." (*Wall Street Journal,* Nov. 1, 2004, p. C.3)

SHORT AGAINST THE BOX. The short sale of a stock owned by the seller, who does not want to close out his or her position.

SHORT INTEREST. The number of borrowed shares that have not been purchased for return to the lender.

SHORT SHRIFT. Ignored; lacking respect.

"Key among the changes was fairer treatment for private enterprises that increasingly underpin growth but often get short shrift from an officialdom and state-banking sector that favor state firms." (*Wall Street Journal,* Oct. 15, 2003, p. A19)

SHORT SQUEEZE. Situation where prices of a stock rise sharply, forcing traders who have SHORTED the stock to buy the stock in order to cover their position, in the process pushing the price of the stock even higher.

SHORT-TERM DISABILITY (STD). Temporarily not able to work.

"I once met an employee who proudly announced to me that she had STD. I beat a retreat, unsure of what sexually transmitted disease she had. Later, I discovered she meant short-term disability." (*Wall Street Journal,* August 1, 1994, p. A14)

SHOT/SHOOT ACROSS THE BOW. A warning, to warn.

"The Chamber's Mr. Bokat said the mutual-fund governance lawsuit is a 'shot across the bow,' signaling to the SEC that the Chamber will challenge the proxy rule if it's adopted." (*Wall Street Journal,* Oct. 27, 2004, p. C.1)

SHOTGUN APPROACH. A marketing campaign without a specific target audience or goal.

"It is critical to target a specific area and not do a shotgun approach to all." (*Summit,* Feb. 2004, p. 11)

SHOT IN THE ARM. Something that helps the company or stimulates action.

SHOUTING MATCH. Loud, noisy argument.

SHOW ME THE MONEY. An exclamation from the film *Jerry Maguire* meaning prove you can deliver on your promise. The phrase has become common in business negotiations.

SHOW STOPPER. An event or situation that captures everyone's attention.

SHOW THE DOOR. Get someone to leave; to dismiss someone.
    "We show them the door. It is the P rule—if performance comes up three times in the first interview, we aren't meant for each other." (*Wall Street Journal,* August 19, 1999, p. C1)

SHRINK. Losses due to shoplifting.

SHYLOCK. Moneylender, especially one who charges exorbitant interest rates (Shylock is a character in Shakespeare's *Merchant of Venice*). See also POUND OF FLESH.

SHYSTER. An unethical business person who attempts to cheat or deceive others.

SICKOUT. When workers by prearrangement CALL IN SICK (a form of union protest).

SIDEBAR. A courtroom discussion among the attorneys and the judge that the jury does not hear; a short news story related to the major story.

SIDE BET. A secondary impact or risk taken when making a business decision.

SIDECAR. New York Stock Exchange CIRCUIT-BREAKER that restricts trading when the S&P 500* index falls 12 points in one day.

SIDE EFFECT. Additional impact or consequence of an action.

SIFING. Abbreviation for structuring information felicitously. To structure information in a way to maximize personal advantage.
    "One breed of businessperson that is particularly skillful in the art of sifing is the management consultant." (*BusinessToday,* Fall 1999, p. 50)

SIGNATURE LOAN. An unsecured loan; a loan not backed by collateral.

SILENT PARTNER. An investor or partner in a business who is not actively involved in the day-to-day management of the business.

SILICON VALLEY. Santa Clara Valley, California, center of the U.S. computer industry.

SIMPLIFIED EMPLOYEE PENSION (SEP) PLAN. Retirement plan to which both the employee and employer can contribute.

SINGLE-DIGIT MIDGET. A company with a stock price below 10 dollars.

"The upshot is that investors are 'shooting the wounded,' dumping their holdings in former high fliers, including eToys and CDnow, and turning them into 'single-digit midgets,' Silicon Valley parlance for companies with droopy share prices." ("Dot-Coms Over a Barrel," *Newsweek,* April 3, 2000)

SINKING FUND. Funds set aside to pay off a bond or preferred stock. Many companies create sinking funds, managed by a custodian, as a means to increase investor confidence and reduce the cost of borrowing.

SINKING INTO THE SUNSET. Slowly disappearing. Products, like records and cassettes, that have reached the maturity stage of the product life-cycle slowly sink into the sunset.

SINK ONE'S TEETH IN TO. Become involved in.

SIN TAX. Taxes on cigarettes and alcohol. The Clinton administration wanted to pay for expanded healthcare coverage through increases in sin taxes.

SIPHON OFF (TO). Remove or steal (usually refers to money).

"Mr. Lohmann says he is seeing support from European clients, though some competitors have already said they are in the blocks to siphon off business from the ailing reinsurer." (*Wall Street Journal,* Sept. 15, 2004, p. A1)

SIT ON ONE'S WALLET. Refuse to purchase or spend.

SIT TIGHT. A directive suggesting that the person be patient.

SITTING DUCK. Defenseless target.

"From the window of his office a few miles from downtown Las Vegas, Mr. Higgins can see the skyline of the Strip, the row of casinos that powers the Nevada economy. 'It's unthinkable that the Strip would ever go dark,' Mr. Higgins said. Still, he added, 'Nevada was a sitting duck.'" (*Wall Street Journal,* Nov. 4, 2002, p. A1)

SITUATION NORMAL, ALL FOULED UP (SNAFU). Half-serious, half-humorous employee comment implying inept management.

SIX OF ONE, HALF A DOZEN OF ANOTHER. It is the same either way; indifference.

SIX SIGMA. A quality management program pioneered by Motorola in the mid-1980s and popularized by General Electric, Microsoft, Honeywell, and others in the 1990s. In statistics, six sigma refers to six standard deviations from quality perfection, or, in practical application, 3.4 defects per million.

SKELETON CREW. A small number of employees left to manage affairs at night or after a company has moved or gone out of business.

SKELETONS IN THE CLOSET. Problems that others are not aware of.

SKIMMING. Pricing policy where a firm initially charges a high price but later gradually lowers the price to increase sales.

SKINNY. The latest information; the truth.

SKULL SESSION. An intense briefing or discussion among members of a business team.

SKY-HIGH. Extremely lofty.

SKYROCKETING. Increasing rapidly.

"The wave of construction fueled skyrocketing investment in making steel, glass, aluminum and cement." (*Wall Street Journal,* Oct. 26, 2004, p. A20)

SKY'S THE LIMIT. Anything you want, there is no limit.

SLAM-DUNK. Something that is easily accomplished (basketball).

"Mr. Ayyagari believes chances are good that the technology will gain acceptance in the market. 'It isn't a slam dunk for power-line connection, but there are a lot of positives for it,' he said." (*Wall Street Journal,* July 24, 2004, p. D7)

SLAP IN THE FACE. An insult.

SLEEPING BEAUTY/SLEEPER/SLEEPING GIANT. A company with many attractive assets but not well known to investors.

SLIPSTREAM (TO). Include something, hoping no one will notice.

SLOWDOWN. A decrease in activity or growth.

SLUSH FUND. Money available to use without review. During the Nixon administration, the Committee to Re-Elect the President was accused of keeping slush funds for campaign efforts, including Watergate.

SMALL BUSINESS ADMINISTRATION (SBA). Government agency that provides information and credit to small businesses in the United States. The SBA has been criticized as a welfare program for corporate America.

SMALL CAP. In the U.S. financial market, small cap companies or mutual funds include those with less than $500 million in value.

SMALL FRY. Unimportant.

SMALL POTATOES. Small amount.
   "Meanwhile, Microsoft's PC-games division will introduce 15 new games and increase its advertising budget for the North American market to as much as $25 million this year from about $20 million last year—small potatoes compared with its Xbox campaign but a boost nonetheless." (*Wall Street Journal,* April 19, 2002, p. A13)

SMART CARD. Similar to a credit card, a smart card contains a microchip with data stored on it. Often, the cards store electronic cash credit. Smart cards are widely used in Europe to pay for telephone calls, vending machine purchases, public transportation, and other services.

SMART MONEY. Informed prediction.

SMIDGE. A very small portion or amount.

SMOKE AND MIRRORS. Deception, illusion.

SMOKING GUN. Evidence of a problem.

"Mr. Hill: There's no smoking gun, no e-mail or memo to support what I'm going to tell you." (*Wall Street Journal,* Jan. 13, 2004, p. C1)

SMOOTH SAILING. Without problems or restrictions.

SNAIL MAIL. U.S. Postal Service mail; any interoffice mail distribution system using paper mailings.

SNAKE-CHECK. Review a plan for hidden consequences.

SNAKE OIL. A product that is represented to do more than it actually will; a misrepresentation.

SNAP UP. To quickly buy when an opportunity arises.

SNEAKERIZATION. The proliferation of choices available for a product or service.

"'I think there will be many choices in the future for the consumer,' he said. 'We call it the 'sneakerization' of the auto industry.... It used to be you had Ked's or Converse or Jack Percell's. Now you have so many choices of tennis shoes it's tough to make a decision.'" ("The drive for change; alternative fuel cars," *Sacramento Business Journal,* Sept. 14, 2001)

SNIPING. Auction technique whereby buyers wait until the last minute to enter their bid.

"Even with all the interest by researchers, some of the questions posed by e-commerce sites remain unresolved. One of them involves the usefulness of 'sniping,' which occurs when a prospective buyer in an auction doesn't get involved in the bidding until the last minute, and then makes an offer the others don't have time to top." (*Wall Street Journal,* Oct. 11, 2004, p. B1)

SNOWBALL (TO). Increase rapidly, get out of control.

"It's snowballing—we're seeing more and more companies reporting their earnings in numerous different ways, and analysts are going along with it." (*Wall Street Journal,* August 24, 1999, p. B1)

SNOW JOB. Persistent persuasion; deception.

SOCCER MOM. A stay-at-home mother of small children.

SOFT CURRENCY. A currency that is not readily accepted for payment in international trade.

SOFT LANDING. An economic slowdown without going into a recession.

SOFT MONEY. Campaign contributions that can be used for a variety of purposes by the political party.

SOIL BANK. Department of Agriculture program that pays farmers not to use part of their land, conserving these resources.

SOMETHING IS ROTTEN IN THE STATE OF DENMARK. Corrupt; not like it should be. The phrase is from *Hamlet* by William Shakespeare.

SONG AND DANCE ROUTINE. Lively sales presentation meant to be entertaining as well as informative.

SORRY. Ineffective; incompetent (Southern).

SOS. International distress signal; abbreviation for "same old shit."

SO-SO. Not very good; barely OK.

SOUND BITE. A short statement quoted in the media.

SOUNDING BOARD. A person or group that provides feedback for ideas.

SOUP-TO-NUTS. Everything.
   "Schwab will pitch itself as a soup-to-nuts provider. At a time when employers are clamoring for more investment options, Schwab will dazzle them with a choice of more than 1,300 funds at 185 fund companies." (*Wall Street Journal,* April 3, 1996, p. C1)

SPAMMING. Usually referring to unsolicited mass marketing via e-mail, but can refer to various forms of harassment inflicted on computer users.
   "Users are going to scream bloody murder" if the pace of spamming picks up, says Alan Mosher, director of research at Probe Group LLC, a Cedar Knolls, N.J., telecom-focused research firm." (*Wall Street Journal,* May, 18, 2004, p. A3)

SPEARHEAD (TO). To lead an effort.

SPECIAL DRAWING RIGHTS (SDRs). International money first created by the INTERNATIONAL MONETARY FUND in the late 1960s. SDRs are considered part of a country's official reserve assets and can be transferred between the country's accounts.

SPIDER. Internet automated search robots.

"Bargain Network deploys automated search robots—known as bots, crawlers, spiders, or scrapers—to hundreds of online retailers and auctioneers." (*Wall Street Journal,* Sept. 16, 2002, p. R13)

SPIFF. A sales commission, often paid by the manufacturer.

SPIM. Instant-messaging SPAM.

"It may be even more annoying than e-mail spam: It's 'spim,' or instant messaging spam." (*Wall Street Journal,* Dec. 3, 2003, p. C5)

SPIN. Sales technique; implication.

SPIN-DOCTORING. See DOCTORING.

SPINNING. A now-illegal practice of directing shares of an initial public offering to insiders.

"H&Q and several other securities firms are under investigation by the Securities and Exchange Commission for 'spinning'—the practice of giving out shares to favored or potential clients in hopes of winning future business. (*Wall Street Journal,* Feb. 8, 1999, p. C1)

SPIN-OFF. A separate product or business created from an existing one.

SPLIT-DOLLAR COMPENSATION. An executive compensation deal where the company pays almost all the premium on a policy that goes into a tax-sheltered annuity. The executive can then borrow from the account without paying interest.

"So-called split-dollar life-insurance policies have become a prime tool to provide tax-free pay and loans to top executives, and, in the process, mask from shareholders the value of large amounts of executive compensation, whether intentionally or not." (*Wall Street Journal,* Dec. 30, 2002, p. C1)

SPLIT RUN. When a marketer places one ad in one segment of a magazine's distribution and another ad in another segment.

SPOILATION. A legal term referring to the destruction, loss, or alteration of evidence.

SPOOFING. A deceptive practice of placing and canceling stock quotes in order to create movement in the price of a stock.

SPOT MARKET. The open market for petroleum or other commodities.

SPREAD. The difference between two prices: in the stock market, the difference between the bid and ask price; in bond markets, the difference between the yield for two securities of different maturities or quality.

SPRINGBOARD. A starting point for change.

SPRING FOR (TO). Pay for.

SPYDER. S&P 500 tracking stock.
"If an investor wants to participate in the performance of the S&P 500 she could buy shares in all 500 of the stocks held in it. Besides a large capital investment this strategy would also incur high commissions. There is a security which tracks the performance of the S&P 500. Its nickname is the Spyders based on its ticker symbol, SPY." ("Wall Street Jargon," about.com Web site, Dec. 12, 2002)

SPYWARE. Software that monitors computing activities, such as Web-surfing and site-surfer patterns, and transmits the information to others. Spyware is sometimes used without the knowledge or authorization of the computer user.
"Some spyware programs reset browser home pages, while others redirect search requests." (*Wall Street Journal,* April 26, 2004, p. R6)

SQUARE ONE. The beginning.

SQUARE PEG IN A ROUND HOLE. Someone or something that does not fit well into the plan or organization.

SQUEAKY-CLEAN. Immaculate; honest.

SQUEEZE OUT. Pressure to eliminate or reduce.

STACK THE DECK/CARDS. Dishonestly prearrange something.

STAGFLATION. A situation in which an economy is experiencing both a lack of economic growth (stagnancy) and inflation.
"One of the dirtiest words in the economic lexicon is making the rounds again: stagflation. Defined as a noxious blend of stagnant growth and rising prices, stagflation last appeared in force in the 1970s." (*Wall Street Journal,* August 16, 2004, p. A2)

STAKE. A financial interest, investment.

STAKE A PLACE (TO). Win the honor of being included.

STAKEHOLDER. Employees, investors, managers, and community members who are affected by the actions of a company.

STALEMATE. A situation in which both parties cannot agree.

STAND ALONE. Act independently.

STANDARD & POOR'S (S&P). One of the two (with Moody's) major investment information and rating services in the United States.

STANDING ROOM ONLY (SRO). Sales technique where buyers are given the impression that there are many other customers waiting in line to purchase the product.

STANDOFF. A situation in which both sides to a negotiation refuse to change their position.

STAR STATUS. Celebrity status.

START UP (TO). To begin.

STARVE-THE-BEAST. To cut taxes with the intent of using the ensuing budget deficits as an excuse to drastically reduce the size and number of services offered by a government.
   "The starve-the-beast doctrine is now firmly within the conservative mainstream. George W. Bush himself seemed to endorse the doctrine as the budget surplus evaporated: in August 2001 he called the disappearing surplus 'incredibly positive.'" ("The Tax-Cut Con," *New York Times,* Sept. 14, 2003)

STAR WARS. Nickname (from the movie of the same name) for the Strategic Defense Initiative, a Defense Department program designed to use satellites with lasers to protect the U.S. from attack. President Ronald Reagan embraced the Star Wars program, spending billions of dollars on it. It is still in the "development" stage.

STATEMENT SHOCK. Consumers' reactions to a huge credit card bill; investors' reaction to declines in the value of their investment portfolio.
   "'Statement shock' afflicts many credit-card users in January after a merry month of charging. So Citibank offers consumers a Credit

Minder record-keeping system, similar to a checkbook's register, to track total spending." (*Wall Street Journal,* Dec. 5, 1996, p. A1)

STATE-OF-THE-ART. Modern, the latest technology.

STATISTICAL MASSAGE. Manipulation of the numbers to show what one wants. See also FORCE THE NUMBERS.

STATISTICAL PROCESS CONTROL (SPC). A variety of statistical measurement techniques to control work processes.

STATS. Statutes (law); statistics (business).

STEALTH MARKETING. Strategy designed to target market customer groups without competitors knowing what one is doing.

STEM THE TIDE. Slow or stop a negative trend.

STEP UP TO THE PLATE. Take responsibility for (baseball).

STICK ONE'S NECK OUT. To take a risk.

STICKER PRICE. List price, full retail price. See also MANUFACTURER'S SUGGESTED RETAIL PRICE.

STICKER SHOCK. Consumer reaction to prices higher than expected.

STICKINESS, STICKY SITE. The ability of a Web site to command attention and keep a viewer at that site.
    "If these companies can bring 'stickiness' to their corner of the Web, their purchases may some day be seen as bargains." (*Wall Street Journal,* Feb. 11, 1999, p. B1)

STICKING POINT. An issue or detail that is preventing negotiations from being finalized.

STIFF. Swindle; refuse to pay; cheap person.

STIRRING THE POT. Mixing things up; causing trouble.

STOCK JOCKEY. Investment analyst, often with little experience. The proliferation of stock market chat rooms on the Internet has increased the visibility of stock jockeys.

STOCK KEEPING UNIT (SKU). Inventory control code.

STOCKLIFTING. Marketing strategy in which a firm buys all the inventory of a competitor's products from a retailer as part of an agreement to get the retailer to carry its products.

STOCK-OUT. When a particular item is not available.

STOCK PARKING. Illegal stock market practice used to hide the identity of the purchaser. During a hostile takeover, the buyer will sometimes not want the target company to know what is happening. Stock parking conceals the actions of the takeover company.

STONEWALL (TO). Refuse to cooperate.
"Because of the legal obligations under Delaware law, it is harder—though clearly not impossible—for companies and their managements to stonewall a hostile bidder." (*Wall Street Journal,* Nov. 8, 1995, p. C1)

STORK PARKING. Reserved parking spaces for expectant mothers.

STORM BACK (TO). Recover, return to the contest.

STRADDLE. Simultaneously sell puts and buy calls in a stock at the same STRIKE PRICE.

STRAIGHT UP. A drink without ice; honest.

STRAIGHT YEARS. Years in a row.

STRANGLE. Simultaneously sell call options or buy put options in a stock at different STRIKE PRICES equally OUT OF THE MONEY.

STRATEGIC ALLIANCE. Usually a temporary partnership between two or more independent companies to achieve mutually beneficial goals.
"Earlier this week, the two companies announced a strategic alliance; as part of the deal, Conoco received a 17.5% interest in the Iraqi venture, making it the first U.S. company with a claim on Iraq's vast oil and natural-gas resources." (*Wall Street Journal,* Oct. 1, 2004, p. A6)

STRAW BOSS. Worker with added responsibilities but without additional compensation or authority.

STRAW MAN. Initial proposal created to elicit responses and changes.

"Using a straw man, the group has something to critique and change as opposed to having a meeting and just asking what should we do." (Mary Grace Allenchey, AT&T, 1996)

STRAW THAT BROKE THE CAMEL'S BACK. Issue or problem that destroys one's patience.

"Ronald Kahn, managing director of the private placement group at Lincoln Partners, says competition from funds sponsored by banks, insurers as well as a handful of existing public funds is already making it difficult for some traditional funds to find attractive deals; the latest crop of public funds could prove to be 'the straw that broke the camel's back.'" (*Wall Street Journal,* May 26, 2004, p. B4G)

STREAMING. Term for putting a stream of bits on the Internet for an audio or video connection.

STREAMLINE (TO). Reduce or cut back.

STREET (THE). Wall Street.

STREET NAME. Securities held in the name of the brokerage house rather than the customer.

STREET SMARTS. Practical experience; a person with street smarts is not easily deceived.

"Bratz dolls are an inch shorter than Barbie, so the rivals can't share their wardrobes. Their name alone symbolizes an irreverent, street-smart attitude that Barbie never possessed." (*Wall Street Journal,* Nov. 29, 2002, p. A11)

STREET SWEEP (TO). To secretly acquire enough shares of stock in a company before making an offer to all shareholders.

"The most effective deterrent to the street sweep is obviously the [poison] pill." (*Wall Street Journal,* Dec. 21, 1999, p. C1)

STRENGTHS, WEAKNESSES, OPPORTUNITIES, AND THREATS (SWOT). Market analysis technique comparing a firm to its competitors.

STRESS PUPPY. Coworker who seems to thrive on being stressed out and whiney.

STRETCH OUT PAYABLES. Pay over a longer period of time.

STRIKE A DEAL. Reach an agreement.

STRIKE OUT. Fail (baseball); initiate a new activity or enterprise.
"'You don't know what is going to stick, and what's not going to stick. The smart companies are able to hit a home run more often than they strike out,' says Joseph Jaffe, founder and president of Jaffe LLC, a Westport, Conn., new-media consultancy." (*Wall Street Journal,* April 15, 2004, p. B3)

STRIKE PRICE. The price at which the stock or commodity underlying a call or put option may be purchased or sold until the option expires.

STRING ALONG. Deceive, to be not fully honest with someone.
"The Bosnian Serbs' prevarication over the peace plan seems to be another attempt to string along negotiations and to sow division between Russia and the West until the Serbs get what they want." (*Wall Street Journal,* July 21, 1994, p. A10)

STRIP (TO). Separate a bond's principal from its interest payments.

STRIP-AND-SELL. Sell off assets.

STRIP MALL. Small shopping mall designed to be convenient to suburban consumers.

STRIPPED-DOWN. Basic model. A product without added features. See also BARE-BONES.
"Mr. Reddy's project, dubbed PCtvt, hopes to deliver systems next year priced at about $250, using low-cost chips from Intel and AMD, stripped-down versions of the Linux operating system or Microsoft Corp.'s Windows, and subsidies from monthly subscription fees." (*Wall Street Journal,* Sept. 2, 2002, p. B4)

STRONG-ARM. To pressure into agreement.

STRONGHOLD. Powerful area.

STRUCTURAL UNEMPLOYMENT. Unemployment due to changes in technology that eliminate the need for some people's skills.

STUDENT LOAN MARKETING ASSOCIATION (SLMA), SALLIE MAE. Federally created stock-held corporation designed to increase the availability of loans for college students. Sallie Mae purchases loans from financial institutions lending to students.

"The company, known as Sallie Mae, said the transition is now expected to occur in 2006, two years before the Sept. 30, 2008, deadline set in the 1996 Student Loan Marketing Association." (*Wall Street Journal*, Jan. 25, 2002, p. A17)

STUMBLING BLOCK. An issue that is preventing completion of an agreement.

STYLIN' DUDS. Nice clothes.

SUBCHAPTER S CORPORATION. Special provisions in the INTERNAL REVENUE SERVICE Code allowing a corporation under certain conditions to be taxed as if it were a partnership, thereby avoiding corporate taxation.

SUBMARINE (TO). To undermine or take attention away from.

"At the same time, companies are submarining in their releases plain-vanilla results, especially if those earnings look worse." (*Wall Street Journal*, August 24, 1999, p. C1)

SUB PAR. Substandard.

SUB-PRIME. High risk. PRIME refers to the prime rate, the interest rate charged to top-quality companies for short-term loans. Sub-prime customers and loans to sub-prime customers are higher risk loans.

"Were it not for the courageous decision by Comptroller of the Currency John Hawke to exempt nationally chartered banks from these state laws, sub-prime mortgage lending might well dry up." (*Wall Street Journal*, Feb. 10, 2004, p. A16)

SUGGING. Sales technique disguised as market research.

SUITOR. Person or company attempting to acquire another company.

SUNBELT. Warmer areas in the United States.

SUNK COST. A cost incurred in the past that should not influence current decisions.

SUNLIGHTING. Doing paid work while taking time away from one's day job.

"Allowing an employee to reconfigure her day can lead to free agency. First, she takes work home and leaves early on certain afternoons. Then she arranges to telecommute three days per week. Then, while she's telecommuting, she begins moonlighting—or 'sunlighting' if she's working on side gigs during the day." (*Free Agent Nation,* 2001)

SUNSET PROVISIONS. Terms written into laws that cause the law to expire unless reinstated by the issuing legislature.

SUNSHINE LAWS. Laws providing for open government. Under sunshine laws, most government proceedings cannot be held in secret.

SUPER. Supervisor.

SUPER BOWL INDICATOR. Stock market phenomenon that if the team from the National Football League wins the Super Bowl, the stock market moves higher.

SUPERMARKET. Mutual fund industry term for selling another firm's mutual funds. Investors can browse and choose among many funds.

SUPER 301. U.S. trade law that identifies countries violating trade agreements and requires sanctions against them unless corrective action is taken.

SUPPLY CHAIN MANAGEMENT. Coordination or control of the distribution system.

SUPPORT LEVEL. Price at which investors come back into the market and buy a stock.

SURE THING. Yes; a certainty.

SURFING THE NET. Exploring the Internet.

SURVIVAL OF THE FITTEST. The strongest competitor will survive. See also ECONOMIC DARWINISM.

SUSTAINABLE DEVELOPMENT. Economic development based on the principles of conservation and use of renewable rather than nonrenewable resources.

SWEAT BULLETS (TO). Be very worried; to work very hard.

SWEAT EQUITY. The time and effort that goes into early stages of a project without compensation.

SWEATSHOP. Low-wage, unhealthy factory, often hiring illegal aliens.

SWEETEN THE DEAL. Increase the offer; make a more attractive offer.
"You had better be prepared to be better next year, and the next year after that; to continually sweeten the deal. Today's consumers expect it." (*Wall Street Journal,* Feb. 12, 1996, p. A14)

SWEETENER. Special bonuses to make an investment more attractive. See also KICKER.

SWEETHEART CONTRACT. A labor contract that favors the employer.

SWEETHEART DEAL. A mutually profitable but illegal arrangement, usually between a business and a government agency.

SWEET SPOT. An ideal situation or event (golf and baseball).

SWIMMING WITH THE SHARKS. Doing business with ruthless or unethical business people.

SWING FOR THE FENCES. To take risks (baseball).
"The Post's attempted scoop illustrates the paper's tendency to swing for the fences under the leadership of Mr. Allan, who came from Australia as editor in 2001." (*Wall Street Journal,* July 7, 2004, p. B1)

SWIPE (TO). Run a credit card through a scanner; steal.

SWIPEOUT. The condition of an ATM or credit card that no longer works because the magnetic strip is worn out.

SWIVEL-CHAIR NETWORK. A computer network requiring multiple terminals or workstations to monitor it.
"A visitor using a corporate Web site may think it's a single, streamlined system, but behind the scenes, people are often manually taking information from one application and entering it into another. Such swivel chair networks, as they have come to be

known, are inefficient, slow, and mistake ridden." ("Your Next IT Strategy," *Harvard Business Review,* Oct. 2001)

SYNERGY. Mutually beneficial interaction, as between components of companies.

"'I thought I'd visit somebody at [Disney-owned] ABC and they'd say, "Of course, your artist can have a special!"' Mr. Goodman recalls. 'But synergy is a two-way street. You still have to bring your partner something they perceive as valuable.'" (*Wall Street Journal,* Oct. 15, 2004, p. B1)

SYNTHETIC LEASE. A financial arrangement allowing a company to get the tax benefits of owning real estate while keeping the debt associated with the real estate off the company's balance sheet.

"Although some companies are pulling out of controversial so-called synthetic leases, many are waiting until the Financial Accounting Standards Board issues a final ruling on the transactions." (*Wall Street Journal,* Oct. 2, 2002, p. B8)

T

TAB. The bill or check, especially for drinks at a bar.

"Congress isn't likely to suspend the law that links Medicare Part B premiums for doctors' care to the program's costs, even though that would make older voters happy. (Medicare beneficiaries, who face a 17% premium increase next year, pay a quarter of the tab.)" (*Wall Street Journal,* Sept. 16, 2004, p. A2)

TAFT-HARTLEY ACT. 1947 law that amended the Wagner Act (1935), protecting the rights of workers to join unions and allowing government injunctions to stop strikes in times of national emergencies.

TAG. Price tag; label; to assign.

TAG LINE. Last few words of a commercial, designed to enhance listener recall.

"As commonplace as branding is today, P&G's brand-focused ads were revolutionary in their era. 'Ivory' and catchy tag lines (such as the '99-44/100% pure' that is still with us) were emblazoned all over the printed ad page, while the Procter & Gamble name itself was displayed discreetly." (*Wall Street Journal,* July 23, 2004, p. W12)

TAIL OFF (TO). Decline.

TAILOR-MADE. Specially designed.

TAILSPIN. A steep decline.

TAKE. Revenue from an event; one's position or understanding of a situation.

TAKE A BATH. Suffer a financial loss. See also TAKE A BEATING.

TAKE A BEATING. Lose; get a bad deal; be crushed.
"For those whose wireless devices could take a beating, Panasonic Computer Solutions Company has introduced the Toughbook CF-Y2, a slim, light notebook computer that offers Intel's latest state-of-the-art mobile technology." (*National Underwriter P&C,* Sept. 13, 2004, p. 31)

TAKE ADVANTAGE OF. Avail oneself of an opportunity, sometimes at the expense of others.

TAKE A FLIER. Make a speculative investment in.

TAKE A HARD LOOK IN THE MIRROR. An examination of current business practices, especially for ethical issues.

TAKE A HIT. Suffer a loss.

TAKE A PASS. Decide against.

TAKE A POSITION. Make an investment in.

TAKE A POWDER. Leave. It is considered crude and unprofessional slang.

TAKE BY STORM. Overwhelm the competition.

TAKE CARE OF BUSINESS. Deal with what needs to be done.

TAKE DOWN A PEG. Deflate or lower someone.

TAKE FIVE. Take a break (may or may not mean a five-minute break).

TAKE FOR A RIDE. Swindle or cheat.

TAKE-HOME PAY. Worker's income after all deductions are taken out.

TAKE IT ON THE CHIN. Be defeated, lose a large amount of money (boxing).

TAKE NO PRISONERS. Management exhortation to be highly competitive.

"In Israel, where the socialist ethos runs deeper than in today's communist China, Mr. Netanyahu says his policies amount to Thatcherism 'with a vengeance': hacking government jobs, curtailing subsidies, cutting taxes and taking no prisoners in confrontations with unions." (*Wall Street Journal*, August 18, 2004, p. A9)

TAKE OFF. To rise quickly.

TAKE ON PARTNERS. Add more owners to a business.

"Drug makers are beginning to look beyond their own labs and take on partners such as biotech mavericks, smaller drug companies and academic researchers." (*Business Week*, Oct. 17, 1994, p. 204)

TAKEOVER. Buying control of another company.

TAKEOVER TARGET. A business investors want to buy.

TAKE THE KNOCK. Sell at a loss.

TAKE THE PACKAGE. Agree to severance benefits being offered by a company.

TALKING HEADS. A derisive advertising term for commercials that consist of a pitch man or woman extolling the virtues of a product.

"When the TV talking heads throw around technical jargon, you don't understand what they're saying. But you're pretty sure it's garbage." (*Wall Street Journal*, July 11, 2004, p. 3)

TALK OUT OF TURN. Speak too candidly.

TALK THE TALK. To be able to speak using the jargon and terminology specific to that industry or situation.

TALK TURKEY. Speak seriously.

"Little Pluto wants to talk turkey about the dangers of plutonium exposure." (*Wall Street Journal,* Jan. 21, 1994, p. B1)

TANK. To fail.

TANK FARM. Collection of oil tanks.

TAP (TO). Access or use as a resource.

TAPE. Ticker tape. Before computers, stock market investors and specialists would watch the tape for the latest prices of stocks.

TAPPED OUT. Broke, penniless, empty; lacking opportunity.
    "Lucent says the trust for management retirees' health care is tapped out." (*Wall Street Journal,* March 29, 2004, p. A1)

TAX BRACKET. The marginal tax rate that applies at each level of income.

TAX BREAK. Any government regulation that reduces the tax burden of specific groups or companies.

TAX HAVEN. Country where individuals are protected from tax scrutiny. The Cayman Islands are known as a tax haven.

TAX HOLIDAY. A period during which a firm is exempt from taxes. Cities and states in the United States will offer a variety of incentives, including tax holidays, as a way to attract new businesses.

TAX IDENTIFICATION NUMBER (TIN). Internal Revenue Service identification number.

TAX SELLING. Selling securities, usually near the end of a year, in order to reduce tax liability.

TAX SHELTER. An investment or expenditure that reduces personal or business taxable income.

TAX-SHELTERED ANNUITY (TSA). Insurance product that allows an investor to avoid or reduce tax liabilities. Taxes are usually deferred until the end of a specified period of time.

T-BILLS. Treasury bills, short-term borrowing instruments of the U.S. government.

TEACHERS INSURANCE AND ANNUITY ASSOCIATION (TIAA). Pension fund for teachers in the United States. In the 1990s, TIAA, like CALPERS*, became an important force in U.S. markets, using its financial power to influence corporate and government policy.

TEAM PLAYER. Someone who works for the betterment of the group (sports). Team players do not ROCK THE BOAT, rarely disagreeing with supervisors.

"The veteran executive, though he had famously pioneered the introduction of the DVD, was regarded as not acting like a team player. (Mr. Lieberfarb says he was a team player for his entire 20-plus year career at Warner Bros., as demonstrated by the strong growth of the studio's home-video division over that time.)" (*Wall Street Journal,* Dec. 11, 2003, p. B1)

TEASER. A low introductory rate on a loan, or a high initial rate on a deposit.

TECHNICAL ANALYSIS. Financial market analysis that focuses on statistical patterns and ignores fundamentals associated with a company.

TECHNOMICS. Economical technology; cheap, accessible technology.

TECHNO-SHIFT IDIOCY. Constant upgrades of technology requiring continuous retraining in order to be able to use the equipment.

TEENIES. Stock market term for sixteenths of a dollar.

TEETERING ON THE BRINK. Almost failing.

"Germany and Japan, according to first-quarter GDP numbers made public last week, are teetering on the brink of recession." (*Wall Street Journal,* May 20, 2003, p. A19)

TEE UP. To initiate (golf).

TELECOMMUTE. Work at home using the Internet and other telecommunication technology.

TELESCOPING. A reduction in the number of shares outstanding by a company in order to raise the price per share. Also called a reverse split.

TELL IT LIKE IT IS. Speak candidly.

TEMPS. Temporary workers.
   "Companies often expand hours and hire temps before gaining the confidence to add to permanent payrolls." (*Wall Street Journal,* Oct. 6, 2003, p. A3)

TEMPUS FUGIT. Time flies (Latin).

TENDER. Sell shares of stock to a buyer.

TENDER FORM. Bid form used for buying U.S. Treasury securities.

TENDER LOVING CARE (TLC). Careful handling.

TENDER OFFER. An offer to buy up shares of a company in order to gain control of the company.

1040. Individual tax return form used by the Internal Revenue Service.

10–K. Annual financial report required for all large, publicly held companies.

1099. Internal Revenue Service form used to report dividend and interest income.

TEN-SPOT. A ten-dollar bill.

1031 EXCHANGE. An exchange of similar properties allowing the owners to avoid paying capital gains. 1031 refers to the Internal Revenue Service code.

TEQUILA EFFECT. The impact of the decline in the Mexican economy (1994) on securities from other Latin American countries.

TESEBONOS. Mexican bonds that are convertible to dollars.
   "In terms of fundamentals, we show that the critical variables in generating the Mexican crisis were the fast rise in US-denominated public debt (tesebonos), the appreciated real exchange rate and the small rises in unemployment and primary deficit." (*Journal of International Money and Finance,* June 2004, p. 595)

TEST THE WATERS. Look for opportunities; experiment.

"'People think they're going to devote themselves to learning to play an instrument, or taking art, or getting a degree in sociology—and they haven't taken any courses,' says Mr. Manheimer. 'They haven't tried that. You'd better test the waters.'" (*Wall Street Journal,* Jan. 4, 2004, p. 2)

TEXAS LEAGUER. A person of minor importance (baseball).

THANK GOODNESS IT'S FRIDAY (TGIF). Expression of relief that the work week is over.

THAT AIN'T PEANUTS. That's a large sum of money.

THAT DOG WON'T HUNT. That idea will not work. A Southernism popularized by President Lyndon Johnson.
"The Massachusetts Democrat insists 'that dog won't hunt.' And this is not a Michael Dukakis unprepared for hand-to-hand combat. His foreign-policy knowledge, complete with the biography—both John Kerry and George W. Bush graduated from Yale in the '60s, one chose to serve in Vietnam, one chose not to—and his personal character is a powerful antidote to any Republican attacks." (*Wall Street Journal,* Jan. 29, 2004, p. A19)

THERE IS NO SUCH THING AS A FREE LUNCH. Everything has a price or opportunity cost. Nobel Prize winning economist Milton Friedman is credited as the original source of this wisdom.

THIN ICE. Unlikely to succeed; dangerous situation.
"In a recent Portals column, Lee Gomes said Microsoft treads on especially thin ice when it waves the innovation flag, because the tech giant usually innovates 'only at the barrel of a gun.'" (*Wall Street Journal,* Oct. 20, 2003, p. R2)

THINKING OUT OF THE BOX, THINKING OUTSIDE THE BOX. Creating new processes, not just changing existing methods.
"'This idea of thinking out of the box is something we've come up with in the '90s,' Ms. Lesonsky says. 'Before that, if you did it, you were branded a freak.'" (*Wall Street Journal,* May 14, 2001, p. R15)

THINK TANK. Institute that studies social or other issues.
"Critics charged the report's findings had been ordered up because the Rotterdam Harbor Authority funded the report and Ms. Kroes served on the think tank's board." (*Wall Street Journal,* Nov. 3, 2004, p. A12)

THIRD DEGREE. Intense questioning.

"The Third Degree: Financial institutions should hold an interrogation, not an interview, with any employee it reasonably suspects has taken funds." (*Savings & Community Banker,* July 1994, p. 45)

360-DEGREE FEEDBACK. Performance appraisal by all of the people one works with, including bosses, peers, subordinates, and customers.

"An unusual experiment in executive coaching, Mr. Porter was testing 360-degree feedback—a popular on-the-job appraisal tool that involves gathering performance ratings not only from managers, but from peers and subordinates as well—as a tool to improve his performance as a husband and father." (*Wall Street Journal,* July 11, 2002, p. D1)

THREE-MARTINI LUNCH. A business meal with large quantities of alcohol to loosen up the customer. During the Carter administration, the term came to represent special tax privileges accorded to business, the ability to include lavish entertainment as a business expense.

"The 15% commission has gone the way of the three-martini lunch, and now agencies are moving to claim a piece of the action from licensing of advertising characters and slogans." (*Wall Street Journal,* Nov. 10, 2000, p. B1)

THREE MILE ISLAND. Location (Pennsylvania) of a 1979 nuclear reactor accident that became a symbol of the dangers of nuclear energy.

THREE-SIX-THREE. Pay three percent on deposits, charge six percent on loans, and make three o'clock tee times. U.S. banking in the "old days" (before 1980) was characterized by three-six-three practices.

THREE STEPS AND A STUMBLE. Stock market theory that stock and bond prices will fall after the third increase in the discount rate by the Federal Reserve.

THREE TAILING. A retail business that operates in three methods, bricks and mortar, catalog, and Internet.

THRIFTS. Savings banks, savings and loans.

THROUGH THE MILL. Subjected to a difficult experience.

"Instead, they're putting the analysts through the mill as third-party witnesses. Their files no doubt contain many documents relevant to Castano's issues, and tobacco executives who have spoken to them might have made comments unrecorded elsewhere but preserved in their notes." (*Wall Street Journal,* Aug. 30, 1995, p. A11)

THROW IN THE TOWEL. Admit defeat (boxing).
"Analysts following Intel have lately been throwing in the towel faster than a palooka's ringside cornerman." (*Wall Street Journal,* July 13, 2004, p. C1)

THROW IT AGAINST THE WALL AND SEE IF IT STICKS. Try a new idea and see if it works.
"'Let's run it up the flagpole and see who salutes?' or 'Throw it against the wall and see if it sticks' or, from my days in England, 'Will the punters buy?'" (*Marketing,* May 3, 2004, p. 17)

THROW MONEY AT. Spend large sums of money in hope of solving a problem.
"Yet there is a constant stampede as potential naming-rights partners and would-be concessionaires line up for the right to throw money into pro football's bulging bank accounts." (*Amusement Business,* Sept. 2004, p. 14)

THROW ONE'S WEIGHT AROUND. Use one's influence.

THUMBS DOWN. A negative response.
"In giving the thumbs down to the depression application, the FDA cited worsening depression in patients and potential biases in the way clinical trials were set up to test the product." (*Wall Street Journal,* August 13, 2004, p. B5)

THUMBS UP. A gesture of approval or success.

TICKER TAPE. See TAPE.

TIDAL WAVE. An overwhelming amount.
"Nearly two decades later, in May 1995, the Microsoft chairman warned employees by e-mail of an Internet 'tidal wave' that threatened to marginalize the company's PC software." (*Wall Street Journal,* July 7, 2004, p. A1)

TIED UP. Very busy.

TIE-IN. Joint promotion; two or more promotion campaigns that are linked together.

"Baskin-Robbins, with the help of Norm Marshall & Associates Inc., a product-placement firm, did a large tie-in with DreamWorks SKG's 'Shrek 2'." (*Wall Street Journal,* Sept. 2, 2004, p. B1)

TIE THE KNOT. To successfully complete a business deal.

TIE UP MONEY (TO). Cause money to be unavailable for use.

TIGER BY THE TAIL. A big, fast moving issue; situation or problem that could easily be lost, with grave consequences.

"Companies moving into groupware with a passion are finding they have a tiger by the tail. Groupware is hard, both technically and culturally." (*Forbes,* June 5, 1995, p. 76)

TIGER ECONOMIES. Any of the growing Asian countries, including Hong Kong, Taiwan, Singapore, and South Korea.

TIGER TEAM. Computer specialists hired to find security flaws in a company's system.

TIGHT-ASS. Person who is inflexible.

TIGHT MONEY. Constrained money supply, resulting in higher interest rates.

TIGHTWAD. A miser, stingy person.

"The Senator brags that he has voted against every tax hike, is a bona fide tightwad on spending, has hewed to the pro-life line and is a national-security hawk." (*Wall Street Journal,* Jan. 13, 2000, p. A23)

TILL. Cash register.

TIME FRAME. A clearly scheduled process with specific beginning and ending points.

TIN CUP. Symbol of poverty and begging.

TINKER (TO). Make small adjustments.

TIN PARACHUTE. A sarcastic reference to the benefits given to lower-level managers when a company is taken over and managers are terminated. Senior managers get a GOLDEN PARACHUTE.

TINSEL TOWN. Hollywood, California.

TIP OF THE ICEBERG. Only a small part of the issue or problem is currently visible. See also ICEBERG PRINCIPLE.

TIREKICKER. Person who inspects a product (car) with little intention of making a purchase at that time.

TOASTMASTERS. Nonprofit organization that helps business people develop their speaking skills.

TOE THE LINE (TO). Follow orders.
"To its credit, Snapple tried to toe the line with regard to discounting and CMAs." (*Beverage World,* Feb. 1995, p. 94)

TOE TO TOE (TO GO). Compete directly and aggressively (boxing).
"If Coke is going to improve in the U.S., as well as overseas, we can go toe to toe." (*Wall Street Journal,* Feb. 26, 1996, B3)

TOKENISM. The hiring or placing of minorities in visible positions to make the company look like it promotes and values its minority employees.

TOMBSTONE. A newspaper advertisement listing the underwriters of new stock.

TONGUE IN CHEEK. Jokingly, not serious.

TOO BIG TO FALL. Idea that some banks and financial companies are so important to economic stability that the government would not let them fail.

TOO RICH FOR MY BLOOD. Too expensive.

TOP BANANA. Leader.

TOP BRASS. Senior executives.
"And just a few weeks ago, Citigroup's top brass said the bank wouldn't be pursuing any 'transformative deals'." (*Wall Street Journal,* August 12, 2004, p. C1)

TOP DOG. Boss.
"In the corporate-fraud cases, the argument is that the top dog was so above the fray that he didn't know what directives were

being issued or carried out by those below him." (*Wall Street Journal,* July 9, 2004, p. B1)

TOP GUN. Important, powerful person.

TOP NOTCH. The best, most important.
"Mr. Mindich hasn't managed money for several years, suggesting he may have challenges starting out with a bang. But investors say he has assembled a top-notch team, including Stuart Hendel, formerly a managing director in Morgan Stanley's prime brokerage division." (*Wall Street Journal,* Nov. 3, 2004, p. B1)

TOP-OF-THE-LINE. The brand leader in a market.
"When I reviewed the first 17-inch widescreen laptop, Apple's top-of-the-line PowerBook, I checked the actual dimensions of airline coach-class trays and found that it would fit, barely." (*Wall Street Journal,* August 5, 2004, p. B4)

TOPPED OUT. Stuck in a position without hope of promotion or opportunity.
"Rallies are meant to be sold now because I believe we've topped out for the year." (*Wall Street Journal,* Nov. 20, 2003, p. C3)

TOPPING THE LIST. Number one, the best, highest priority.

TOPSY-TURVY. Disorderly.
"Topsy-turvy trading during the day reflected investor uncertainty." (*Wall Street Journal,* Dec. 5, 2003, p. C1)

TORPEDO. An inept employee who quits to work for a rival company. Also, to secretly undermine a competitor.
"An incompetent coworker leaving—with some encouragement— for a competing company is a torpedo." ("When 'e' Was Just a Letter," *Chief Executive,* Jan. 1, 2001)

TOTAL QUALITY MANAGEMENT (TQM). A management strategy for continuous quality improvement in all organizational processes.
"Almost two-thirds of the Chinese manufacturers say they follow a 'total quality management' philosophy." (*Industry Week,* Nov. 2004, p. 35)

TOTAL RETURN. A measure of the return on an investment calculated by adding capital gains, foreign exchange gains, and dividend or interest yield.

TOUCH ALL BASES. Consult with everyone involved in a decision.

"A conversation with Thomas A. Golub, president and chief executive officer of Atlanta's Hobbs group touches all the bases you would expect to touch with the head of a prominent US brokerage firm." (*National Underwriter,* August 13, 2001, p. 21)

TOUCH BASE. Consult with casually (baseball). See also RUN BY.

"In the wake of the recent publicity, the company says it decided to contact the National Highway Traffic Safety Administration to touch base with them and give them the information we have." (*Wall Street Journal,* Oct. 26, 2000, p. A3)

TOUGH NUT TO CRACK. Difficult person or problem.

TOUGH THING TO DO. Very difficult.

TOURIST TRAP. A cheap, tasteless tourist attraction.

"Believe it or not, some of these folksy sites are still going strong. In an age of killer whales, theme parks and cheap air travel to out-of-state tourist meccas, these highway tourist traps of yesteryear are finding ways to survive—and at a profit." (*Wall Street Journal,* July 15, 1998, p. T1)

TOXIC WASTE. A financial market term referring to investments that are unattractive due to certain underlying provisions or risks making them generally illiquid and lacking transparency. Toxic waste is often associated with collateralized mortgage obligations.

T-PLUS THREE. Stock market settlement rule: trade day plus three days.

TRACKING STOCK. The stock of one part of a company issued by the parent company that trades independently of the parent company.

TRACK RECORD. Past performance.

"And while it would be a huge vote of confidence for anybody who is brought in, by the same token, it's a remarkable track record you would be expected to uphold." (*Wall Street Journal,* Nov. 5, 2004, p. C1)

TRACTION. Influence; progress.

TRADE FLAT. Securities that trade without accrued interest. Convertible bonds, preferred stocks, and bonds in default usually trade flat.

TRADING COLLAR. Trading restrictions used by the New York Stock Exchange, limiting program trading to trades going against the trend in the market when there is a significant rise or fall in the market.

"Trading collar: If the Dow Jones Industrial Average rises or falls 180 points, the exchange slows down program trading by requiring that orders relating to the 'index arbitrage' form of program trading go against the trend of the market." (*Wall Street Journal,* July 24, 2002, p. C1)

TRADING LIMIT. The maximum daily fluctuation allowed on futures contracts. Trading limits are imposed by each major exchange.

TRAFFIC BUILDER. Marketing promotion designed to generate more customers.

"Many supermarket chains have added the trees as well, often propping them up by the front door near the Salvation Army kettle. 'Trees are a great traffic builder' that also turn a profit, says Mike Gettler, vice president of merchandising for Lowe's Cos., Wilkesboro, N.C., which has 638 home-improvement stores in 40 states." (*Wall Street Journal,* Dec. 19, 2000, p. B1)

TRAILERS. Commercials that run before movies.

TRANCHE. A part of an overall investment. For example, investors can purchase the interest income, repayment of principal or options associated with a loan.

TRAVEL DAZZLE. Efforts to impress the boss during a day he or she travels with you.

TRAVERSALITES. Intersections in corporate mergers (like synergies), partnerships.

TREASURY SHARES. Shares of stock issued but held by the company. Treasury shares are often shares that have been repurchased by the company, reducing the number of shares outstanding.

TREASURY STOCK. Stock held by the company. Treasury stock is sometimes used to thwart a hostile takeover.

TREES DON'T GROW INTO THE SKY. Stock prices have stopped going up.

TREEWARE. Printed material.

TRENCHES. The workplace (World War I).
"In the print campaign that starts tomorrow, EDS strikes a dogged posture toward its work and recent troubles. One ad shows a bull preparing to charge. The text alludes to EDS's actions to fix poorly managed contracts that have led to its financial setbacks: 'One thing we've learned after 42 years in the trenches, you never back down from a tough challenge.'" (*Wall Street Journal,* May 10, 2004, p. B4)

TRIAL BALLOON. An experiment or an idea proposed to see how other people respond.

TRIAL PERIOD. Time allowed to test and try the product.

TRICKLE-DOWN THEORY. Economic idea (especially associated with the Reagan administration) that benefits to the wealthy eventually benefit poorer groups.
"He feels the pain of the less fortunate, but he is a firm believer in the 'trickle down' theory of social welfare." (*Wall Street Journal,* Nov. 14, 2000, p. A24)

TRIM THE FAT. Reduce excess employees or costs; budget cutting.
"No matter how fast Chairman and Chief Executive Paul Norris moves to trim fat and accelerate earnings growth, he can't outrun the company's past." (*Wall Street Journal,* March 16, 2000, p. 1)

TRIPLE WITCHING DAY. The third Friday in March, June, September, and December, when three types of options expire on the same day.
"Trading was brisk because Friday was what is called a triple-witching session, the quarterly expiration of index futures and index and stock options" (*Wall Street Journal,* Sept. 21, 2002, p. B3)

TROJAN or TROJAN HORSE. A software program, often a game or other useful program, with hidden and potentially damaging features. Trojans often evade computer security systems by tricking users into authorizing access to their computer systems. Trojan horse is a reference to the ancient military tactic described in *The Iliad* and *The Odyssey* whereby Greek soldiers entered Troy concealed in a large, hollow horse.

TROLLING. Making COLD-CALLS, soliciting new business (fishing).

TROOPS. Workers.

"Assistant Attorney General Anne K. Bingaman's antitrust troops are looking into whether, as rivals and PC makers allege, Microsoft Corp. is using anticompetitive tactics with their new software, Windows 95." (*Business Week,* July 10, 1995, p. 100)

TRUMP (TO). To overwhelm or outmaneuver the competition.

TRUST SLUG, TRUST FUND BABY. A person who has grown lazy and unmotivated from living off a trust fund.

"Clients want their wealth to give their children opportunities they did not have themselves when they were young. But they also fear their children will turn into trust slugs, dependent on family money, with no incentive to follow a career, Cooper says." ("Newly Rich Fear Spoiling Kids," *Reuters,* Feb. 19, 2000)

TRY TO TAME THE MARKET. Make money from investments.

TUNNEL VISION. Limited perception or understanding.

"Avoiding tunnel vision requires broadening one's view. The classic mistake is to fall in love with a specific technology." (*Datamation,* Feb. 15, 1995, p. 88)

TURF. One's domain.

"These changes were greeted in part by the usual mutterings from RIAs who feel Schwab is trampling yet again on their own turf." (*Financial Planning,* April 1, 2004, p. 1)

TURKEY. A poorly performing investment, decision, or product line.

"Mexico's economy: A real turkey?" (*The Economist,* August 5, 1995, p. 68)

TURKEY TROT. Shuffling ineffective employees from one part of the company to another by managers who are not willing to terminate them.

"A turkey trot is the practice of transferring a marginal, incompetent, or problem employee from one department or job to another." (*Across the Board,* Nov./Dec. 1994, p. 52)

TURN A SOW'S EAR INTO A SILK PURSE. Make a bad business profitable.

TURN BACK THE CLOCK. Go back to earlier times.

"But if the company's executives could somehow get the young wizard to flick his wand and turn back the clock to the days before AOL Time Warner was mashed together in a series of ill-fated mergers, AOL's value could rise out of its current depths." (*Wall Street Journal,* Jan. 31, 2003, p. C1)

TURNING POINT. The beginning of a new time or era.

TURNKEY. A project delivered ready for use.

"They began marketing themselves as a turnkey, outsourcing company to handle all the manufacturing for bigger players." (*Wall Street Journal,* March 2004, p. B4)

TURN-OF-THE-MONTH (TOM) EFFECT. Stock market phenomenon in which prices tend to go up because investors receive cash to put into the market.

"However, we find a significant turn-of-the-month effect in both stocks and bonds and show that investors may be able to enhance the performance of their retirement portfolios." (*Journal of Economics and Finance,* Spring 2000, p. 64)

TURN ON. Cause excitement or pleasure; introduce people to something new.

TWADDLE. Financial salesmanship.

"Twaddle is irrelevant, erroneous, or irresponsible financial information." (Bill Holland, KNSD-TV, August 16, 1996)

TWEAK (TO). Manipulate; make slight adjustments to.

"We enable customers who would like to do their own development. And we can tweak the monopolist. That's always fun and not a bad strategy if you're a small company." (*Wall Street Journal,* July 8, 2004, p. B5)

TWEEDS-TO-RICHES. The process whereby an academic takes his or her research and parlays it into a successful company.

"An academic whose expertise is in parallel algorithms and applied mathematics, Leighton is at first glance an unlikely candidate for an Internet tweeds-to-riches success story." ("Akamai's Algorithms," *Technology Review,* September 2000)

24/7 (TWENTY-FOUR/SEVEN). Twenty-four hours a day, seven days a week, to be continuously available.

20-20 HINDSIGHT. To learn something afterward or too late to be useful.

TWIN DEFICITS. The combined federal budget and trade deficits.

TWISTING. Unethical insurance industry strategy of persuading clients to cash in one investment and purchase another, making commissions for the agent.

"A the behest of his trusted insurance agent, Pickering was buying and selling one annuity after another in a deceitful industry practice called 'twisting'." (*AARP Bulletin,* Nov. 2002, p. 25)

TWOFERS. Two for the price of one.

2/10, NET 30. Two percent discount when a bill due in thirty days is paid in ten days.

"I knew I was beginning to understand business when I found myself telling a customer that my terms were 2/10, net thirty." (Rebecca Folsom, Sunshine Productions, 1995)

TWO-WAY STREET. Both parties should participate or benefit.

TYING. Making the sale of one item or service contingent on the purchase of another.

"The National Association of Securities Dealers said it is investigating a widespread but controversial banking practice in which loans to companies are made only if the borrowers agree to give the lender lucrative, fee-generating investment-banking business. While laws formally prevent banks from initiating such an arrangement, known as tying, many banks have found loopholes to the laws." (*Wall Street Journal,* Sept. 17, 2002, p. C2)

TYPE A. Aggressive, compulsive (personality).

U

UMBRELLA. Overall group or organization; something that supports or protects all involved.

UNBRIDLED OPTIMISM. Uncontrolled enthusiasm, feeling good. Owners of new businesses and inventors of new products frequently are blinded by unbridled optimism.

"It added that Mr. Stellato initially didn't seek to leave after allegedly blowing the whistle but instead expressed 'unbridled optimism' about Knight's future." (*Wall Street Journal,* Sept. 24, 2004, p. C3)

UNBUNDLE. Separate the costs of the various operations in a business.

UNCLE SAM. The United States government. During the War of 1812, a New York pork packer named "Uncle Sam" Wilson shipped so many barrels of pork to troops with his first two initials on each barrel that his name came to symbolize the U.S. government itself.

UNDERCUT. Price lower than competitors.

"The U.S. charges that European government subsidies have allowed Airbus to undercut Boeing prices, giving Airbus an unfair advantage in the marketplace and harming the U.S. aerospace industry." (*Wall Street Journal,* Nov. 8, 2004, p. A.3)

UNDERDOG. A firm that is not expected to be a major competitor.

UNDERPERFORM. Stock market analyst's rating suggesting the stock or bond will not appreciate as fast as the overall market. An underperform rating is a sell recommendation.

UNDER THE GUN. Under pressure to deliver or perform.

UNDER THE TABLE / COUNTER. Secret, illegal. The phrase is associated with bribes passed under the table, the opposite being an ABOVE BOARD agreement.
"The suits accuse the brokers of failing 'to adequately disclose ... under-the-table payments or kickbacks' received from insurers. As a result, they allege, "defendants are able to reap tens of millions of dollars in additional fees while purporting to provide independent and unbiased brokerage advice." (*Wall Street Journal,* August 11, 2004, p. C3)

UNDERTIME. Time spent during the workday on personal affairs to make up for workplace demands. The opposite of overtime.
"It may be the worst-kept secret in the workplace: People are working more undertime—stealing time off during the day to compensate for heavier workloads and more stress. Undertime can take many forms, from hours spent away from the office on errands or shopping to chunks of time spent at your desk surfing the Internet." (Sue Shellenbarger, "Why You Can Hit the Gym—but Not Get a Manicure—on Company Time," *Wall Street Journal,* April 18, 2002)

UNDERWATER OPTIONS. Stock options in which the strike price (the price at which the employee can exercise the option to buy the shares) is higher than the current stock price.
"Confronted with the shortcomings of their options strategies, tech companies might be expected to look around for alternatives. But they're not. The few companies that are talking publicly about dealing with their employees' underwater options are desperately looking for ways to dial back the clock to the way things were before the Nasdaq bear arrived." ("The Party's Over," *Fortune,* June 26, 2000)

UNDERWRITE. To purchase securities at set price from an issuer and then resell the securities in the financial market.

UNDERWRITERS LABORATORIES (UL). Company that tests and reviews the safety of electrical products.

UNEARNED INCOME. Income received in advance of providing the service or delivering the product.

UNFUNDED DEBT. Short-term debt, usually maturing within one year.

UNHEARD OF. Never happened in the past.

UNIFORM RESOURCE LOCATOR (URL). An Internet address.

UNILATERAL TRANSFERS. Gifts and income transfers out of a country, often to families in workers' home countries.

UNINSTALLED. Euphemism for being terminated.

UNIT. A security that includes more than one class of securities. Units often combine shares of stock and warrants to purchase additional shares.

UNIT BALANCE. Total number of mutual fund shares.
   "Jargon: unit balance. Translation: total number of shares." (*Wall Street Journal,* Jan. 4, 1999, p. R8)

UNITED PARCEL SERVICE (UPS). A large, privately held package delivery company headquartered in the United States.

UNITED WAY. Cooperative nonprofit organization that solicits donations from local businesses and distributes the funds to local charities.

UNLOAD. Get rid of, dispose of. Managers try to unload unwanted products, divisions, or employees.
   "If you wait too long to unload your stocks, you could get caught up in one of these rotten patches and find yourself selling shares at fire-sale prices." (*Wall Street Journal,* Nov. 7, 2004, p. 3)

UNLOCK DATE. The date following an initial public offering of stock when the company's insiders, management, employees, and large shareholders are allowed to sell their shares on the open market.

"At day 181, the fire hose hits. Everyone and his brother is unlocked. If the stock is at lofty levels, they will blow out, or try to, all at the same time. It is uncommon for any stock to trade up when shares are unlocked. Shorts try to outguess the market and short stocks ahead of the unlock date, figuring they will buy distressed shares lower." ("IPO = Inefficient Public Offering," TheStreet.com, August 11, 1998)

UNQUALIFIED OPINION. An independent auditor's opinion of a company's records.

UNWIND A DEAL. To cancel or withdraw from.

UP AND RUNNING. Now working, newly operational.

UP A TREE, UP A CREEK (WITHOUT A PADDLE). A difficult situation, predicament. Like a stranded animal, managers sometimes find themselves up a tree.

UP FOR GRABS. Available. In a dynamic, changing economy, new opportunities are up for grabs.

UP FRONT. In advance; honest, open.

"So it soon could pay for itself, especially after getting a rebate up front." (*Wall Street Journal,* Oct. 31, 2004, p. 10)

UP-FRONT MONEY. Money paid in advance. When making sales to new customers or expensive customized products, businesses often require up-front money.

UPGRADE. Improve. In airline travel, to switch from economy to higher-class seating.

UPSCALE. Superior, better quality, often more expensive.

"The target population was defined for the study as educated, upscale professionals in the state of Iowa." (*Association for Computing Machinery,* July 2004, p. 73)

UPSELL. Persuading customers to buy more expensive models or versions of a product than they originally intended to purchase.

UP TICK/UPSWING. An increase in stock market prices or the economy in general.

UP TO PAR. Meets standards. An analogy to golf, where par is considered the normal number of strokes to take on a hole.

"For our own gift hunt, we went looking for heirloom-quality frames in sterling silver. (No 'World's Best Mom' numbers for us.) To make sure the presentation was up to par, we shopped at catalogs such as Tiffany and Martha by Mail that we assumed would have pretty, Mom-pleasing gift wrap." (*Wall Street Journal,* May 3, 2002, p. W10)

UP TO THE MINUTE. The latest, most current.

USED CAR SALESMAN. Fast-talking promoter.

"'The financial-aid administrators are very sensitive to being treated as used-car salesmen,' said Mark Kantrowitz, publisher of Finaid.com, a financial-aid Web site." (*Wall Street Journal,* April 29, 2003, p. D2)

USE LIFE. The expected productive life of a depreciable asset.

USER-FRIENDLY. Designed for easier use. The term is frequently used in discussions of computer software, but manufacturers are redesigning many products to be more user-friendly as a means to increase customer satisfaction.

USURY. Lending money at extremely high interest rates. Many states have usury laws limiting the interest rate that can be charged. The Bible has admonitions against usury.

V

VALUE CHAIN. The stages a product goes through in an organization from development through sale, and the value added at each point in the process.

VALUE INVESTING. Investment strategy focusing on assets that are currently undervalued. Measuring value is difficult, and often there are reasons a company, stock, or other asset is priced less than comparable investments. Value investing is considered a conservative, long-term investment strategy.

VANILLA MODEL. Standard, ordinary. A product with few amenities is called a vanilla model. See also PLAIN-VANILLA AND STRIPPED-DOWN.

VAPORWARE. Products, usually computer software or hardware, announced as if imminent when they are actually in early formative stages. The products may or may not ever make it to market in any form similar to the original announcements. The practice can be used to gain various marketing and competitive advantages.

"Indeed, Microsoft has been criticized in the past for offering up 'vaporware': announcements of products far from being ready to market." (*Wall Street Journal,* June 23, 2000, p. B6)

VEEPERS. Virtual personalities. Using online software and photographs of themselves or others, people can create scripts and have the virtual character appear to say the script.

"The user stores a digital photo at the Bud Light Internet site, and writes a script of what the veeper should say. After some adjustments, the resulting character will appear to be live, with eyes that blink and lips that move in synch with its voice." (*Wall Street Journal,* Sept. 17, 2002, p. B1)

VEER OFF COURSE. Go the wrong way.

VEG OUT (TO). Relax, to "vegetate."

"'Nothing personal, I just want to veg out and watch TV tonight,' he says." (*Wall Street Journal,* Nov. 27, 1997, p. B1)

VELOCITY. In economics, the turnover rate of the money supply.

VENN DIAGRAM. A graphic means to represent interactions among sets, displaying this information in a manner that can be read easily.

VERTICAL INTEGRATION. The expansion of a company, either upward or downward in the process from production to sale. Vertical integration expands company control of production, distribution, and retailing.

VESTED/VESTING. Having worked for a company the minimum amount of time necessary to qualify for various benefits.

"The 'EPS Challenge Option Grants' promised 350 shares of fully vested stock options at a strike price of $62.50 a share for all employees—and many more shares for executives—if the company reached annual earnings-per-share of $6.46 by Dec. 31, 2003, twice the figure for 1998." (*Wall Street Journal,* Sept. 23, 2004, p. A1)

VESTED INTEREST. Personal financial involvement.

VET (TO). To investigate or review a proposal or business deal.

VIG. A small fee charged to a seller or buyer by a third-party whose software or technology was used to implement the transaction.

"The word vig is short for *vigorish,* which is bookie slang for a fee that's charged on each bet placed. (It can also mean interest paid on a loan.) It's origin seems to be the Yiddish word *vyigrysh,* meaning 'profit or winnings.'" (Wordspy.com, August 9, 2004)

VIRAL MARKETING. Word-of-mouth advertising using the Internet. Like a computer virus, information is rapidly forwarded among Internet users, reaching thousands and millions of people in a short period of time.

"Creators of the buzz phrase 'viral marketing' don't know jack about it compared to two people who inadvertently put the Internet community's newfangled term for word-of-mouth advertising to work and received millions of dollars in pledges without even trying." (*DM News,* Jan. 25, 1999, p. 1)

VIRTUAL COMPANY. A company that develops and markets products but subcontracts production to other companies.

VIRTUAL EARNINGS. Creative reporting of a firm's business results. During the technology boom in the late 1990s, many new technology companies had no profit and resorted to a variety of accounting techniques to generate interest among investors.

"Investors are increasingly seeing 'virtual earnings' for virtual companies." (*Wall Street Journal,* August 24, 1999, p. C1)

VIRTUAL PRIVATE NETWORK. Electronic private communication system.

VIRUS. A computer program, commonly transmitted through e-mail, that spreads quickly from computer to computer. Viruses can be pranks or destructive, disabling computers and slowing the Internet.

VISIBILITY. The extent to which it is possible to anticipate a future trend or situation; the "distance" that it is possible to "see" into the future; ability to be easily noticed or recognized.

"Analysts became audibly agitated during Wednesday's call when, after pressing for more information on the company's long-term prospects, Koogle said that Yahoo, like many other companies, was unsure about how 2001 would turn out. 'We simply don't have good visibility on the back half of the year,' Koogle said." ("Yahoo: 'Sad, Mad, Scared,'" *Wired News,* March 8, 2001)

VISIBLE SYMBOL. Something one can see.

VISION CONGRUENCIES. Thinking the same way.

VISION STATEMENT. Management's prediction of the future or hopeful plan for the future.

"As part of its strategic rollout, the hospital's 1,100 workers were given blue ribbons to affix to the bottom of their ID cards, bearing the slogan 'It All Begins With Me!' the hospital's new 'vision statement.'" (*Wall Street Journal,* Oct. 16, 2002, p. B1)

VISION THING (THE). Coined by President George H.W. Bush in the 1992 election, when criticized that he lacked vision or clear goals. The term has been used by many writers when debating whether President George W. Bush does or does not have a vision for the future of the country.

"No one can accuse Hillary Clinton of lacking the vision thing. The First Lady was elected to public office on Tuesday and by Friday was rewriting the Constitution." (*Wall Street Journal,* Nov. 13, 2000, p. A36)

VOLDIS. Abbreviation for volume discounts. Many companies offer lower prices for large-volume orders.

VOLUNTARY EXPORT RESTRAINT (VER). Trade restrictions an exporting country agrees to, fearing imposition of import restrictions by the other country.

VOLUNTARY REDUCTION IN FORCE (VRIF). Management's first method of DOWNSIZING. U.S. companies offer their employees incentives in order to achieve voluntary reductions in force.

VOODOO ECONOMICS. Coined by George H.W. Bush in the 1980 election, when challenging candidate Ronald Reagan's proposal to cut taxes, increase defense spending, and balance the budget at the same time; suggesting that these goals could only be simultaneously accomplished by using voodoo.

"'The paradoxical lesson of the '80s is that when marginal rates are too high, cutting them is—thanks to the resulting economic growth—a win-win policy for both taxpayers and the treasury,' Mr. Baker wrote. 'This is not voodoo economics; it's hard, cold reality.'" (*Wall Street Journal,* Jan. 13, 2004, p. A14)

VOTING STOCK. Stock that includes the right to vote on the company's business.

VULTURE FUND. An investment fund that speculates in companies or real estate holdings that have declined significantly in value.

"The Aladdin is in bankruptcy proceedings in Las Vegas. Marriott's main rival, Starwood Hotels & Resorts Worldwide Inc., has linked up with restaurateur Robert Earl and New York vulture fund Bay Harbour Management LC as the so-called stalking-horse bidder for the Aladdin, with a deal that would cost less than half the $1.4 billion originally invested in the property." (*Wall Street Journal,* June 2, 2003, p. B5)

W

WAFFLE. To be indecisive or undecided.

WAGE FREEZE. No raises for employees. During recessions many U.S. companies announce wage freezes.

WAKE-UP CALL. An event that changes one's assumptions or direction.

WALK AWAY FROM. To discontinue involvement in or negotiations.

WALKING PAPERS. Notice of job dismissal. See also PINK SLIP.
"It was possibly a crummy solution even if it might yet pass muster with the IRS—a question still up in the air. But last week Messrs. Bill Esrey and Ron LeMay were given their walking papers merely out of fear that the IRS might rule against them." (*Wall Street Journal,* Feb. 12, 2003, p. A17)

WALK ON WATER. When one can do no wrong. An analogy to the biblical story about Jesus; the phrase is often used to describe some-one who thinks highly of him- or herself.

"Told by the instructor 'you have to sell yourself,' he decided to be 'more confident' in his next job interview. He still didn't get the job. Mr. Cooper says he later was told that one of the managers in the session thought he acted like he 'could walk on water.'" (*Wall Street Journal,* April 2, 2001, p. A1)

WALK THE PLANK. Take on a dangerous project or situation that could end one's career.

"So far, only Gonzalez's associates have been forced to walk the plank. Naturally, these scandals have not exactly bolstered Gonzalez's reputation with the voters of Spain." (*Global Finance,* June 1995, p. 49)

WALLFLOWER. An investment or person who is largely ignored by others.

WALLPAPER. Securities that have no value; the background pattern on a computer screen.

WALLPAPER A MEETING. Include supporters in the meeting.

WALL STREET. The financial district in lower Manhattan, New York City. Wall Street got its name in the seventeenth century, when settlers erected a wall to keep pigs out of their crops.

WAL-MART EFFECT. The economic impact of a Wal-Mart store opening in a community, often forcing smaller competitors out of business and driving down wages, and broader effects such as helping to keep inflation low and productivity high.

"At Wal-Mart, 'everyday low prices' is more than a slogan; it is the fundamental tenet of a cult masquerading as a company. Over the years, Wal-Mart has relentlessly wrung tens of billions of dollars in cost efficiencies out of the retail supply chain, passing the larger part of the savings along to shoppers as bargain prices. New England Consulting estimates that Wal-Mart saved its U.S. customers $20 billion last year alone. Factor in the price cuts other retailers must make to compete, and the total annual savings approach $100 billion. It's no wonder that economists refer to a broad 'Wal-Mart effect' that has suppressed inflation and rippled productivity gains through the economy year after year." ("Is Wal-Mart too powerful?" *Business Week,* Oct. 6, 2003)

WAMPUM. The use of high-priced shares of an Internet company as a form of currency to acquire other businesses. Wampum was a Native American term for money.

WAR CHEST. Financial resources of a company.

"Meanwhile, Mr. Bollore is likely to tighten the screws on Havas's senior management further. According to one person close to the businessman, Mr. Bollore had a war chest of around 1 billion euros from his investments." (*Wall Street Journal,* Oct. 13, 2004, p. C5)

WARM-CHAIR ATTRITION. The loss of workplace productivity due to employees who dislike their jobs and are just waiting for the opportunity to quit and move on to something better.

"Surveys indicate that more than a third of American workers have already mentally checked out of their current jobs, waiting to pounce on the next opportunity, he said. 'We call it warm-chair attrition, and a lot of employers are going to get caught short by it.'" ("Workplace forecaster predicts skilled-worker drought," *Dallas Morning News,* Oct. 3, 2003)

WARM FUZZIES. Verbal compliments; good memories.

"It wasn't a great combo: The machine spat kernels well beyond our bowl (one flew 8 feet) before finally churning out a few handfuls of dry corn. We were left with a lot of no-pops—we counted 320—and few nostalgic warm fuzzies." (*Wall Street Journal,* Jan. 10, 2003, p. W9C)

WARRANT. Option to purchase shares of stock in a company for a specified period of time. Many U.S. companies with less than INVESTMENT-GRADE financial ratings offer warrants with their debt securities.

WAR STORIES. Tales of how things used to be, often long-winded stories by senior employees and of little interest to the younger staff members. War stories often begin with "I remember when..."

WASH. Situation where one outcome cancels another—for example, when an increase in sales to one customer offsets a loss of sales to another.

WASH SALE. When an investor sells an asset at a loss and then repurchases the asset within 30 days.

"A wash sale typically occurs when an investor sells a stock or some other security at a loss and buys the same stock with 30 days before or after the sale." (*Wall Street Journal,* May 1, 2003, p. D2)

WATCHDOG. Person or group that scrutinizes the actions of business or government. See also NADER'S RAIDERS.

"The Marsh board gets low marks from corporate watchdogs who track board governance. Corporate Library grades the Marsh board a "D" on a scale of A to F, meaning it ranks below 80% of the roughly 2,000 boards that Corporate Library studies." (*Wall Street Journal,* Oct. 22, 2004, p. A1)

WATCH LIST. Companies under review by investment brokers or ratings agencies due to signs of pending changes.

WATERING HOLE. A bar.
"I could find only three skimpy beer references to Elvis. One was a decade-old *Los Angeles Times* profile of a dying Hollywood watering hole called the Formosa Cafe in which the writer asserted that 'this, after all, is the bar where Elvis drank beer' without saying any more about it." (*Wall Street Journal,* Oct. 8, 2004, p. W1)

WAVER. A release from a contract.

W-CUBED. Whatever, wherever, and whenever you want it. To emphasize the importance of customer service, managers will claim their mantra is W-cubed.
"So instead of subscribing to some a la carte, 24-hour channel, you'll just get the show you want on demand, whenever you want it. It will be W-cubed, whatever, wherever, and whenever you want it." (*Wall Street Journal,* Feb. 16, 1995, p. A14)

WEALTH EFFECT. An increase in consumer spending based on an increase in wealth created by the escalating value of stock market portfolios.
"Big portfolio gains by investors in recent years have created what economists call the 'wealth effect,' which has boosted consumer spending, the single biggest factor that has driven the US economy. The 'wealth effect' means simply that when investors feel more secure about their wealth, they spend more." ("Market economy," *Boston Globe,* Oct. 25, 1998)

WEAR MANY HATS. Have many different responsibilities.
"U.S. Troops Wear Many Hats in Kosovo—GIs Act as Mayors of Towns, Organize Trash Pickups, Patrol Dangerous Streets" (*Wall Street Journal,* August 13, 1999, p. A9)

WEARS OFF. Does not work after a while.

WEATHER THE STORM/TASK (TO). Survive.

WEED OUT (TO). Pick out and eliminate.
"P's shares Friday rose 4% to 126.43 euros ($155.11) in Frankfurt, and its American depositary shares were up 5% on the New York

Stock Exchange, as investors ticked off possible benefits for SAP of an Oracle-PeopleSoft deal. The tie-up would weed out a key competitor to SAP and might allow SAP to poach PeopleSoft customers unhappy about being forced to switch to Oracle's systems." (*Wall Street Journal,* Sept. 13, 2004, p. C1)

WELFARE STATE. Conservative Americans' perception that the United States is moving toward socialism.

"Alan Greenspan nicely teed up the 'ownership society,' presumed theme of George Bush's convention speech Thursday night. Mr. Bush will rightly emphasize the positive, but he'll be offering a way to deal with the pending crash of the welfare state, topic of the Fed chairman's widely noted talk last Friday." (*Wall Street Journal,* Sept. 1, 2004, p. A13)

WELL-HEELED. Affluent.

"Nordstrom, whose department stores are popular with well-heeled shoppers, saw comparable-store sales gain by 7.2%." (*Wall Street Journal,* Sept. 23, 2004, p. C1)

WETBACK. An ILLEGAL ALIEN in the United States, usually describing someone who has crossed the Rio Grande from Mexico into the country.

"In 1995 the number of illegals apprehended fell by 75% to just under 250,000 and the Immigration and Naturalization Service declared: The so-called 'wetback' problem no longer exists.... The border has been secured." (*Wall Street Journal,* Nov. 9, 1995, p. A20)

WHAT LINE ARE YOU IN? What is your work/business?

WHAT MAKES HIM/HER TICK? What motivates the person?

WHEELER DEALER. A fast-talking and often shifty salesperson or entrepreneur. Wheeler dealer can refer to both ethical and less-than-ethical business people.

WHEN PIGS FLY! Never!

"Other managers share the sentiment. 'This is a year when pigs can fly,' says Jeff Van Harte, manager of the $150.9 million Transamerica Premier Equity Fund, up 16.86% this year through Sept. 30. 'People shouldn't be too surprised by what's happened so far this year, but they shouldn't get greedy either. If you own a fund that's up 40%, you might want to take some money off the table.'" (*Wall Street Journal,* Oct. 6, 2003, p. R3)

WHERE THE ACTION IS. The center of activity. It is important for CORPORATE LADDER–climbing workers to be where the action is. An assignment that takes an employee away from the center of activity is being SENT TO SIBERIA.

WHIPSAW. Move violently; organized labor's description of the practice by companies of creating plant-against-plant competition for survival. The threat of closings is used to extract concessions from workers.

"These types of market storms 'come and go,' says the 40-year-old Mr. Lavan, who runs Salomon Brothers Short/Intermediate U.S. Government Fund. But this one has been 'a class-five hurricane.' The whipsaw has rattled investors who flocked to bonds in the wake of the stock swoon early this decade, and threatened to rock some Wall Street trading houses, which had come to depend on a healthy bond market for a chunk of their profits." (*Wall Street Journal,* Sept. 15, 2003, p. C1)

WHISPER CIRCUIT. A network in which people trade gossip, innuendo, and other unsubstantiated data, particularly within the investment community.

"Meanwhile, Epinions.com has kept up constant reconnaissance on the competitors it will be jockeying with this fall, despite those competitors' best efforts to keep their strategies secret. The Valley has what it calls the 'whisper circuit,' which is not so much wild gossip as the ability to call in old favors and threaten to pull people's teeth. A lot of whisper-circuit surveillance leaks out the back door of companies through their engineers, who often refuse to lie on principle or are very bad at it when they try." ("Instant Company," *New York Times,* July 11, 1999)

WHISPER EARNINGS. Unpublished but widely circulated rumors regarding the expected earnings of a company.

WHISPER NUMBER. An unofficial forecast of a company's earnings estimated by analysts covering a stock.

"Intel's earnings were far ahead of the $ 1.07 a share expected by Wall Street analysts surveyed by First Call. The results even surpassed the "whisper number" of $ 1.10 a share circulated among traders following Intel's news in November that its results would be higher than analysts were projecting." ("Profits at Intel, Yahoo Beat Wall St. Forecasts," *Los Angeles Times,* Jan. 13, 1999)

WHISTLE BLOWER. A person who reports unethical activity to authorities. U.S. laws protect workers from retaliation by employers, but whistle blowers are often ostracized by management and fellow employees.

"A price-fixing probe in the chemical industry has widened into a series of global inquiries involving Dow Chemical, DuPont, Bayer and other companies, helped in part by amnesty for whistle-blowers. U.S. and European investigators are looking into alleged conspiracies to fix prices in a half-dozen chemicals used in plastics, rubber and synthetics." (*Wall Street Journal,* June 22, 2004, p. A1)

WHISTLING PAST THE GRAVEYARD. To act bravely.

WHITE ANGLO-SAXON PROTESTANT (WASP). Caucasian-American of European descent, some WASPs perceive themselves as the aristocracy of America.

"Unlike the country's old money, bound by convention, WASP reflexes and diminishing resources, the rich today are defining a different style of monied life." (*Mediaweek,* Nov. 7, 1994, p. SS14)

WHITE BOX. Generic computer.

"In targeting dealers, the Austin Texas, concern is hoping to edge in on a market where the biggest brands still lose some of their business to 'white boxes,' the no-name computers put together from parts from various suppliers and tailored to a customer's specific needs." (*Wall Street Journal,* August 20, 2002, p. B1)

WHITE-COLLAR. Executives, managers, professional employees.

"White-collar workers are defined as 'salaried exempt'—salaried employees who aren't executives and for whom overtime pay isn't required by the Fair Labor Standards Act—and by some lights they shouldn't complain." (*Wall Street Journal,* Oct. 26, 2004, p. B1)

WHITE-COLLAR CRIME. Crimes, often financial, committed by professional workers.

"According to a recent Office of Technology Assessment (OTA) report, the idea that computers armed with artificial intelligence (AI) can curb the money laundering that accompanies drug trafficking, prostitution, and white-collar crime is fraught with technical, political, legal and cost obstacles." (*Computerworld,* Sept. 18, 1995, p. 12)

WHITE FLAG. Symbol of surrender.

WHITE KNIGHT. Good guy; in finance, a friendly buyout.

"Management at Harbin welcomed the takeover by Anheuser-Busch. Peter Lo, Harbin's chief executive, said Wednesday, 'The SABMiller offer was wholly unsolicited and not welcomed by the management or employees of Harbin. I am therefore delighted that Anheuser-Busch has stepped in as a white knight with a counter-bid.'" (*Wall Street Journal,* June 4, 2003, p. A3)

WHITE-KNUCKLE. Tense, stressful.

WHITE PAPER. A position paper, often used in political debates.

WHITE SALE. A special promotion of bedding products and towels.
"Both domestics and housewares are among the most price com-petitive categories at retail, and one finely-timed and well-focused white sale can make all the difference." (*Stores,* August 1994, p. 46)

WHITE-SHOE FIRM. A closed, "country club–like" firm.
"Online stock trading, gathering steam among individual inves-tors, is attracting interest from an unlikely source: white shoe securities firm Goldman, Sachs & Co." (*Wall Street Journal,* Feb. 22, 1999, p. C1)

WHITTLE AWAY. Slowly reduce/shrink. Like a craftsman carv-ing a piece of wood, managers may choose to slowly rearrange or reduce a department or division.

WHO-KNOWS-WHAT. An unknown.

WHOLE BATTERY. Many, a lot of different impacts.

WHOLE NINE YARDS. The total thing, full details.

WHOLE SHEBANG. The entire thing.

WHOOPS. Washington Public Power Supply System. WHOOPS became (in)famous in the 1980s for its inept management of multiple nuclear power plant development projects, resulting in default on its bonds, the largest default in municipal bond history in the United States.

WIDGET. Generic for a firm's product. A favorite term used in economics classes.
"It's little wonder that tech companies are reticent about their use of ODMs—or of outsourced manufacturing in general. If I buy a widget from Acme Corp., I assume Acme made it, and I may even be willing to pay more for it as a result. But if I were to learn that Acme is simply reselling someone else's widgets and that Acme's rival has the same product for less money, I might well take my widget dollars elsewhere." (*Wall Street Journal,* July 19, 2004, p. B1)

WIDOW-AND-ORPHAN STOCK. A relatively low-risk stock that pays a high dividend.

WI-FI, WIRELESS FIDELITY. A high-speed wireless data service. Wi-Fi allows multiple users to connect to the Internet without a cable connection.

"Wi-Fi, for Wireless Fidelity, is a high-speed wireless data service. For less than $200, consumers can beam their existing high-speed Internet signals wirelessly throughout their households." (*Wall Street Journal,* Sept. 25, 2002, p. R4)

WIGGLE ROOM. Having options or flexibility.

WILLY LOMANS. Salespeople. Willy Loman is the central character in Arthur Miller's play, *Death of a Salesman.*

"'The dominant image of the American salesperson is still Willy Loman from Arthur Miller's play, Death of a Salesman: the sad-sack peddler pushing items of dubious value on unsuspecting people,' says Gene Siskel, film critic for the Chicago Tribune." (*Sales & Marketing Management,* Oct. 1993, p. 142)

WINDOW DRESSING/UNDRESSING. The addition/removal by a mutual fund manager of one or more poorly performing stocks just prior to a performance review date.

"In the investment world, there remain plenty of impenetrable phrases which make sense only to those in the know. A new one crossed my desk the other day. It was 'window undressing'. Like much, but by no means all, investment jargon, it originated in the US. The term applies to the practice of fund managers dumping unsuccessful investments before a review date. Thus, a fund manager might sell technology stocks on which there is a big loss immediately ahead of a quarterly review period so they do not appear on the portfolio valuation." ("Investment View," *Money Marketing,* April 5, 2001)

WINDOW OF OPPORTUNITY. Short period of time when one has the chance to take advantage of a situation.

"The ring-tone market will 'be a big business for the next few years and then it's going to go away,' says veteran music attorney Jay L. Cooper, who represents artists such as Sheryl Crow and some ring-tone companies. But, he adds, if companies don't take advantage 'while you have this window of opportunity, you're losing millions of dollars a day.'" (*Wall Street Journal,* Sept. 13, 2004, p. A1)

WING IT. Do something without a set plan.

WIN-WIN. Beneficial to both parties.

WIRED. Connected to the Internet; hyperactive, often induced by caffeine.

WISH LIST. Resources a division or company would like to have.

WONK. An expert in a narrow area of knowledge.

WON'T FLY. Will not work, will not be approved.

WOODEN NICKELS. See DON'T TAKE ANY WOODEN NICKELS.

WOODSHED (TO BE TAKEN TO). Be verbally chastised.

WOODSTOCK GENERATION. Anti–Vietnam War teenagers in the 1960s. The 1969 rock music festival in Woodstock, New York, symbolized this generation's challenge of existing values and policies.

WORD-OF-MOUTH. Information passed from person to person. In the United States, an estimated 80 percent of professional positions are filled through word-of-mouth.

WORD ON THE STREET. The current rumor being disseminated.

WORD-SALAD SPAM. E-mail messages using long strings of nonsensical words to get past antispam filters.
"Word-salad spam has become especially problematic in the last year, say antispam software companies. The technique of stringing together gibberish phrases was devised specifically to dodge a sophisticated type of screening technology, known as a Bayesian filter, which gained popularity in 2003." (*Wall Street Journal,* May 28, 2004, p. B1)

WORK A CROWD. Impress people at a gathering by moving around the room meeting and greeting people.
"Endless Referrals discusses how to work a crowd, practical and sensible follow-up techniques and clever strategically designed promotional pieces." (*Managers Magazine,* April 1995, p. 4)

WORKAROUND. An ingenious, undocumented way to solve a problem.
"I only ran into one problem with the Verizon service. On one occasion, when I lost the connection, the software wouldn't let me reconnect until I rebooted the computer. But this didn't occur on the two other times I lost the connection, and Verizon says there's a workaround for the problem." (*Wall Street Journal,* April 8, 2004, p. B1)

WORKER BEES. Low-level employees who do repetitive tasks. In the technology industry, worker bees are computer programmers and other technical people who sit at a computer all day.

WORKING CAPITAL. Money available to finance current operations.

WORK LIKE A DOG. Work very hard.

"All sorts of advertisers now use the same theme: We know you work like a dog, so we work like dogs for you." (*Adweek,* May 22, 1995, p. 20)

WORKLOAD COMPRESSION. Office humor for a situation in which there is a lot of work to be done in a short period of time.

WORK OUT. Sell by the end of the trading day at any price. See also BE FLAT. Also to restructure a problem loan so that the borrower will not default.

WORK-OUTS. Intense, structured conferences where managers respond to employee problem-solving proposals.

WORKPLACE SENSITIVITY. Awareness of topics and language that are particularly offensive to minorities and ethnic groups.

WORLD BANK. See INTERNATIONAL BANK FOR RECONSTRUCTION AND DEVELOPMENT.

WORLD INTELLECTUAL PROPERTY ORGANIZATION (WIPO). United Nations agency established to oversee intellectual property rights.

WRAPAROUND MORTGAGE. A mortgage agreement that creates a second mortgage that includes the existing first mortgage. A wraparound mortgage allows the borrower to keep the existing rate charged on the first mortgage.

WREAK HAVOC. Make a mess, do damage.

WRINKLE (NEW). A new or different idea or feature.

"It's not as if the Oil for Food-related documents in question could be shared with either Congress or Mr. Volcker but not both. But this latest hush letter adds a new wrinkle, stating twice that the U.N. demands control of 'documentation or information' (emphasis added). Translation: Shut up or we'll sue." (*Wall Street Journal,* May 11, 2004, p. A18)

WRITE DOWN. Reduce the book value of an asset to reflect its current market value.

WRITE OFF. Give up on; in accounting, to remove from a balance sheet because it no longer has value.

"The Yankees will have to write off some of their high-priced pitchers as poor investments, though it's not clear which ones (except for you, Javier Vazquez). The team plainly needs another starter, a left-handed reliever and a center fielder—a very modest rebuilding campaign." (*Wall Street Journal,* Oct. 22, 2004, p. A16)

WRITTEN ON ICE. A gift, loan, or agreement that will be forgiven or forgotten.

X

X/XD. Ex-dividend. A stock trading with the dividend designated to the seller.

XEROID. A person who works for Xerox Corporation. Xerox employees refer to themselves as Xeroids, implying that they are like robots.

"They were stymied by 'Xeroids'—veterans of the hugely successful electro-mechanical copier business who saw electronics as more threat than opportunity." (*Business Week,* Feb. 13, 1989, p. 92)

X OUT (TO). Delete words from a contract. A phrase frequently used by lawyers.

Y

YANKEE BOND. A bond issued by non-U.S. entities trading in the U.S. stock market.

"Indeed, as part of Friday's deal, Indonesia promised to seek similar rescheduling terms from private creditors, such as the London Club of nongovernmental lenders. But the Paris Club agreement notably excluded government-guaranteed payments worked out as part of an earlier restructuring of the foreign debts of Indonesian banks, as well as Indonesia's $400 million Yankee bond." (*Wall Street Journal,* April 15, 2002, p. A12)

YEAR-END CLOSE. Business completed by the end of the year.

YELLOW GOODS. Products bought only rarely that offer high profit margins to retailers.

YELLOW SHEETS. U.S. National Quotation Bureau lists of over-the-counter corporate bonds.

YELLOW UNION. A company-controlled union with no real interest in representing the workers.

YES MAN. An employee whose main function is to endorse a supervisor's decisions. In many management environments, these people are easily identified by the deference they show to superiors and the condescending manner shown to subordinates. See also ASS-KISSER.

"The alleged WorldCom fraud, moreover, contains several notable 1990s boomtown traits. One is the young chief financial officer closely tied to the superstar CEO. The CFO is supposed to be a corporate truth-teller, not a yes man. Yet WorldCom's CFO, 40-year-old Scott Sullivan, rose in the company as chairman Bernard Ebbers's right-hand man." (*Wall Street Journal,* June 27, 2002, p. A20)

Y.E.S. UNIT. Your Extra Salesperson, fact sheet on a retail shelf that pulls down like a shade.

YETTIE. A young person who creates or manages a technology company. From the phrase young, entrepreneurial, tech-based twenty-something.

"He carries a black computer bag stitched with a company name, has tightly cropped hair, wears tiny black glasses and frequently talks into a mobile phone about a double-chip switching router. Everyone has met him: he is a yettie, a Young, Entrepreneurial, Tech-based Twenty-something, and can be found tapping into his Psion while sipping a vodka and cranberry in a bar near you." ("Enter the abominable yettie," *Sunday Times [London],* Feb. 13, 2000)

YIELD TO CALL. The percentage rate of return on a bond if held to the call date. Many bonds have call provisions allowing the issuer to redeem them prior to the maturity date. This allows the issuer to re-finance if interest rates decline.

YIELD TO MATURITY. The percentage rate of return on a bond if the investor holds the bond to the maturity date.

YOU BET. An affirmation meaning surely or certainly. It is considered casual and less-than-professional speech.

"'We haven't been able to raise the $200 million,' said Jim Kim, an adviser to WHO Director General Jong Wook Lee, and a participant in the public-private fund-raising plan. He said if public-health systems in developing countries aren't improved, 'is the world in trouble? You bet.' China is believed to be the breeding ground for SARS, new flu viruses and other deadly bugs." (*Wall Street Journal,* Oct. 10, 2003, p. A8)

YOUR MILEAGE MAY VARY. Buyer beware, the information may be less than honest or accurate.

YO-YO. To destabilize deliberately a business relationship by increasing or decreasing orders or frequently changing other arrangements; as with the toy, the business is kept on a string, going up and down.

YO-YO STOCK. A stock that fluctuates wildly with no apparent stable pattern.

"Textile industry sales usually follow a yo-yo path with a down year following a good one, but the industry broke tradition with its second consecutive good year in 1993." (*Textile World,* June 1994, p. 23)

YUPPIE. A "young urban professional." A popular, uncomplimentary characterization of young American business people in the 1980s. It implied that these people were especially mercenary.

"China's cheese market is still tiny, with estimated annual retail sales this year of about $31 million, says market researcher Access Asia Ltd. in Shanghai. And most of the cheese sold to Chinese is in the form of slices, not fancier varieties with visible mold and rinds. (Frontier does ship finer cheeses like Brie to China, but Mr. Kumar says they're 'niche products' for the rare yuppie or expatriate buyer.)" (*Wall Street Journal,* Dec. 11, 2003, p. B1)

Z

ZERO. A person with no recognized ability.

ZERO-BASED BUDGETING. A management policy that calls on all programs to justify every aspect of their funding at the start of each year. The idea behind this policy is that nothing is sacred and all expenditures must be continually justified.

"Zero-based budgeting is a means of rooting out waste by challenging each component of overhead on an annual basis." (*D&B Reports,* Sept./Oct. 1991, p. 48)

ZERO-COUPON BONDS. A bond that does not pay periodic interest but instead is sold at a discount from its face value. The value of the bond increases as the bond approaches maturity.

ZERO-DRAG WORKER. People who are not encumbered by family responsibilities and therefore can work long hours.

"The ideal zero-drag employee is young, unmarried and childless with no responsibilities and an eagerness to do well." ("Wedded to workplace," *Boston Globe,* March 11, 2001)

ZERO POPULATION GROWTH (ZPG). When a country's birth rate equals its death rate. In the 1970s ZPG was a popular political and social goal among environmentalists in the United States.

ZERO-SUM GAME. A management game theory in which advantages to one party are exactly equal to the disadvantages suffered by another. The term was popularized by Lester Thurow's 1985 book, *Zero-sum Solution.*

"World trade is not a zero-sum game, but beneficial to all who engage in it. Why else would rational humans do it, and why else would the history of world economic development be told in terms of the search by traders and investors for new opportunities?" (*Wall Street Journal,* Nov. 25, 2003, p. A19)

ZILCH. Zero, nothing.

"Ms. Burzynski, who has a calm, maternal demeanor herself, knew zilch about technology. 'My strength is building organizations,' she says. She expanded Molly Maids by focusing on front-line workers, giving health benefits and providing English classes to improve retention." (*Wall Street Journal,* Feb. 3, 2004, p. B7)

ZILLION. An exceedingly large, indeterminate number. See also JILLION.

"The idea that there are zillions of Chinese eagerly rushing out to buy anything from an offshore company at fat profits is pure bunk." (*Forbes,* Jan. 31, 1994, p. 140)

ZINGER. A quick and sharp response or retort.

"When Kerry threw zingers at the president, however, which he did on numerous occasions despite his calls for bipartisanship, he was greeted with prolonged cheers." (*U.S. News & World Report,* Aug. 9, 2004, p. 26)

ZIP. Zero. See also ZILCH.

ZOMBIE BONDS/BORROWERS. Bonds that were thought to be valueless (dead) for which trading resumes. The term was first attributed to traders at Goldman Sachs, a large New York investment company.

"Japan's third-largest retailer, which overexpanded in the go-go 1980s, the company has long been considered an indicator of how serious the nation's banks are about dealing with what are known here as 'zombie' borrowers. At the urging of a protective government, banks kept Daiei on life support for years." (*Wall Street Journal,* August 11, 2004, p. C1)

ZOMP. Nickname used by insurance companies for zero money down and deferred monthly payments.

ZULU TIME. Time standard used in global satellite systems; Greenwich mean time.

ACRONYMS

ABC	Activity-based costing
ACH	Automated clearing house
ACRS	Accelerated cost recovery system
AGI	Adjusted gross income
AICPA	American Institute of Certified Public Accountants
AKA	Also known as
AMEX	American Stock Exchange; American Express credit card
AMT	Alternative minimum tax
ANOVA	Analysis of variance
AON	All-or-none order
AP	Associated Press
APR	Annual percentage rate
ARM	Adjustable rate mortgage
ASAP	As soon as possible
ASCII	American National Standard Code for Information Interchange

ASP	Application service provider
ASQC	American Society for Quality Control
AT&T	American Telephone and Telegraph
ATM	Automated teller machine
AV	Audiovisual
BA	Bachelor of arts (degree)
B&B	Bed and breakfast
BBB	Better Business Bureau
BLM	Bureau of Land Management
BLS	Bureau of Labor Statistics
BOP	Balance of payments
BRICs	Brazil, Russia, India, and China
BS	Bachelor of science (degree); bull shit
BTB, B2B	Business-to-business
BTW	By the way
BWQ	Buzzword quotient
CAD	Current account deficit
CAD/CAM	Computer-aided design/manufacturing
CALPERS	California Public Employees' Retirement System
CAPM	Capital asset pricing model
CATS	Certificates of accrual on treasury securities
CBOE	Chicago Board of Options Exchange
CBOT	Chicago Board of Trade
CBS	Columbia Broadcasting System
CBT	Computer-based training
CC	Copy correspondence
CCC	Civilian Conservation Corps
CD	Certificate of deposit
CDMA	Code-division multiple access
CD-RW	CD re-writeable
CE	Capital expenditures
CEA	Council of Economic Advisers
CEO	Chief executive officer
CEU	Continuing education unit
CFC	Chartered financial consultant

CFO	Chief financial officer
CFS	Chronic fatigue syndrome
CIF, c.i.f.	Cost, insurance, and freight
CMO	Collateralized mortgage obligation
COD	Cash on delivery
COE	Corps of Engineers
COLA	Cost of living adjustment
CP	Commercial paper
CPA	Certified public accountant
CPI	Consumer Price Index
CPM	Cost per thousand
CSMS	Customer Satisfaction Measurement Survey
CTR	Click-through rate
CU	Consumers Union
CV	Curriculum vita
CYA	Cover your ass
DAC	Deferred acquisition cost
DAP	Developmental action plan
D&B	Dun and Bradstreet
DBA	Doing business as; doctor of business administration
DD	Due diligence
DIDMCA	Depository Institutions Deregulatory and Money Control Act
DINK	Double-income no kids
DJIA	Dow Jones Industrial Average
DM	Deutsche mark
DMA	Direct Marketing Association
DNC	Do not call
DOA	Dead on arrival
DOL	Department of Labor
DOMA	Die or move away
DQYDJ	Don't quit your day job
DRIP	Dividend reinvestment plan
DSO	Day sales order
EBITDA	Earnings before interest, taxes, deprecation, and amortization

ECU	European currency unit
EDGAR	Electronic data gathering analysis and retrieval system
EDGE	Enhanced data (rates for) global evolution
EEOC	Equal Employment Opportunity Commission
EFTS	Electronic Funds Transfer System
EIS	Environmental impact statement
EM	Electronic mail
EMEA	Europe, Middle East, and Africa
EOM	End of the month
EP	European plan; extended play
EPA	Environmental Protection Agency
EPS	Earnings per share
ERISA	Employment Retirement Income Security Act
ERP	Enterprise resource planning
ESOP	Employee self-ownership plan
ETA	Estimated time of arrival
EU	European Union
EULA	End-user license agreement
FAB	Features, advantages, benefits
FAQ	Frequently asked question
FASB	Federal Accounting Standards Board
FCC	Federal Communications Commission
FDIC	Federal Deposit Insurance Corporation
FEB	Feature, evidence, benefit
FEMA	Federal Emergency Management Agency
FHA	Farmers Home Administration
FHLB	Federal Home Loan Bank
FHLMC	Federal Home Loan Mortgage Corporation, "Freddie Mac"
FICA	Federal Insurance Contribution Act
FIFO	First in, first out accounting system
FNMA	Federal National Mortgage Association, "Fannie Mae"
FOB	Free on board
FOIA	Freedom of Information Act
FOMC	Federal Open Market Committee
footsie	Financial times-stock exchange 100 share index

FRB	Federal Reserve Board, "Fed"
FSBO	For sale by owner
FSLIC	Federal Savings and Loan Insurance Corporation
FTC	Federal Trade Commission
FUBAR	Fouled up beyond all recognition
FUD	Fear, uncertainty, and doubt
FWIW	For what it's worth
FY	Fiscal year
FYI	For your information
G-7	Group of seven
GAAP	Generally accepted accounting principles
GAO	General Accounting Office
GATT	General Agreement on Tariffs and Trade
GDP	Gross domestic product
GG	Got to go
GIC	Guaranteed investment contract
GIF	Graphics interchange format; global income fund
GM	General manager; General Motors
GNMA	Government National Mortgage Association, "Ginnie Mae"
GO bond	General obligation bond
GOP	Grand old party (Republican party)
GPRS	General packet radio service
GS	General service (rating)
GTC	Good till canceled
HLM	Honorary life member
HMO	Health maintenance organization
HR	Human resources; House of Representatives
HUD	Department of Housing and Urban Development
HUT	Households using television
IBIDAT	Income before interest, depreciation, and taxes
IBRD	International Bank for Reconstruction and Development, World Bank
ICANN	Internet Corporation for Assigned Names and Numbers
ICC	Interstate Commerce Commission
ICP	Internet content provider

ID	Identification
IM	Instant messaging
IMC	Integrated marketing communication
IMF	International Monetary Fund, "the Fund"
IMHO	In my humble opinion
IPO	Initial public offering
IRA	Individual retirement account
IRC	Internal Revenue Code
IRIF	Involuntary reduction in force
IRR	Internal rate of return
IRS	Internal Revenue Service
ISM	Institute for Supply Management (formerly NAPM, National Association of Purchasing Management)
ISP	Internet service provider
ITM	In the money
JC	Junior college
JD	Juris doctor (degree)
JIT	Just-in-time
JPEG	Joint Photographic Experts Group
JTPA	Job Training Partnership Act
KISS	Keep it simple, stupid
KKR	Kohlberg, Kravis, Roberts
KO	Knock out
K&R (insurance)	Kidnap and ransom insurance
LAN	Local area network
LBO	Leveraged buyout
LDC	Less developed country
LEAPS	Long-term equity anticipation securities
LIBOR	London Inter-Bank Offered Rate
LIFO	Last in, first out
LOB	Line of business
LOC	Letter of credit
LOL	Laughing out loud; lots of luck
LP	Limited partnership

M1, M2	Measures of the money supply
MA	Master of arts (degree)
M&A	Merger and acquisition
MAP	Modified American plan
MBA	Master of business administration (degree)
MBI	Management by intimidation
MBO	Management by objectives
MBWA	Management by walking around
MERC	Chicago Mercantile Exchange (nickname)
MFN	Most favored nation
MIS	Management information system
MIT	Massachusetts Institute of Technology
MITI	Ministry of International Trade and Industry (Japan)
MLP	Master limited partnership
MLS	Multiple listing service
MMS	Multimedia messaging service
MNC	Multinational corporation
MO	Modus operandi
MRO	Maintenance, repair, and operations (supplies)
MS	Master of science (degree)
MSRP	Manufacturer's suggested retail price
MTBU	Maximum time to belly-up
NAFTA	North American Free Trade Agreement
NAICS	North American Industrial Classification System
NASDAQ	National Association of Securities Dealers Automated Quotations
NAV	Net asset value
NBC	National Broadcasting Corporation
NC	No charge
NCUA	National Credit Union Administration
NDA	Non-disclosure agreement
NIC	Newly industrialized country; network interface card
NIH	National Institutes of Health
NIMBY	Not in my backyard
NLRB	National Labor Relations Board

NOW	Negotiable order of withdrawal; National Organization of Women
NPV	Net present value
NSF	Not-sufficient funds
NYSE	New York Stock Exchange
OAG	Official Airline Guide
OAS	Organization of American States
OASDI	Old age, survivors, and disability insurance (Social Security)
OASIS	Ordering and shipping improvement system
OB	Or better; out-of-bounds
OE	Operating expenses
OECD	Organization for Economic Cooperation and Development
OEM	Original equipment manufacturer
OIG	Office of Inspector General
OMB	Office of Management Budget
OPM	Other people's money; Office of Personnel Management
OS	Operating system
OSHA	Occupational Safety and Health Administration
OT	Overtime
OTC	Over the counter
OTOH	On the other hand
P-to-P, P2P	Peer to peer; path to profitability
P3P	Platform for privacy preferences
PAC	Political action committee
PBGC	Pension Benefit Guarantee Corporation
PC	Politically correct; personal computer
PDA	Personal digital assistant
P/E	Price/earnings ratio
PI	Performance improvement
P&I	Principal and interest
PIK	Payment in kind
PIN	Personal identification number
PITI	Principle, interest, taxes, and insurance
P&L	Profit and loss

PLC	Product life cycle
PLS	Please
PO	Purchase order; post office; piss off
POP	Point-of-purchase
POS	Point of sale
PPC	Pay per click
PPI	Producer price index
PR or pr	Public relations
PS	Postscript
PSA	Public service announcement
PUR	People using radio
PVC	Poly-vinyl chloride
QA	Quality assurance
Qs	Nasdaq 100 tracking stock
QT	Quiet
R&I	Read and initial
R&D	Research and development
RAM	Random access memory
REIT	Real Estate Investment Trust
RICO	Racketeer Influenced and Corrupt Organization Act
RIF	Reduction in force
RJR	R. J. Reynolds Tobacco Company
ROI	Return on investment
ROM	Random operating memory
ROTFL	Rolling on the floor laughing
RPM	Revolutions per minute
RR	Railroad
RTC	Resolution Trust Corporation
RTF	Rich text format
RTW	Right to work
SBA	Small Business Administration
SDR	Special drawing rights
SDRAM	Synchronous dynamic random access memory
SEC	Securities and Exchange Commission
SF	Sinking fund

SIC	Standard industrial classification
SIPC	Securities Investor Protection Corporation
SITCOM	Single Income, Two Children, Oppressive Mortgage; situation comedy
SKU	Stock keeping units
S&L	Savings and loan
SLMA	Student Loan Marketing Association
SMS	Short messaging service
SMSA	Standard Metropolitan Statistical Area
SNAFU	Situation normal, all fouled up
SOB	Son of a bitch
SOMO	Sell one, make one
SOP	Standard operating procedure
SOTA	State-of-the-art
SOX	Sarbanes-Oxley Law
S&P	Standard & Poor's
SPC	Statistical process control
SRO	Standing room only
SSA	Social Security Administration
STD	Short-term disability
SWAG	Scientific wild-ass guess
SWOT	Strengths, weaknesses, opportunities, and threats
T&A	Tits and ass
TAFN	That's all for now
TAT	Turn around time
TBA	To be announced
TCP/IP	Transmission control protocol/internet protocol
TGIF	Thank goodness it's Friday
TI	Texas Instruments Corporation
TIAA	Teachers Insurance and Annuity Association
TIN	Tax identification number
TLC	Tender loving care
TM	Trademark
TOM	Turn-of-the-month
TQM	Total quality management

TSA	Tax-sheltered annuity
TTYL	Talk to you later
UAW	United Auto Workers
UCE	Unsolicited commercial e-mail
UMW	United Mine Workers
UPC	Uniform practice code
UPS	United Parcel Service
USB	Unique selling proposition; universal serial bus (drive or port)
USCC	United States Chamber of Commerce
USPS	United States Postal Service
VA	Veterans Administration
VALS	Values and lifestyles
VAT	Value-added tax
v.f.d.	Value for duty
VIP	Very important person
VM	Voice mail
VP, VEEP	Vice president
VPN	Virtual private network
VRIF	Voluntary reduction in force
WACC	Weighted average cost of capital
WAP	Wireless application protocol
WASP	White Anglo-Saxon Protestant
WHOOPS	Washington Public Power Supply System
Wi-Fi	Wireless Fidelity
WIPO	World Intellectual Property Organization
WOMBAT	Waste of money, brains, and time
WOOFYS	Well-off older folks
WPA	Works Projects Administration
WSJ	*Wall Street Journal*
WYSIWYG	What you see is what you get
X/XD	Ex-dividend
YMMV	Your mileage may vary
ZPG	Zero population growth

BIBLIOGRAPHY

Bennet, Steven. *Guide to Management and Technology*. Amsterdam: Information Innovation, 1994.

Burke, David. *Biz Talk 1: American Business Slang & Jargon*. Los Angeles: Optima, 1993.

Chapman, Robert L. *New Dictionary of American Slang*. New York: Harper & Row, 1986.

CNNMoney.com business glossary.

Downes, John and Jordan Elliot Goodman. *Dictionary of Finance and Investment Terms,* 4th ed. New York: Barrons, 1995.

Gozzi, Raymond, Jr. *New Words and a Changing American Culture*. Columbia: University of South Carolina Press, 1990.

Green, Jonathon. *Dictionary of Jargon*. New York: Routledge & Kegan Paul, 1987.

Green, Tamara. *The Greek & Latin Roots of English*. New York: Ardsley House, 1990.

IMUSERS.com, Internet shorthand.

Investopedia.com.

Makkai, Adam, ed. *Dictionary of American Idioms,* 2nd ed. New York: Barrons, 1987.

Netlingo.com.

Pritchett, Thomas K., Betty M. Pritchett, and Caroline M. Fisher. *Study Guide for Schoell-Guiltinan Marketing,* 5th ed. Boston: Allyn and Bacon, 1992.

Reed, Stanley Foster. *The M&A Deskbook.* New York: McGraw-Hill, 2001.

Schaaf, Dick and Margaret Kaeter. *BusinessSpeak.* New York: Warner Books, 1994.

Techweb.com/encyclopedia.

Wentworth, Harold and Stuart Berg Flexner. *Dictionary of American Slang,* 2d ed. New York: Thomas Crowell, 1975.

Wordspy.com.

About the Author

W. DAVIS FOLSOM is Professor of Economics and Marketing, University of South Carolina, Beaufort. He is the author of several books, including *American Business Language* and *NAFTA Law and Business*, and editor of *The Encyclopedia of American Business*.